GANGSTERS

GANGSTERS

igloobooks

igloobooks

This edition published 2012
by Igloo Books Ltd
Cottage Farm
Sywell
NN6 0BJ
www.igloobooks.com

A copy of the British Library Cataloguing-in-Publication
Data is available from the British Library

SHE001 1112
2 4 6 8 10 9 7 5 3
ISBN: 978-0-85734-795-4

Written by Michael Newton
Design by Cara Rogers

Printed and manufactured in China

Contents

Introduction	7	Paul Castellano	62
Itzhak Abergil	8	Mickey Cohen	64
Tony Accardo	8	Vincent Coll	66
Joe Adonis	11	Joe Columbo Snr.	67
Evsei Agron	13	Frank Costello	69
Joe Aiello	14	Raffaele Cutolo	71
Yaakov Alperon	16	Moe Dalitz	72
Albert Anastasia	17	Jack Diamond	73
Ramon Arellano Félix	19	Jack Dragna	75
Gaetano Badalamenti	21	Du Yuesheng	76
Joe Barboza	22	Rayful Edmond III	77
Antonio Bardellino	24	Pablo Escobar	78
Clyde Barrow and Bonnie Parker	25	Demetrius Flenory	82
Sam Battaglia	29	Rolando Florián Féliz	83
Marcos Arturo Beltrán Leyva	32	Frankie Fraser	84
Donovan Bennett	34	Jimmy Fratianno	85
Charles Binaggio	35	Carmine Galante	87
Griselda Blanco	37	Joey Gallo	89
Joe Bonanno	38	Carlo Gambino	92
Klaas Bruinsma	41	Juan García Abrego	96
Angelo Bruno	42	Vito Genovese	97
Lepke Buchalter	45	Sam Giancana	99
Ali Budesh	47	Detlef Gloutsbach	102
James Bulger	48	Waxey Gordon	103
James Burke	50	John Gotti	105
Tommaso Buscetta	51	Danny Greene	110
Martin Cahill	52	Joaquín Guzmán Loera	111
Alaattin Çakici	53	George Enrique Herbert	114
Al Capone	55	Dawood Ibrahim	115
Vicente Carrillo Fuentes	59	Pappu Kalani	116
Alfonso Caruana	61	Harry Kalasho	117

Contents

Khun Sa	118	Paul Ricca	175
Reginald and Ronald Kray	120	Salvatore Riina	178
Vladimir Kumarin	124	John Rosselli	181
Meyer Lansky	125	Arnold Rothstein	182
Luciano Leggio	126	Alex Rudaj	184
Carlos Enrique Lehder Rivas	129	Nicky Scarfo	185
Salvatore Lo Piccolo	130	Dutch Schultz	188
Frank Lucas	134	Bugsy Siegel	191
Tommy Lucchese	136	Klaus Speer	194
Lucky Luciano	138	Tony Spilotro	195
Owney Madden	141	Stanko Subotić	198
Carlos Marcello	143	Omid Tahvili	199
Juan Ramón Matta-Ballesteros	145	Ömer Topal	199
Frank McErlane	146	Johnny Torrio	200
Jacques Mesrine	147	Roger Touhy	202
Sergei Mikhailov	151	Santo Trafficante Jr.	204
Semion Yudkovich Mogilevich	152	Robert Trimbole	205
Diego Montoya Sánchez	153	Yves Trudeau	206
Lewis Moran	155	Francis Vanverberghe	207
Nam Cam	156	Calogero Vizzini	210
Frank Nitti	158	Curtis Warren	211
Manuel Noriega	159	Adam Worth	212
Khozh-Ahmed Noukhayev	164	Frankie Yale	213
Raymond Patriarca Snr.	165	Yoshio Kodama	216
Quirino Paulino Castillo	166	Gaetan Zampa	217
Santiago Luis Polanco Rodríguez	167	Zhenli Ye Gon	219
Bernardo Provenzano	168	Abner Zwillman	222
Chotta Rajan	171	Picture credits	224
Željko Ražnatović	172		

PAGE 1: Reggie and Ronnie Kray, pictured after 36 hours spent being interviewed by the police regarding the murder of George Cornell.

PAGE 2: John Gotti, pictured leaving Brooklyn Federal Court.

Introduction

Organized crime has existed throughout history. Every society in every age has harbored groups created to provide illegal goods and services. Whatever the type of product – a form of vice (commercial sex, illicit gambling, banned intoxicants), forbidden weapons, stolen merchandise sold cheaply and untaxed, or transportation to another country without proper documents – it is available for customers with ready cash in hand.

America presents a case in point. During the 19th century, street gangs battled for turf and ethnic pride, selling their services to urban politicians and receiving the protection of corrupt police. When Prohibition outlawed alcoholic beverages in 1920, small-time local thugs became millionaires with international connections, quenching a vast nation's thirst. With repeal in 1933, they turned to gambling, earning billions over the next four decades. The early 1970s brought 'war on drugs' and a new Prohibition that enriched old and new mobsters alike, while traditional rackets – prostitution, extortion, gun-running, wholesale theft and fraud – continued unabated. Everywhere worldwide, it was the same, with variations on a common theme.

Gangsters, by definition, operate in gangs. The oldest syndicates – Persia's Federation of Assassins (formed in 1090) and India's Thuggee (active from the 1600s through the 1870s) – were cults that used religion as a mask for crime. China's Triad societies date from 1644, initially pledged to unseat the Qing dynasty, unwilling to disband when it collapsed in 1912. Japan's Yakuza syndicates arose from an 18th-century merger of gamblers and swindlers. Italy's Camorra dates from 1735, while the Sicilian Mafia is more recent, publicly named for the first time in 1863. In France, the Unione Corse seems to be a 20th-century creation, as are Italy's Stidda, Ndrangheta and Sacra Corona Unita. Russia's "vory v zakone" the elite of Russian crime, developed under Soviet rule but only expanded worldwide from the 1970s onward.

Organized crime can only exist through corruption of public officials. Bribery of local police, judges and lawmakers is a global phenomenon. America's Central Intelligence Agency has forged alliances with gangsters since its creation in 1947, using them as Cold War shock troops against communists, employing mafiosi in bungled attempts to assassinate Cuba's Fidel Castro during 1960–63, and recruiting drug-traffickers to finance covert operations such as the 'Contra' war against Nicaragua's government in the 1980s. Mexico's Federal Judicial Police were disbanded to eradicate corruption in 2002, while its successor, the Federal Investigations Agency, was scrapped for the same reason in May 2009.

Gangsters exist because they meet society's illicit needs and dark desires. Beyond that, they provide free entertainment with their reckless, outrageous and often bloody exploits. Some are cast as modern 'Robin Hoods' while still alive. Many others are romanticized on film after their deaths. Their victims, for the most part, are forgotten, or dismissed as worthless ciphers, if they dwell within the underworld milieu.

Bugsy Siegel once remarked, inaccurately, that 'We only kill each other.' Mickey Cohen played the same refrain, insisting that 'I never killed nobody who didn't deserve it.' But gangster Harry Pierpont may have said it best, addressing the prosecutor at his 1934 murder trial: 'You'd probably be like me if you had the nerve.'

BELOW: Mafia boss Paul Castellano leaving Federal Court after posting $2 million bail in February 1985.

Itzhak Abergil

While gangsters of Jewish ancestry rose to prominence in the United States during the 19th century, Israeli police date the first significant appearance of organized crime in their country from the 1980s. One of six major syndicates founded during that era was the Abergil crime family, led by ruthless brothers Avraham, Itzhak, Meir and Ya'kov Abergil. The gang's activities – staunchly denied by all its principals – reportedly include drug trafficking, loan-sharking, extortion and illegal gambling, with discipline enforced by murder. In 2008, the US State Department ranked Itzhak Abergil and his 'Jerusalem Network' among 40 top importers smuggling illegal drugs into America.

Protestations of innocence notwithstanding, elder brother Ya'kov paid the price for an underworld lifestyle in June 2002, when rival mobsters gunned him down in Tel Aviv, before the horrified eyes of his family. Itzhak then assumed command of the family business, directing his brothers and various cohorts in the smuggling of cocaine, hashish and Ecstasy into Europe and the United States. Expansion to America found the gang collaborating with established syndicates such as the Mexican Mafia and California's Vineland Boys. Bank fraud was another lucrative pastime, as detailed by Trade Bank clerk Etti Alon in April 2002. Alon told Tel Aviv police that she had embezzled NIS 250 million ($67 million) from the bank on behalf of the Abergil crime family, a confession that prompted indictment of Itzhak and brother Meir in Los Angeles, on July 13, 2002.

California prosecutors blame the Abergils for killing Israeli drug dealer Sami Atias in Los Angeles, on August 31, 2003, dismissing Itzhak's vague defense that he had never personally set foot in the US. Rival mobsters respond in kind, as in 2005, when gunmen strafed a party attended by Itzhak in Ramle, Israel, killing two female bystanders. Such mistakes are depressingly common, as when Abergil gunmen fired on a beachside restaurant in Bat Yam, killing innocent diner Margarita Lautin in July 2008. On that occasion, the brothers allegedly planned to kill three of their own family associates, but succeeded only in wounding one – Rami Amira – while the other targets escaped injury.

Israeli police charged Itzhak and Meir in that case, but avoided the expense of trial by extraditing them to the US in August 2008, with three alleged accomplices, to face trial on drug-trafficking charges. Meanwhile, brother Avraham, known as 'Ibi,' remains incarcerated in Israel, charged with multiple drug offenses and conspiracy to commit murder. While congratulating themselves on the apparent dismantling of one syndicate, Israeli police remain embroiled in conflict with other organized gangs, including both native mobsters and immigrants from the former Soviet Union.

Tony Accardo

Future mafioso Antonino Leonardo Accardo, alias Anthony Joseph Accardo, was born on Chicago's Near West Side to Sicilian immigrant parents on April 28, 1906. Expelled from school at age 14, he joined the local Circus Cafe Gang and began compiling a record of juvenile crimes. In 1926, at the height of Chicago's liquor wars, Accardo was recruited for Al Capone's mob by triggerman Vincenzo Gibaldi, AKA 'Machine Gun Jack McGurn.' His zeal for slugging adversaries with a baseball bat earned Accardo the nickname 'Joe Batters,' while the press dubbed him 'Big Tuna' for his catch on a later deep-sea fishing expedition.

FBI bugs caught Accardo on tape, boasting of his personal involvement in the 1928 murder of New York mafioso Frankie Yale and in the 1929 St. Valentine's Day Massacre that ultimately led to Al Capone's downfall. Capone's tax-evasion conviction meant promotion for Accardo, who attained the rank of *caporegime* (captain) under successor Frank Nitti. In 1943, after Nitti's alleged suicide and the imprisonment of reigning Outfit leaders for their roles in a Hollywood extortion scheme,

BELOW: Tony Accardo pleads the Fifth Amendment during a Senate Committee hearing on July 11, 1958.

Accardo filled the power vacuum as Chicago's latest godfather. Predecessor Paul Ricca, himself incarcerated in the Hollywood case, once observed that Accardo 'had more brains for breakfast than Capone had all day.'

Accardo's empire in the late 1940s included an estimated 10,000 gambling dens in Chicago alone, plus control of Continental Press – the national race-wire service used by America's illicit bookmakers – seized from founder James Ragen in June 1946. When legal casinos sprouted from the desert sands of Las Vegas, Nevada, most bought their slot machines from a company owned by Tony Accardo. In Kansas and Oklahoma, where sales of alcohol were banned long beyond Prohibition, Accardo and the Outfit supplied thirsty patrons with untaxed liquor.

In November 1957, the infamous Mafia meeting at Apalachin, New York, finally forced FBI headquarters to acknowledge organized crime's existence. Seeking a lower profile, Accardo chose flamboyant underling Sam Giancana to succeed him as boss by year's end, but Giancana's antics forced him to flee the country in 1966, whereupon Accardo resumed command of the family through appointee Joseph Aiuppa. Anyone who doubted Accardo's authority, however, made a grave mistake.

In January 1977, while Accardo vacationed in California, six foolish burglars looted his suburban home. It took a year for Outfit soldiers to identify the thieves, but vengeance was swift thereafter. Bernard Ryan died by gunfire on January 20, 1978. Automobile trunks yielded the mutilated corpses of Steven Garcia on February 2, Vincent Moretti and Donald Swanson on February 4 and John Mandell on February 20. Gunmen caught lone survivor John McDonald in a North Side alley, in April 1978.

Legal problems dogged Accardo and his family during the godfather's declining years. A middle-aged nephew, John Simonelli, faced indictment on auto theft charges in February 1983. Congress cited Accardo himself for contempt in February 1984, when he refused to testify at hearings on labor racketeering despite a grant of legal immunity. Alleged poor health spared him from jail, but niece Sheila Simonelli was less fortunate, arrested on charges of trying to sell $23.5 million in stolen securities. In August 1991, a federal court denied Accardo's bid to dodge payment of $60,000 in overdue taxes and penalties. Congestive heart failure killed the aged mafioso on May 22, 1992.

Joe Adonis

A prime mover in the foundation of American organized crime, the mobster known as Joe Adonis or 'Joey A' was born Giuseppe Antonio Doto in Montemarano, Italy, on November 22, 1902. His parents emigrated to Brooklyn, New York, in 1915, and young Giuseppe wasted no time on formal education, preferring to roam the mean streets as a sneak thief and pickpocket. Always a vain ladies' man, Adonis reportedly got his nickname from an infatuated Ziegfeld Follies dancer in the early 1920s. Good friend Lucky Luciano once saw Adonis preening before a mirror and asked him, 'Who do you think you are, Rudolph Valentino?' The gangland Adonis smiled and replied, 'For looks, that guy's a bum!'

Adonis and Luciano sold bootleg liquor together in Prohibition, while Adonis doubled as an enforcer for mafioso Frankie Yale's gambling operations in Brooklyn. When rivals Salvatore Maranzano and Giuseppe 'Joe The Boss' Masseria battled for control of America's Mafia in the 'Castellammarese War' of 1929–31, Adonis followed Luciano into Masseria's camp, then reportedly joined the firing squad that executed 'Joe the Boss' at a Coney Island restaurant on April 15, 1931. Luciano next eliminated Maranzano – last of the American Mafia's stodgy 'Mustache Petes' – on September 10, 1931, and thereafter remodeled organized crime along corporate lines.

Joe Adonis claimed a seat on the new syndicate's board of directors, overseeing a territory that spread from Broadway and Midtown Manhattan to neighboring New Jersey, run from his modest headquarters at Joe's Italian Kitchen in Brooklyn. Investigators named him as the mafioso in charge of supervising Albert Anastasia, second in command with Lepke Buchalter of the contract killers known collectively as 'Murder Incorporated.'

Lucky Luciano's imprisonment in 1936 left Adonis and Frank Costello as New York's dominant mafiosi, increasingly subject to government scrutiny. Turncoat gunman Abe 'Kid Twist' Reles named the leaders of Murder Inc. in 1939, sending Lepke to the electric chair, but his murder in November 1941 foiled plans to prosecute Adonis and Anastasia. In 1950, the US Senate's Kefauver Committee grilled Adonis on his criminal activities, and while he refused to answer any questions, the exposure produced an indictment for illegal gambling in New Jersey. Adonis pled guilty in 1951 and received a two-year prison sentence.

While he was incarcerated, Immigration agents 'discovered' that Adonis had never applied for US citizenship. Branded an illegal and undesirable alien in

LEFT AND BOTTOM: A New York City Police mugshot of gangster Joe Adonis after his arrest in December 1937.

BELOW: Adonis, who prided himself on his good looks, was a key player in the growth of modern organized crime in the United States in the 1930s.

1953, Joe fought deportation in court for three years, then finally returned to Italy in 1956, settling outside Milan in a luxurious villa with frequent visits from Lucky Luciano. He attended Luciano's funeral in January 1962, bearing a floral wreath with the legend 'So Long, Pal.'

Italian authorities remained extremely suspicious of Adonis, and a police flying squad raided his villa on November 26, 1971, transporting him to an isolated mountain shack for interrogation. The ordeal proved too much for Joe, who suffered a heart attack and died before physicians could help him. After years away from the United States, he was buried at Madonna Cemetery in Fort Lee, New Jersey.

Evsei Agron

Little is known of Evsei Agron's early years, beyond reports that he was born in St. Petersburg, Russia, in 1932. At some point he joined, the criminal *Bratva* ('Brotherhood') as a 'thief in law' – the equivalent of a Mafia 'made man' in Russian organized crime – and reportedly served seven years in prison on a murder charge. Despite Soviet restrictions on emigration, applied most strictly to Jews, Russian authorities were probably relieved when Agron left the country in 1971, to settle in Hamburg, Germany. Over the next four years he ran a thriving prostitution ring, biding his time, waiting for better opportunities.

American President Gerald Ford opened a window for Agron on January 3, 1975, when he signed the Jackson-Vanik Amendment denying 'most favored nation' trading status to countries with restrictive immigration policies. By year's end, some 5,200 Russian Jews reached the United States, and one of them was Evsei Agron, arriving in New York City on October 8, 1975. Settling in the Russian expatriate community of Brighton Beach, on Coney Island, where he operated from an office at the El Caribe Country Club, Agron quickly gathered a personal army of Russian ex-convicts, former KGB agents and athletes gone to seed.

Initially, Agron – nicknamed 'The Little Don' – specialized in blackmail and extortion, mimicking 'Black Hand' terrorists who preyed on early Italian immigrants in America. His approach was straightforward: pay, or die. In one notorious case, he threatened to kill a young bride on her wedding day unless her parents paid Agron $15,000. Enforcers like Benjamin Nayfield, who once stabbed an unarmed victim to death in broad daylight and then persuaded 18 witnesses to testify that it was 'self-defense,' kept objections to a minimum.

In 1980, following an ambush that left him hospitalized, Agron forged an alliance with local mafiosi for mutual benefit. Italian mobsters guarded Agron during his convalescence, then joined him in sales of stolen, untaxed diesel fuel and heating oil for homes. Paying a 'street tax' of two cents per gallon to the Mafia – versus state and federal taxes of 28 cents per gallon – Agron banked millions of dollars per year, reportedly costing the state of New Jersey alone some $1 billion in tax revenue.

Such profits sparked competition, and Agron soon faced incursions on his turf from Israeli mobster Boris Goldberg. Agron survived a second shooting in January 1984, but a tense meeting with Goldberg that May resolved nothing. On May 4, 1985, Agron left his apartment, bound for Manhattan, but never reached his car. A lurking gunman opened fire at close range, striking Agron twice in the head. This time the wounds were fatal. Presumed conspirator Boris Goldberg enjoyed his success until 1989, when federal prosecutors indicted him on a list of charges including armed robbery, arms dealing, attempted murder, drug trafficking and extortion. Conviction on those charges left Goldberg in custody until July 2000.

A

Joe Aiello

Born in 1891 at Bagheria, Sicily, Giuseppe Aiello was one of ten sons in a thriving extended family. Siblings and other relatives preceded him in emigrating to America, and by the time Giuseppe arrived in July 1907 the family had grocery-related business interests both in New York City and Chicago. Aiello – often known as 'Joe' – joined fellow Sicilian Antonio 'The Scourge' Lombardo to import cheese and pursue 'Black Hand' extortion schemes until Prohibition started a liquid gold rush in 1920. Over the next decade, the Aiellos sold tons of sugar to illegal distillers bossed by the six Genna brothers, in Chicago's Little Italy.

On the side, Joe Aiello dreamed of dominating the Mafia, operating in those days through a Sicilian benevolent society, the *Unione Siciliana,* run from New York by mobster Frankie Yale. Chicago's *Unione* president, Michele 'Mike' Merlo, kept peace in Little Italy while generally favoring bootleggers Johnny Torrio and Al Capone. Since neither of them were Sicilians, Aiello regarded Merlo as a traitor. Matters might have improved for Aiello in November 1924, when Merlo

ABOVE: The last known photo of the American mafioso, Joe Aiello. He strove for many years to become *Unione* president, but his reign was all too brief.

LEFT: An official holds up the coat, riddled with 37 bullet holes, worn by Joe Aiello when he was slain by Capone assassins.

died from cancer. Aiello compatriot, Mike Genna, briefly assumed the presidency, then died in a shootout with police on June 13, 1925. Successor Samuel 'Samoots' Amatuna lasted until November 13, when he was shot in a barbershop.

Tony Lombardo replaced Amatuna as *Unione* president, but soon snubbed his old partner Aiello in favor of the Johnny Torrio-Al Capone alliance. Frankie Yale, now hostile to Capone, supported Aiello's bid for

the *Unione* presidency in January 1928, but Lombardo won re-election.

Capone gunmen killed Yale in New York on July 1, 1928, and Aiello retaliated by slaying Lombardo and one of his bodyguards in Chicago on September 7. *Unione* president successor Pasqualino 'Patsy' Lolordo survived

BELOW: Crowds gather outside the buildings where Aiello was murdered on October 23, 1930.

until January 8, 1929, when gunmen murdered him at his home.

Meanwhile, Aiello tried to kill Capone directly, importing a series of gunmen who failed to do the job. Eight died between May and September 1927 alone, followed by two of Aiello's own brothers on November 10. Aiello then bribed Capone's favorite chef to poison Big Al, but the cook squealed instead, and Capone soldiers strafed the Aiello Brothers Bakery on January 5, 1928. Joseph Giunta, a secret Aiello ally, succeeded Patsy Lolordo as *Unione* president in early 1929, recruiting Mafia assassins Alberto Anselmi and Giovanni Scalise to murder Capone, but Al uncovered the plot and held a banquet in Giunta's honor on May 8. There, Capone and Tony Accardo beat the trio to death with baseball bats.

Giunta's murder finally allowed Joe Aiello to assume the *Unione* presidency, but he spent most of his reign in hiding from Capone assassins. When the Chicago Crime Commission published its first list of 'public enemies' in April 1930, Aiello was unlucky No. 13. Six months later, on October 23, Capone machine-gunners ambushed Aiello outside the home of *Unione* treasurer Pasquale 'Presto' Prestogiacomo. Hit 59 times, Aiello was dead on arrival at Garfield Park Hospital.

Yaakov Alperon

Residents of Israel have long been accustomed to bombings and other acts of terrorism. Still, the explosion that killed one victim and wounded three more on November 17, 2008, at the crowded Tel Aviv intersection of Yehuda HaMaccabi Street and Namir Road was different. No radical Palestinians were involved, and the dead man – 53-year-old Yaakov Alperon – was named by police as a leading figure in organized crime.

Alperon was the son of Jewish immigrants from Egypt, born on February 18, 1955, and raised in a small flat in Giv'at Shmuel. With his rowdy brothers and other teenage hoodlums, Alperon extorted money from local shops, gradually extending his influence throughout the Tel Aviv Metropolitan Area known as Gush Dan. In 1993, police charged Yaakov and two of his brothers – Nissim and Zalman – with extortion, winning conviction of all three at trial. Yaakov was sentenced to 54 months in prison, but maintained control of the organization then ranked as Israel's third-largest crime family.

Beset by rivals on every side, the Alperons fought sporadically with syndicates led by Itzhak Abergil, Asi Abutul, Amir Mulner and Zeev Rosenstein. An attempt on brother Nissim's life in December 2003 led police to arrest four Belarusian hitmen three months later, catching them with an arsenal of guns, explosives and shoulder-launched missiles. Yaakov Alperon met with Amir Mulner on January 2, 2006, to discuss a truce, but wound up stabbing Mulner in the throat. After an interval in hiding, Yaakov and brother Reuven surrendered to authorities, faced with charges of 'making threats, attempted assault and intentionally damaging a car.'

Two months later, in March 2006, Yaakov faced additional charges of brandishing a knife during a brawl with rival gangsters in a Tel Aviv restaurant. Convicted of that offense on February 6, 2008, Alperon paid a NIS 20,000 ($5,400) fine and received an 18-month suspended prison sentence.

Between his latest indictment and wrist-slap punishment, police said Alperon had launched a new vendetta against the syndicate run by adversary Itzhak Abergil. According to the daily newspaper *Haaretz,* in July 2007, authorities collected 'credible intelligence' regarding Alperon's employment of two contract killers from the Russian Commonwealth of Independent States, hired to liquidate Abergil. The feud surfaced in January 2007, when Yaakov Alperon, brother Aryeh and several of their thugs assaulted Abergil and cohort Mottie Hassin outside Abergil's residence, the Sha'arei Ha'ir building in Ramat Gan. February brought charges against Aryeh Alperon and two cohorts for assault and causing grievous injuries to Abergil and Hassin. On the day charges were filed, Abergil emerged from court to find Alperon waiting with friends, one of whom struck Abergil again.

In July 2007, police trailed a carload of Abergil soldiers to a neighborhood inhabited by Nissim Alperon, blocking the vehicle before their trap was sprung. One of the gunmen, Avishai Balkar, opened fire on the officers,

wounding one before he was killed by return fire, his companions arrested.

No charges have been filed in Yaakov Alperon's slaying, but family members vow to avenge his murder. Thousands attended Alperon's funeral at Ra'anana Cemetery on November 18, 2008, where one of his sons pledged, 'We will find the man who did this. I'll send this man to God. He won't have a grave because I'll cut off his arms, his head, and his legs.'

Albert Anastasia

The future 'Lord High Executioner' of America's Mafia was born Umberto Anastasio in Tropea, Italy, on September 26, 1902. He emigrated to New York with brother Anthony (born in 1906) around 1917, altered his name, and soon began running extortion rackets on Brooklyn's waterfront. In 1920, Anastasia murdered longshoreman Joe Torino and received a death sentence, but that verdict was overturned when key witnesses recanted their testimony – then disappeared before Anastasia's scheduled retrial. Thus he adopted a lifelong motto: 'No witnesses, no case.'

Upon release from prison, Anastasia joined the Mafia family led by Giuseppe 'Joe the Boss' Masseria, serving under *caporegime* Lucky Luciano. During Masseria's bloody war against rival Salvatore Maranzano, Anastasia followed Luciano's lead to modernize the Mafia by ousting stodgy 'Mustache Petes.' He was part of the four-man firing squad that executed Masseria on April 15, 1931, and subsequently shared command of the modern syndicate's 'Murder Incorporated' hit team with labor racketeer Louis 'Lepke' Buchalter, dispatching expert killers to liquidate targets from coast to coast.

Formally assigned by Luciano to Vincenzo Mangano's crime family, Anastasia waited two decades before he rebelled. Mangano vanished forever on April 19, 1951, while his brother was murdered in Brooklyn the same

LEFT: A grim-faced Albert Anastasia arrives at the Supreme Court in December 1952 to answer questions before the New York State Crime Commission.

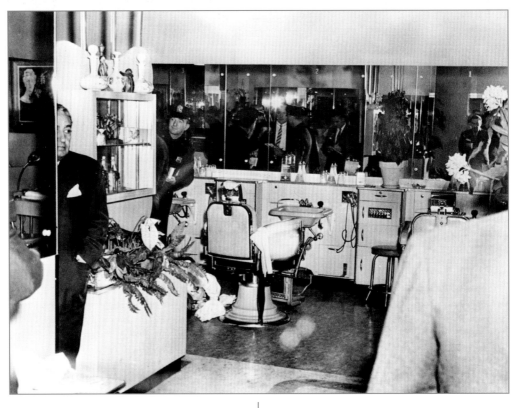

ABOVE: A scene from the Park Sheraton barbershop on October 25, 1957, following Anastasia's murder.

day. Anastasia persuaded New York's other Mafia bosses that the Manganos had planned to kill him, thereupon receiving permission to rule the family. Unfortunately, his mercurial temper – some said raving insanity – produced multiple murders and sparked friction with powerful mobsters including Vito Genovese and Meyer Lansky. Anastasia, now dubbed 'The Mad Hatter,' was so erratic that he once ordered the slaying of a civilian who turned in one of the FBI's Ten Most Wanted fugitives, then executed the hitman who carried out his impulsive order.

By 1957, Anastasia had his eye on Lansky's gambling empire in Cuba, demanding a piece of the action. He also swore vengeance against Genovese for a botched attempt to kill friend Frank Costello on May 2. Someone beat Anastasia to the punch on October 25, 1957, when two masked gunmen shot Albert dead in the barbershop of the Park Sheraton Hotel (now the Park Central).

Brother Anthony 'Tough Tony' Anastasio made peace with Genovese and was permitted to retain control of Brooklyn's waterfront. By 1962, suspecting Genovese of plotting against him, he approached FBI agents and offered to turn informer. However, cancer claimed his life on March 1, 1963, before the deal bore fruit.

Ramón Arellano Félix

Born in Tijuana, Mexico, on August 31, 1964, Ramón Arellano Félix joined brothers Benjamín, Eduardo, Francisco, Javier, Miguel and Ramón – plus four sisters – to create the drug-trafficking Tijuana Cartel in 1989; it was formed from remnants of the fractured Guadalajara Cartel led by lately-imprisoned uncle Miguel Ángel Félix Gallardo. Headquartered 25 km (16 miles) south of San Diego, California, the cartel smuggled tons of cocaine, heroin and marijuana into the United States over the next two decades, killing hundreds of victims in the process.

Active in 15 of Mexico's 31 states, the Tijuana Cartel conducts itself with ruthless violence. On September 17, 1997 – the day before Ramón Arellano Félix earned a spot on the FBI's Ten Most Wanted list as an international fugitive – cartel assassins slaughtered 12 residents of Ensenada. The murdered were said to be relatives of a drug dealer who owed the cartel money for a shipment. Such flamboyant crimes had a price, as police on both sides of the border focused on cartel leaders.

Brother Francisco was an early casualty, serving ten years in a Mexican prison (1994–2004), then was caught at sea with another drug shipment and extradited to the US in September 2006. Despite a June 2007 guilty plea

BELOW: An undated photograph of brothers Benjam□n (left) and Ram□n Arellano F□lix, prime movers in the Tijuana Cartel.

to charges of drug trafficking, he was released to Mexico in March 2008.

American prosecutors indicted brothers Benjamín and Ramón in May 2000. On February 10, 2002, police surprised Ramón in Mazatlán, killing him after he wounded an officer. Benjamín was captured alive on March 9, 2002.

Despite arrests at the top, the Tijuana Cartel remained active – and deadly. On April 26, 2008, cartel soldiers fought a pitched battle with rivals in the streets of Tijuana, leaving 17 gunmen dead and six more wounded. Police identified two of the dead as Arellano hitmen, based on trademark gold rings depicting Saint Death, a ghoulish figure erroneously thought by some gangsters to offer protection from harm. April's massacre brought Tijuana's drug-related murder toll to 190 for the year. Another 57 died within a single week of September 2008, including 12 corpses dumped together at an elementary school on September 29.

Mexican soldiers caught brother Eduardo Arellano Félix in Tijuana on October 26, 2008, whereupon control of the cartel passed to nephew Luis Sánchez Arellano. In retaliation, the syndicate declared open war on law enforcement officers. In February 2009, cartel soldiers broadcast threats against two specific Tijuana policemen, accompanied by drug ballads, then killed both officers within hours, followed by sarcastic radio 'condolences.' Another seven Tijuana policemen were gunned down together on April 28, 2009. Luis Sánchez Arellano remains at large.

BELOW: Mexican police guard the Federal Agency Investigation building in April 2002. Government and police officials were arrested on suspicion of corruption involving the Tijuana Cartel.

Gaetano Badalamenti

The mafioso known as 'Don Tanino' was born at Cinisi, in the Sicilian province of Palermo, on September 14, 1923. He was the last of nine children, discouraged from schooling by parents who put him to work on their hardscrabble farm at age ten. Conscripted into military service at 18, Badalamenti deserted in July 1943, when Allied troops invaded Sicily. His first known civilian offense came in 1946, when he was charged with kidnapping and conspiracy. The next year, police added a murder charge. Badalamenti fled, trailing an older brother to America, but narcotics officers arrested and deported him in 1950.

By then, Italian prosecutors had forgotten his youthful **indiscretions.** They also failed to press charges when Badalamenti was caught smuggling cigarettes in 1953, and again in 1957. Safe in Cinisi, he married, founded a construction business and bribed officials to build Palermo's new Punta Raisi Airport nearby. Aside from the windfall for his firm, the airport offered endless possibilities for theft and smuggling.

A car bomb killed top Cinisi mafioso, Cesare Manzella on April 26, 1963, clearing the throne for Badalamenti. At a time when Italian police were at war with the Mafia, seeking revenge for a bombing that killed seven officers in Ciaculli on June 30, 1963, Badalamenti earned appreciation from the *Carabinieri* (Italian police) by eradicating violence and street crime in Cinisi. With his base of operations secure, Badalamenti broadened his interests to include wholesale drug trafficking between Sicily and the United States.

RIGHT: A library photograph of Gaetano Badalamenti from the 1950s. The Sicilian mafioso had strong links to New York's Bonnano crime family.

In 1975, with Salvatore Catalano from New York's Bonanno crime family, Badalamenti established a network nicknamed the 'Pizza Connection,' since drugs were shipped to and distributed from pizzerias across the United States. Over the next nine years, the syndicate earned an estimated $1.65 billion from sales of cocaine and heroin. The operation's first snag occurred when Italian police caught mobsters smuggling large quantities of cash through Palermo's airport. An alert put FBI agents and New York police on the case, producing indictments of Badalamenti and 31 other defendants. Twenty-two of those accused were captured in America, while wiretaps led agents to arrest Badalamenti in Madrid, Spain.

The Pizza Connection trial in New York spanned 17 months, from October 24, 1985, to March 2, 1987, costing prosecutors $50 million. Only 22 of the original defendants were in court when trial began; nine others eluded arrest, while one died from natural causes. During the trial itself, another defendant was killed, with yet another wounded by unknown assailants. Turncoat Sicilian *pentitos* (repented criminals) Tommaso Buscetta

and Salvatore Contorno joined the list of prosecution witnesses, describing machinations of the smuggling ring in Italy. Jurors finally convicted 18 defendants, including Gaetano Badalamenti, who received a 47-year prison term. Badalamenti's son, Vito, was acquitted and later deported.

Still, Badalamenti's troubles were not over. A second federal jury convicted him of money laundering on June 22, 1987, adding another 45 years to his sentence. In 1999, an Italian court tried Badalamenti *in absentia* for the murder of journalist Mino Pecorelli, killed on March 20, 1979, to prevent publication of a Mafia exposé in the magazine *Osservatorio Politico*. The court acquitted Badalamenti and four codefendants, but Badalamenti's acquittal was reversed on appeal, on November 17, 2002, as allowed by Italian law. In yet another strange twist, Italy's Supreme Court once again cleared Badalamenti in that case, on October 30, 2003.

It hardly mattered, as the aging mafioso faced effective life imprisonment in the United States. On April 29, 2004, he died from heart failure at the Devens Federal Medical Center in Ayer, Massachusetts.

Joe Barboza

The former whaling port of New Bedford, Massachusetts, hosts a large Portuguese-American community. One of America's most notorious contract killers, Joseph Barboza, was born there on September 20, 1932, the second child of an alcoholic ex-convict and small-time boxer who abandoned his family in 1944. Barboza's simian appearance, complete with fang-like teeth and growling voice, earned him derisive nicknames as 'The Animal' and 'Wild Thing,' which were mirrored in outbursts of violence. A typical incident occurred in Revere, Massachusetts, where Barboza slapped an elderly man in a barroom. Chastised by mafioso, Henry Tameleo and ordered to keep his hands off the tavern's patrons, Barboza then bit the man's ear before telling Tameleo, 'I didn't touch him with my hands.' Later, undocumented stories claimed that Barboza cannibalized some of his murder victims.

In 1949, Barboza led a gang of teenage burglars who were dubbed 'The Cream Puff Bandits' after vandalizing restaurants with whipping cream. Arrested for that spree in 1950, Barboza drew a five-year sentence and apparently forged his first links to New England's Mafia while imprisoned. A brief escape in 1953 increased

his sentence, ending with parole in 1958. Barboza's reputation for violence, both in prison and the free world, made him useful to the Mafia family led by Raymond Patriarca from Providence, Rhode Island. While barred from full Mafia membership by his Portuguese lineage, Barboza still served Patriarca as a loan shark and enforcer,

ABOVE: Barboza testifies before a Washington DC House Crime Committee regarding unsolved murders in May 1972.

linked to 26 known murders.

Barboza's most notorious hit occurred on March 12, 1965, when he and others shot Teddy Deegan in Chelsea, Massachusetts. Local FBI agents were warned of the slaying two days in advance, but did nothing to stop it for fear of exposing paid informers, whose number included Deegan's murder accomplice, Vincent Flemmi. An FBI memo dated June 9, 1965, read: 'From all indications, [Flemmi] is going to continue to commit murder...The informant's potential outweighs the risks.' Police arrested four suspects for Deegan's murder in 1967, and convicted them at trial in August 1968, based on false testimony from Barboza – by then, a government informer. After the trial, Agent Paul Rico laughed at how 'funny' it was to frame 'four pigeons' for a crime they did not commit.

Barboza's shift from hitman to state's witness came in June 1967, after a year of tension between himself and members of the Patriarca family. His high profile in Boston and his arrogant disdain for certain mafiosi soured Barboza's relations with the syndicate. When police arrested Barboza on weapons charges in October 1966, Patriarca not only declined to post $100,000 bail, but apparently murdered two friends of Barboza's who tried to raise the money. Barboza sat in jail until December, when he was convicted and received a five-year sentence. Six months later, Vincent Flemmi's brother tipped Barboza to a contract on his life and Barboza promptly joined the ranks of FBI informers. By October 1967, his testimony had produced indictments naming Patriarca and eight others as slayers of three murder victims.

In exchange for his cooperation, Barboza was freed in March 1969 and relocated to California, where he enrolled in culinary school – and continued killing. In 1971, he pled guilty to second-degree murder and was sentenced to five years at Folsom Prison. There, he dabbled in poetry, composing odes with titles such as 'Boston Gang War' and 'The Mafia Double Crosses.' Paroled in October 1975, Barboza rented a cheap apartment in the name of 'James Donati' and befriended a transplanted Boston thug named James Chalmas. It was his last mistake, as Chalmas evidently tipped New England mafiosi to their target's whereabouts.

On February 11, 1976, Barboza left Chalmas's apartment in San Francisco, California, and was approaching his car when four close-range shotgun blasts snuffed out his life. Although armed with a pistol, Barboza had no chance to fight back. An FBI bug later caught Massachusetts mafioso Ilario Zannino boasting that Barboza was killed by one J.R. Russo.

Barboza's death solved nothing for the men whom he had framed, with FBI complicity, in 1967. Henry Tameleo died in prison during 1985, followed by Louis Greco ten years later. Joseph Salvati was paroled in 1997, while Peter Limone remained in custody until 2001, when a federal court vacated his conviction and Salvati's. Both sued the FBI and won their case in July 2007, receiving damages in the amount of $101.7 million.

As for the G-men who participated in the frame-up, Agent John Morris escaped prosecution because the statute of limitations had expired on his offenses. Agent Paul Rico died in 2004, while awaiting trial for the 1981 murder of Oklahoma businessman Roger Wheeler. Agent John Connolly was convicted of bribery and racketeering in 2002, receiving a ten-year sentence. In 2008, he stood trial for arranging the 1982 murder of government witness John Callahan in Florida. Jurors convicted Connolly on November 6, 2008, and he received a 40-year sentence on January 15, 2009.

Antonio Bardellino

Camorra boss, Antonio Bardellino was born in 1945 at San Cipriano d'Aversa, in the Italian province of Caserta. He founded the Casalesi clan, based in Casal di Principe, midway between Naples and Caserta, but cultivated relationships with other Camorra families nationwide. Police informer Pasquale Galasso described Bardellino as 'the reference point of all Camorra clans, even the ones that could not stand him. With his charisma he managed to maintain a certain equilibrium in Campania.' Bardellino also broke with Camorra tradition by maintaining links to the Sicilian Mafia, a fact that led to difficulty for him in the 1980s.

His first Mafia alliance involved the Porta Nuova family of Giuseppe 'Pippo' Calò, who allegedly performed a blood-oath ceremony granting Bardellino full Mafia membership in 1975. From smuggling cigarettes, Bardellino soon progressed to trafficking in heroin and cocaine. His Sicilian drug-running partners included Gaetano Badalamenti, Stefano Bontade, Tommaso Buscetta, Rosario Riccobono and Salvatore Riina. Unfortunately for Bardellino, Bontade's murder on April 23, 1981, launched Sicily's so-called 'Second

Mafia War' – the 'first' having occurred in 1961–63, claiming 68 lives – and disrupted the flow of illicit drugs until peace was restored with Riina's Corleonesi Mafia faction triumphant.

Sicily's war reverberated on the mainland, as Salvatore Riina urged the Camorra's Nuvoletta clan to murder rival, Tommaso Buscetta. Lorenzo Nuvoletta passed the contract to longtime smuggling partner Bardellino, but Antonio dragged his feet out of friendship for Buscetta, allowing the target to flee Italy and hide out in Brazil. Captured there in 1982, Buscetta would return to Italy as a police informer, with disastrous results for the Mafia.

Bardellino, fearing retribution from the Nuvoletta family, likewise took his leave of Italy, embarking on a flight through Spain, Brazil and the Dominican Republic. Early in 1983, he sought a truce, arranging to meet with Aniello Nuvoletta in Zurich, Switzerland, but police were waiting at the site and took Nuvoletta into custody. Spanish authorities arrested Bardellino in Barcelona, during November 1983, then unexpectedly released him on bail, whereupon he vanished. Soon afterward, gunmen killed Ciro Nuvoletta on the family's farm at Marano di Napoli, northwest of Naples. Two months later, another raid slaughtered eight members of the Nuvoletta-allied Gionta clan and wounded 24 at the Circolo dei Pescatori in Torre Annunziata.

With victory in hand, Bardellino pursued a new spirit of cooperation between underworld families with creation of *Nuova Famiglia* (the 'New Family'). Designed to counter the rising power of the New Camorra Organization founded by Raffaele Cutolo, *Nuova Famiglia* combined Bardellino's clan with surviving Gionta and Nuvoletta family members, Carmine Alfieri's family from Saviano, Pasquale Galasso's gang in Naples, Luigi Vollaro's family from Portici and Michele Zaza's Mafia-allied Camorra clan, also active in Naples.

The power of that combination still could not protect Bardellino from prosecution, however. New indictments drove him from Europe in 1987, settling at Buzios, Brazil, a seaside resort two hours north of Rio de Janeiro. It was there, on May 26, 1988, that police claim Bardellino was murdered by right-hand-man Mario Iovine. The story remains unconfirmed, since Bardellino's corpse was never found and Iovine himself was slain in Portugal, in 1991.

Clyde Barrow and Bonnie Parker

Clyde Chestnut Barrow was born outside Telico, Texas, on March 24, 1909. He learned to steal from older brother Marvin, known as 'Buck,' and rarely tried his hand at honest work. One such effort, as a delivery boy for Western Union, introduced Clyde to Ted Hinton, later a member of the posse that would track Barrow to his death. Clyde logged his first arrest in 1926, for failure to return a rented car, then another with Buck for stealing turkeys. A two-year string of burglaries, hold-ups and car thefts finally sent him to prison in April 1930. Barrow may have committed his first murder there, of an inmate who raped him, but no charges were filed. Paroled in February 1932, he returned to Dallas and met the love of his life.

Bonnie Elizabeth Parker was born in Rowena, Texas, on October 1, 1910. Her father died in 1914, whereupon her mother moved the family to West Dallas. Bonnie excelled in school, but married hoodlum Roy Thornton in September 1926. He abandoned her in January 1929 and later went to prison, but they never divorced. Meeting Clyde at a relative's home, soon after his parole, she fell madly in love and devoted the rest of her short life to him, logging her first arrest after a bungled burglary in April 1932.

Days later, on April 30, Clyde and unidentified accomplices killed merchant J.N. Bucher during a hold-up in Kaufman, Texas. Bonnie rejoined him in June, after a grand jury declined to indict her for burglary.

On August 5, police in Stringtown, Oklahoma, confronted Clyde and two cohorts, Raymond Hamilton and Everett Milligan, for drinking bootleg whiskey at a dance. The three opened fire, killing Sheriff C.G.

Maxwell and Deputy Eugene Moore. The gang killed a fourth victim, Howard Hall, on October 11, 1933, while stealing $28 and some groceries from his shop in Sherman, Texas. The year ended badly on Christmas Day, as Clyde and accomplice W.D. Jones stole a car in Temple, Texas, killing owner Doyle Johnson. Eleven days later, Clyde, Bonnie and Jones walked into a trap which had been set for other criminals in Tarrant County, Texas, where Clyde killed Deputy Sheriff Malcolm Davis.

Buck Barrow left prison on March 22, 1933, with a full pardon but no thought of reform. Accompanied by wife Blanche, he joined Clyde, Bonnie and Jones in Joplin, Missouri. The reunion was rowdy, including drunken late-night parties and the accidental discharge of a Browning Automatic Rifle Clyde while cleaning in their apartment. Neighbors summoned police, who arrived on April 13, thinking they had found a group of bootleggers. Instead, they stumbled into sudden death, as gunfire claimed the lives of Newton County Constable, Wes Harryman and Joplin Detective and Harry McGinnis. The gang escaped with minor wounds, leaving behind a cache of evidence including Buck's release papers and marriage license, undeveloped photos – including a now-famous shot of Bonnie with a cigar – and one of her poems, 'The Story of Suicide Sal'.

Instantly famous, the gang embarked on a dead-end

ABOVE: American outlaw Bonnie Parker playfully points a shotgun at her partner Clyde Barrow in 1932.

releasing them unharmed. On June 10, 1933, Clyde crashed their car outside Wellington, Texas, leaving Bonnie's right leg badly burned. A farmer's family offered some help, and was repaid when Jones accidentally blasted the hand of one family member with a shotgun.

While hiding out in Fort Smith, Arkansas, Buck and Jones staged an abortive robbery in nearby Alma, killing Marshal Henry Humphrey on June 26. Propelled into flight once more, the gang checked into a tourist court near Platte City, Missouri, on July 18. Suspicious owner Neal Houser tipped police, whose arrival the following day sparked another pitched battle. The gang wounded three officers and escaped once more, but Buck and Blanche were wounded, with Buck shot through the head. Surprised again on July 24, while camped at an abandoned amusement park outside Dexter, Iowa, Clyde, Bonnie and Jones escaped with wounds, while Buck and Blanche were captured. Buck died on July 29, while Blanche later received a ten-year sentence for attempted murder of an officer wounded in the Platte City shootout.

odyssey that carried them from the Midwest to Texas and back again, executing small-time robberies along the way, sometimes abducting witnesses and then

The violent trek wore on. Bonnie and Clyde were wounded again in an ambush on November 22, 1933, while visiting relatives near Sowers, Texas. Six days later a

Dallas grand jury indicted Bonnie and Clyde for murder. On January 16, 1934, the gang staged a prison break in Texas, liberating inmates Ray Hamilton and Henry Methvin while fatally wounding Major Joe Crowson. Prison authorities then hired ex-Texas Ranger Frank Hamer to track the gang without regard to jurisdiction and bring them to heel.

On April 1, 1934, Barrow and Henry Methvin killed highway patrolmen H.D. Murphy and Edward Wheeler at Grapevine, Texas. Dallas papers headlined the story, including false reports that Bonnie stood over the bodies, spraying them with bullets. Public hostility increased on April 6, when the gang killed Constable William Campbell near Commerce, Oklahoma, also wounding the chief of police.

Meanwhile, Frank Hamer tracked Henry Methvin to his Louisiana home and coerced Methvin's father into arranging a trap for Bonnie and Clyde. Hamer's party – including Ted Hinton and four other officers – arranged a highway ambush outside Gibsland, using Methvin's father as bait. When Bonnie and Clyde arrived on May 23, 1934, the six riflemen fired without warning, riddling Clyde's car and its occupants with more than 180 bullets. Both died without reaching their weapons, which included several automatic rifles, sawn-off semi-automatic shotguns and assorted pistols.

While Bonnie and Clyde did 'go down together' as predicted in one of her poems, they were buried miles apart. Her headstone

RIGHT: Frank Hamer (bottom right) and his law enforcement posse who were responsible for shooting and killing the notorious outlaws.

BELOW: Bonnie Parker, posing with pistol and cigar. This photograph was one of several recovered from a raid on the gang's apartment in April 1933.

bears an ironic inscription: 'As the flowers are all made sweeter by the sunshine and the dew, so this old world is made brighter by the lives of folks like you.'

Gang member W.D. Jones received a 15-year sentence for his crimes in October 1934. Ray Hamilton died in the electric chair at the Texas State Penitentiary in Huntsville on May 10, 1935. Henry Methvin served ten years of a life sentence, paroled in 1946, then passed out drunk on railroad tracks in April 1948 and was crushed by a passing train.

Sam Battaglia

The Battaglia brothers – Augie, Frank, Paul and Salvatore – were products of Chicago's Little Italy, born in the early years of the 20th century. Salvatore, known as 'Sam,' joined the growing family on June 30, 1908, and did not hesitate to follow his brothers' felonious footsteps when he was able. All joined the Forty-Two Gang, which produced such leading lights of the Chicago syndicate as Tony Accardo and Sam Giancana, with Paul serving as leader for a time and later operating a saloon.

Sam joined the bootlegging gang led by Johnny Torrio and Al Capone in 1924, earning his nickname 'Teets' in his role as a collector of overdue cash from gamblers, whom he would threaten to 'bust in da teets [teeth].' Arrested 25 times during his long career and, suspected of seven murders, Battaglia first made headlines on November 17, 1930, when he robbed Mayor William Thompson's wife of jewelry valued at $15,500 and disarmed police bodyguard Peter O'Malley. Two weeks later, on December 1, he was jailed as the getaway driver for a gang that robbed a local high-stakes poker game, leaving one of the gamblers dead.

Battaglia was free on bail when he tried to rob a speakeasy on New Year's Eve and shot Detective Martin Joyce. His next arrest involved the kidnapping of wealthy auto dealer, Louis Kaplan for $100,000 ransom, but Battaglia beat that charge – and the rest – with assistance from syndicate lawyer and fixer Sidney Korshak.

Two of his brothers were less fortunate. Augie died in a 1931 shootout with Chicago police, during one of the Windy City's many labor wars, with Sam and Frank forced to attend their brother's funeral in handcuffs. Paul turned to armed robbery at Prohibition's end, unwisely targeting bookmakers protected by The Outfit. Frank Nitti ordered his death in 1938, and Paul was snatched from the street on August 27, shot twice in the head, then

ABOVE: Sam Battaglia invoked the Fifth Amendment 60 times during questioning by the Senate Labor Rackets Committee in July 1968.

tossed from a speeding car.

On August 18, 1943, police stopped Battaglia and Marcello 'Marshall' Caifano in Chicago, cruising in a rented car. A search of the vehicle revealed a rifle, sawn-off shotgun, five pistols and a hand grenade. The case was dropped when both mobsters denied any knowledge of the weapons, claiming they had not examined the car's trunk upon taking delivery. Thereafter, Outfit soldiers made a point of driving rented cars when they embarked on shady errands.

By 1950, Sam Battaglia was known in Chicago as

an overseer of The Outfit's narcotics traffic, a multi-millionaire in his own right and proud owner of a lavish Illinois horse-breeding ranch. Local operations included control of illegal gambling on Chicago's West Side, and in the suburbs of Bellwood, Elmwood Park, Melrose Park and Schiller Park. On the 'legitimate' side, Battaglia's crew owned an auto dealership on North Cicero Avenue, where the unsolved theft of 300 cars in one night resulted in bankruptcy and a huge insurance payoff. In 1958, Battaglia risked a citation for contempt of Congress, pleading the Fifth Amendment 60 times to avoid answering questions posed by the US Senate's Select Committee on Improper Activities in Labor and Management. Charges were not pursued, however, and Chicago associates claimed Battaglia was less concerned about self-incrimination than public embarrassment from his mangling of proper English.

Some observers thought Battaglia might be next in line to rule The Outfit in 1966, when FBI surveillance hounded boss Sam Giancana into Mexican exile, but war nearly erupted when Fiore 'Fifi' Buccieri made incursions into Battaglia's North Side gambling preserve. Tony Accardo and Paul Ricca called a meeting to negotiate a truce, but the gathering almost dergenerated into bloodshed when underboss Joseph 'Mr. Clean' Ferriola took Fiore's side and Battaglia loyalist Felix 'Milwaukee Phil' Alderisio threatened to tear Ferriola apart 'limb by limb.'

Battaglia was briefly distracted from the action in Chicago during May 1966, when a grand jury indicted his son, Sam Joseph, for violating the Universal Military Training and Service Act. Specifically, authorities charged that young Battaglia lied repeatedly to his draft board between February and December 1964, concealing evidence of a divorce that would have made him eligible for military service. Sam senior retained Washington celebrity attorney Edward Bennett Williams to defend his wayward boy, but all in vain.

BELOW: 'Teets' Battaglia in handcuffs after being indicted on extortion charges in 1966.

On February 7, 1968, Sam Joseph received a two-year prison term, eligible for parole if and when he agreed to military induction. The US Court of Appeals rejected Sam Joseph's challenge to that sentence in March 1969.

Meanwhile, father Sam had more legal problems of his own. Late in 1966, federal prosecutors indicted him on charges of extorting $48,500 from a Chicago construction firm. Convicted at trial on May 8, 1967, Battaglia was held in jail as 'dangerous to the community' pending fruitless appeal of his conviction. Diagnosed with terminal cancer in 1973, Battaglia was paroled on August 29 and died at his home in Oak Park, Illinois, on September 8.

Marcos Arturo Beltrán Leyva

The eldest of five brothers, born on September 27, 1961, at Badiraguato, in the Mexican state of Sinaloa, Marcos Arturo Beltrán Leyva launched the family tradition of drug trafficking as a member of the Sinaloa Cartel, founded by Pedro Avilés Pérez in the early 1970s. Federal police killed Avilés in September 1978, and the Beltrán Leyva brothers – including Alfredo, Carlos, Héctor and Mario Alberto – subsequently abandoned successor Joaquín Guzmán Loera to create their own cartel in Sinaloa, fielding an army of 1,000 gunmen to defend their turf.

While the syndicate produces its own heroin, marijuana and methamphetamines, cocaine is purchased from Colombia's Norte del Valle Cartel, presently led by fugitive Carlos Alberto Rentería Mantilla. Sidelines include human trafficking, money laundering, extortion, gun-running, ransom kidnapping and contract murders.

The organization's development followed the usual course of corruption and mayhem, including hundreds of homicides. Sinaloa's murder rate soared from 215 in 1987 to an average 650 per year through the 1990s, with victims including 47 attorneys, 40 state policemen and 12 university professors, plus hundreds of farmers, merchants and suspected drug traffickers. Recipients of payoffs from the Beltrán Leyva Cartel range from local police to the highest ranks of government. One identified collaborator was Noé Ramírez Mandujano, Mexico's top drug-enforcement officer from 2006 to August 2008, who received $450,000 per month to warn the cartel of impending raids.

RIGHT: Marcos Arturo Beltrⁿn Leyva made a career of drug smuggling, people trafficking, money laundering, extortion, gun-running, ransom kidnapping and contract murders.

Despite that help, the cartel took its first serious hit on January 20, 2008, with the arrest of Alfredo Beltrán Leyva on charges of plotting to murder Federal Police commissioner Édgar Eusebio Millán Gómez and other high-ranking officials. Alfredo's brothers blamed Sinaloa Cartel leader Joaquín Guzmán Loera for the arrest and sent a team of 15 soldiers to kill Guzmán's son at a Sinaloa shopping mall. Thereafter, Marcos Beltrán Leyva forged a mutual-defense alliance with *Los Zetas*, a team of Mexican army deserters initially fielded by the Gulf Cartel as elite contract killers. Alliance with the Gulf Cartel itself soon followed, with the Beltrán Leyva Cartel joined in battle against its Sinaloa rivals and La Familia Michoacána, another drug syndicate based in the state of Michoacán.

As violence flourished, on May 30, 2008, US President George W. Bush named Marcos Beltrán Leyva and his network as special targets under the Foreign Narcotics Kingpin Designation Act of 1999. Under that law the government may freeze assets, deny visas and take other punitive actions against any individual found transacting business of any kind with identified drug 'kingpins.' Unimpressed by that announcement, or the reward of 30 million pesos ($2.35 million) offered in Mexico for the capture of any Beltrán Leyva brother, Marcos and *Los Zetas* continued their violent rampage along the US-Mexican border, reducing some smaller communities to the status of virtual ghost towns.

On December 11, 2009, a strike force of Mexican marines sought to capture Marcos in Ahuatepec, near Cuernavaca, where he had staged a Christmas party featuring singer Ramón Ayala, balladeers Los Cadetes

BELOW: The bloody aftermath of a raid by Mexican Navy and Army in December 2009 which led to the death of Beltrⁿn Leyva.

de Linares and two dozen prostitutes. Beltrán escaped in the ensuing battle, which left three of his gunmen and an innocent bystander dead, while the raiders seized $280,000 in cash, 20 guns and 1,700 rounds of ammunition.

Five days later, another military squad traced Marcos to a posh apartment in Cuernavaca, touching off a 90-minute firefight. Beltrán's soldiers lobbed grenades and telephoned for reinforcements, finally requiring an army tank and helicopter to end the standoff. When the smoke cleared, Marcos and three cohorts were dead from marine gunfire, while a fourth committed suicide. A marine, Melquisedet Angulo Córdova, also died in the shootout. On December 22, one day after his funeral, cartel gunmen murdered several members of Angulo Córdova's family.

Eight days later, on December 30, police in Culiacán stopped Carlos Beltrán Leyva for a traffic violation, seizing a rifle, pistol, ammunition and cocaine from his vehicle. Despite a false driver's license in the name of 'Carlos Gámez Orpineda,' he was identified and remains in custody. Command of the cartel then passed to 45-year-old Hector Beltrán Leyva, still at large. Outstanding rewards for his capture include 26 million pesos ($2.1 million) from the Mexican government and $5 million from the US State Department.

Donovan Bennett

Jamaican gangster Donovan Bennett, nicknamed 'Bulbie' for reasons still unclear, was born in Spanish Town, west of Kingston, sometime in 1964. As a youth, he joined a local gang known as Clans Massive, one of several 'Yardie' syndicates said to control Jamaica's illicit drug trade. The Yardie (or 'Yawdie') term initially applied to residents of Trenchtown, in West Kingston, a housing project erected for homeless victims of Hurricane Charlie in 1951, but now is broadly applied to organized gangs – sometimes also called 'posses.'

While details of his early life are vague, reports claim that Bennett rose to command Clans Massive after murdering his predecessor, Derrick 'Puppy String' Eccleston, on May 12, 1993. Despite heightened police scrutiny, Bennett led his fellow Clansmen in a war against Spanish Town rivals from the One Order Gang ruled by Andrew 'Bun Man' Hope. While that campaign was in progress, Bulbie's soldiers fattened their warchest by extorting funds from taxi drivers and other commercial targets in Clarendon, May Pen, Old Harbour, Portmore and St. Catherine. By the time he fled to Britain under an assumed name in 2001, investigators pegged Bennett's personal fortune at $100 million and ranked him as Jamaica's most-wanted fugitive.

In his absence, Superintendent Kenneth Wade documented evidence of Clans Massive's collaboration with the People's National Party, a socialist movement that claimed affiliation with 32 separate criminal posses.

The SLP's primary rival, the Jamaica Labour Party, responded in kind by employing members of 14 posses to stage riotous demonstrations on election days. Bulbie himself was less concerned with politics than profit, and the lure of money drew him back to Jamaica in 2004, where he resided quietly in Rock River, Clarendon.

Police found him there on October 30, 2005, surrounding Bennett's home at the climax of a long search dubbed 'Operation Kingfish.' Officers ringed the house at 5:00 a.m. and called for Bulbie's surrender, but Bennett and a chauffeur-bodyguard known only as 'Nathan' responded with gunfire. After an extended battle, the house fell silent. Police stormed the building, discovering Bennett and Nathan dead, each clutching a pistol. Bennett's weapon, a .50-caliber Desert Eagle Action Express automatic, ranks among the most powerful handguns on Earth. While scouring the house, officers found an uninjured woman hiding in one of the home's seven bedrooms and briefly detained her for questioning.

Bennett's death provoked violent demonstrations in Spanish Town, where residents blocked streets, fired on police and burned effigies of National Security Minister

Dr. Peter Phillips. In Clarendon, meanwhile, Bulbie's neighbors were stunned to discover that Jamaica's most-wanted outlaw had lived among them. They were troubled by reports that Clans Massive planned to kill ten local residents in retaliation for Bennett's slaying.

Charles Binaggio

Future mobster Charles Binaggio was born in Beaumont, Texas, on January 12, 1909, and moved to Kansas City, Missouri, with his family, as a child. Living on the heavily Italian North Side, he witnessed both the classic 'Black Hand' extortion rackets and the rising power of mafioso John Lazia, who controlled most organized crime in Kansas City by the 1920s, collaborating with political boss Tom Pendergast and his Jackson County Democratic Club. As a teenager Binaggio found work in one of Lazia's gambling clubs, advancing in the mob from there.

In 1930, war erupted between Lazia's family and the Denver Mafia led by Joe Roma. That December, Denver police raided an apartment occupied by Binaggio and two other Missouri mafiosi, seizing a small arsenal and charging all three with weapons violations. Those counts were reduced to vagrancy, and Binaggio remained in Denver through early 1931, when officers detained him a second time. Back in Kansas City by summer, he was jailed on July 22 after a shootout that killed Prohibition agent Curtis Burke. Those charges were again reduced to vagrancy after police determined Burke was shot by roving bandit 'Pretty Boy' Floyd.

Lazia's control of Kansas City slackened in 1933. FBI agents suspected him of plotting the Union Station massacre which killed four lawmen on June 17, and another firefight on August 12 – between Lazia's soldiers and rivals led by Joe Lusco – left Lazia lieutenants Sam Scola and Gus Fascone dead. In early 1934, jurors convicted Lazia of tax evasion, and while he appealed his one-year sentence, the war with Lusco continued. Drive-by gunmen murdered Lazia on July 10 and, while police grilled Joe Lusco, the crime remains officially unsolved. Binaggio served as one of his mentor's pallbearers three days later, subsequently elevated to Mafia underboss serving Charles 'Charley the Wop' Carollo. Federal jurors did Binaggio a favor on

October 30, 1939, convicting both Carollo and Tom Pendergast on tax evasion charges. Both were imprisoned, leaving underboss Binaggio to rule the roost.

His reign was nearly disrupted in November 1941, when Binaggio struck and killed a middle-aged pedestrian with his car. Manslaughter charges were dismissed, and while employment of a full-time chauffeur solved his driving problems, Binaggio faced other difficulties. Feds arrested him, with 12 others, for liquor law violations on December 21, 1943. Jurors acquitted Binaggio, but he was suspected of killing a key prosecution witness. Binaggio also dabbled in politics. His hand-picked slate of candidates were beaten at the polls in 1944, and Binaggio was implicated in a 1946 voting scandal – until thieves blew the election board's safe and stole hundreds of suspect ballots on May 28, 1947. Between those events, in 1945, Binaggio was arrested once more for operating a gambling casino, the Green Hills Country Club, in Missouri's Platt County. Detained with his father-in-law and four other associates, Binnagio avoided prosecution. He helped elect Governor Forrest Smith in 1948, based on Smith's promise to permit wide-open gambling in Kansas City and St. Louis, but Smith reneged after he was inaugurated and appointed law enforcement agents hostile to the Mafia.

Smith's campaign investors – Charles 'Trigger Happy' Fischetti of the Chicago Outfit chief among them – were not pleased. Matters went from bad to worse in 1950, with the creation of the US Senate's Special Committee to Investigate Crime in Interstate Commerce, led by Estes Kefauver. Republican committee members sought to focus on crime in traditional Democratic preserves such as Kansas City, where the late Pendergast machine had groomed and promoted sitting president Harry Truman from a local judgeship to the White House. Binaggio, who operated from an office at the First Ward Democratic Club near downtown Kansas City, was an irresistible target.

Someone, somewhere, determined that he should not have the opportunity to testify. On the night of April 5, 1950, Binaggio left bodyguard/chauffeur Nick Pena at a mob-run tavern, announcing that he had to deal

ABOVE: Mrs Charles Binaggio, wife of the slain mobster, is led from church following his funeral in April 1950.

with certain business at the Democratic Club. Soon after 8:00 p.m. a neighbor of the club heard gunshots, but failed to alert police. Eight hours later a passing pedestrian noted that the club's front door was open, with a sound of running water audible inside. When officers arrived, they found Binaggio and underboss Charles 'Mad Dog' Gargotta dead, each shot four times in the head with two different .32-caliber pistols. Their executioners remain unidentified today.

With Binaggio's murder, control of Kansas City passed to a Mafia board known locally as 'the Five Iron Men.' According to published reports, their number included Sicilian-born James Balestrere, former Lazia rival Joseph DeLuca, Joseph 'Scarface' DiGiovanni, his brother Peter DiGiovanni and native New Yorker Anthony Robert Gizzo. Three of the five – Balestrere, DeLuca and Gizzo – died from natural causes during 1952–53, leaving Nicholas Civella to command the family until his 1977 conviction for illegal gambling.

Griselda Blanco

Born on Colombia's Caribbean coast, on February 15, 1943, Griselda Blanco moved to Medellín with her family at age three. Her father soon abandoned his wife and children, while Griselda's mother drowned her sorrows in liquor, becoming an abusive alcoholic. Decades later, in the 2008 film *Cocaine Cowboys II: Hustlin' with the Godmother,* ex-lover Charles Cosby claimed that Griselda kidnapped a boy from Medellín's slum at age 11, demanding ransom, then shot her victim when no payment was forthcoming. Employed as a child prostitute by age 14, Blanco graduated to drug smuggling after she emigrated to Queens, New York, in the early 1970s.

In time, Griselda's Medellín connections made her one of America's top cocaine importers, variously known as 'Mama Coca' and *La Madrina* ('The Godmother'). On the domestic front, despite overt bisexuality, Blanco married three times – and allegedly killed all three husbands, thus earning another nickname: 'The Black Widow.' Those unions produced four sons, the youngest of whom – Michael Corleone Blanco – she named for a fictional character from *The Godfather* novel and films. (Blanco also named her German shepherd 'Hitler.') Three of her boys would ultimately be imprisoned in America, then deported to Colombia where rival mobsters killed them on arrival.

Following a 1975 indictment for drug smuggling in New York, Blanco fled south to Florida and established a new syndicate in Miami. There, she assembled a private army known as *Los Pistoleros,* with membership restricted to gunmen who committed murder and presented Blanco with a severed portion of the victim's corpse. Deemed responsible for some 200 homicides in Miami and environs, including some victims slain for sport when she indulged her personal whims as a serial killer, Blanco amassed a fortune used to support her obsession with jewelry and nubile young women. All of her drug 'mules' were female, shuttling between Colombia and the US in lingerie designed by Blanco, sporting pockets for cocaine.

On July 11, 1979, three of Blanco's gunmen staged a massacre at Miami's Dadeland Mall, killing two rivals and wounding four bystanders with machine-gun fire. That incident made Blanco a primary target for local police and the federal Drug Enforcement Administration's Central Tactical Unit, but pervasive corruption and fear still shielded Blanco. In 1982, while stalking rival dealer Chucho Castro, Blanco's gunmen accidentally killed Castro's two-year-old son. A year later, after executing competitors Alfred and Grizel Lorenzo, lead assassin Jorge Ayala angered Blanco by leaving the couple's three children alive. Her rage persuaded Ayala to turn state's evidence as a means of self-preservation, but Blanco's erratic behavior – smoking an estimated $7 million worth of crack cocaine, compelling men at gunpoint to have sex with her – already marked the beginning of her downfall.

In 1984 Blanco moved her headquarters to Irvine, California, where DEA agents arrested her the following year. Extradited to Florida, she received a ten-year sentence for drug trafficking, then was indicted for murder in 1993. A 1998 plea bargain added 20 years to her sentence, but she was still paroled and deported to Colombia on June 6, 2004. A photo snapped at Bogotá's airport in May 2007 indicates that Blanco may still be alive.

Joe Bonanno

Giuseppe Bonanno was born into a Mafia family in Castellammare del Golfo, Sicily, on January 18, 1905. His father brought the family to New York City in 1908, running a tavern and a pasta factory in Brooklyn, then returned to Sicily in 1912 to escape escalating tension with the rival Buccellato family. Giuseppe enrolled at the Joeni Trabia Nautical Institute in Palermo, hoping to pursue a naval career, but his anti-fascist activities led to expulsion and drove him back to the US in 1924. He entered Florida illegally, from Cuba, then returned to New York at the time Prohibition turned small-time gangsters into millionaires.

O n arrival in Manhattan, Bonanno joined the crime family led by fellow Castellammarese Salvaltore Maranzano. His business acumen impressed the would-be 'Boss of Bosses,' whose ambition sparked a war with rival Giuseppe 'Joe the Boss' Masseria for control of New York – and, by extension, of the Mafia throughout America. Masseria underboss Lucky Luciano engineered his leader's murder in April 1931, then learned that Maranzano planned to kill him over Luciano's refusal to abandon Jewish allies Meyer Lansky and Bugsy Siegel. Luciano struck first, using soldiers provided by Lepke Buchalter, and thus eliminated Maranzano on September 10, 1931.

LEFT: Joe Bonanno surrenders to federal authorities in New York in May 1966 after a 19-month worldwide manhunt.

RIGHT: Bonanno became rich on the illegal profits of Prohibition after arriving in America for the second time in 1924.

BELOW: A chart created by the Senate crime committee in 1963 showing the structure of the Bonanno mafia family.

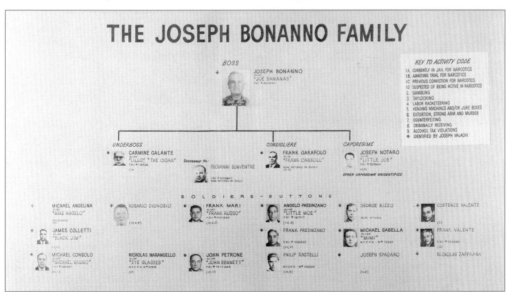

THE JOSEPH BONANNO FAMILY

ABOVE: Salvatore (Bill) Bonanno, son of mafia don Joe, talks with an FBI agent following his arrest in December 1964.

naturalization in 1953, citing a $450 fine imposed for violating federal labor laws a decade earlier, but the case was dismissed. Four years later, decades of underworld peace began unraveling with an attempt on the life of mafioso Frank Costello in May 1957, the barbershop murder of Albert Anastasia in October and a police raid at Apalachin, New York, in November that saw 63 mafiosi arrested and their national network exposed. Bonanno skipped that meeting, but three of his *caporegimes* – Giovanni Bonventre, Natale Evola and Anthony Riela – were briefly detained.

In October 1963, informer Joe Valachi named Bonanno as a top mafioso and aired his 'Joe Bananas' nickname in televised testimony before the US Senate. Around the same time, Bonanno conspired with Joseph Magliocco, boss of the former Profaci Family, to kill New York bosses Carlo Gambino, Gaetano 'Tommy' Lucchese and Stefano Magaddino in a ruthless power play to seize control of the Mafia. Magliocco assigned the murder contracts to underboss Joe Colombo, who seized a golden opportunity for advancement by informing the prospective targets of Magliocco's treachery. The Mafia's ruling commission summoned Bonanno and Magliocco to explain themselves, but Bonanno refused to appear. Magliocco, meanwhile, confessed and blamed Bonanno for the plot, escaping with a $50,000 fine and forced retirement, climaxed by a fatal heart attack on December 28, 1963.

With Bonanno still missing, the commission expelled him *in absentia* and placed Gaspar DiGregorio in charge of Bonanno's family. Thus began the 'Banana War,' also dubbed 'The Banana Split,' as a faction led by Joe Bonanno and son Salvatore fought to regain control

Although Bonanno was steeped in Old World traditions of Mafia 'honor' and 'respect,' he accepted the victory of Luciano's rebels and emerged from the Castellammarese War as head of a new family, one of five created by Luciano to rule New York in a spirit of mutual cooperation.

To avoid future legal problems, Bonanno left America in 1938, then re-entered legally via Detroit and applied for US citizenship, which was granted in 1945. Immigration officials sought to revoke Bonanno's from DiGregorio. Joe disappeared on October 21, 1964, conveniently snatched from a Manhattan street at gunpoint on the eve of his scheduled testimony before a federal grand jury. While reporters speculated on his chances of survival, Salvatore 'Bill' Bonanno carried on the fight, himself nearly killed in a machine-gun ambush in January 1966, with over 500 shots fired. Joe Bonanno resurfaced in May 1966, claiming that he was 'held captive' upstate for 19 months by cousin Stefano Magaddino's family in Buffalo, but most crime historians regard the abduction as a sham. Bonanno's soldiers were holding their ground when he suffered a heart attack in February 1968, thereafter agreeing to leave New York and retire in Tucson, Arizona.

Bonanno had barely arrived in the desert when a series of bombings and shootings occurred, targeting his home and that of Detroit mafioso Peter Licavoli. Journalists predicted a new gang war in the making, but when Tucson police caught the bombers, they were identified as local hoodlums hired by FBI agent David Hale. The attacks, orchestrated by Hale in the hope of provoking bloodshed between rival Mafia families, cost Hale his job, but left him at liberty without prosecution.

Bonanno logged his only felony conviction on September 2, 1980, when jurors in San Francisco found him guilty of interfering with a federal grand jury investigation of his sons. He ultimately served eight months, but not before completing his memoirs, titled *A Man of Honor*, published in 1984. Son Bill followed his father's lead, publishing *Bound by Honor* in 2000. Joe Bonanno died in Tucson, from heart failure, on May 12, 2002.

Klaas Bruinsma

Future drug lord Klaas Bruinsma was born in Amsterdam on October 6, 1953, the son of a Dutch father and a British mother. It was the third marriage for Anton Bruinsma, wealthy head of a beverage factory, and doomed to fail. In the late 1950s, Bruinsma's mother returned to England, leaving Klaas and three siblings in care of their father's housekeeper Fokje, who doubled as Anton's mistress. In 1964, Anton moved the family to affluent Blaricum, in North Holland, where he forced the children to clean his factory's bottles on Sundays and took Klaas sailing in storms on the North Sea 'to make him tough.' Klaas responded by smoking hashish and selling it to other teenagers, logging his first arrest on September 4, 1970. Unimpressed by a judge's warning in that case, Klaas became a chronic truant and began selling drugs full-time after his expulsion from school.

Already demonstrating the organizational skill that would later see him dubbed *De Dominee* ('The Minister'), Bruinsma delegated sales to cohort Thea Moear and other underlings. Still, he was caught with 100 kg (220 lb) of hashish in 1976 and served three months of a six-month sentence, emerging from jail to continue operations under the alias 'Frans van Arkel.' The ID switch apparently confused police, as Bruinsma and Thea Moear recruited a new band of smugglers and dealers to move their product. Mobster Etienne Urka from Suriname soon joined the team, while Andre Brilleman was employed as Bruinsma's personal bodyguard. Syndicate expansion included purchase of two office buildings in Amsterdam for 300,000 guilders ($150,000), and acquisition of several 'coffee shops' where hashish was sold.

Late in 1979 police charged Bruinsma with smuggling 1,500 kg (3,300 lb) of hashish into Holland from Pakistan. Conviction brought an 18-month sentence, of which Klaas served 12, released in December 1980. He immediately set about expanding his network, ultimately smuggling drugs to Belgium, France, Germany and Scandinavia. He laundered money through legitimate investments and trained a private army to deal with stubborn competition. Bruinsma himself led a raid against Pietje Pieterse in 1983, after Pieterse stole 600 kg (1,320 lb) of hashish from Bruinsma's transporters. The resultant shootout left one man dead, while Bruinsma suffered three bullet wounds. He found himself sentenced to five years in prison on January 31, 1984, reduced to three years on appeal in December 1984.

Upon his parole in 1987, Bruinsma reorganized his syndicate once again, with Etienne Urka supplanting Thea Moear as his primary partner. British ex-convict Roy Francis Adkins took charge of drug smuggling, with continuing emphasis on hashish and marijuana, while Bruinsma launched a new sideline in gambling machines, supervised by associates Sam Klepper and John Mieremet. Internal discipline was rigid, as when suspected embezzler Andre Brilleman was murdered, encased in concrete, and dropped into the River Waal. Pocketing millions of guilders per day by some estimates, Bruinsma spoke of retiring after one last, great score, but police captured his 40,000 kg (44 ton) shipment of hashish in February 1990, upon arrival in the Netherlands.

Bruinsma took the loss badly, using cocaine and laying fruitless plans to blackmail other criminals while Etienne Urka assumed effective command of the syndicate. In spring 1990, while relaxing at his Yab Yum brothel in Amsterdam, Bruinsma quarreled with Roy Adkins and they came to blows. Although peace was restored, some observers suspected Bruinsma when Adkins was shot dead at the American Hotel in Amsterdam on September 28, 1990.

Time ran out for Bruinsma on June 27, 1991, as he left a bar at the Amsterdam Hilton Hotel. Martin Hoogland, a Dutch ex-policeman-turned-contract killer, accosted Bruinsma and shot him three times, killing him instantly. While Hoogland claimed the shooting capped a private quarrel, speculation persists that orders came from rival drug lord Johan Verhoek, or a Yugoslavian syndicate seeking revenge for Bruinsma's murder of their boss. At trial in 1993, Hoogland received ten years for killing Bruinsma and ten more for the slaying of drug dealer Tony Hijzelendoorn. While serving time in an open facility, he was gunned down by persons unknown on March 18, 2004.

After Bruinsma's murder, associates Sam Klepper and John Mieremet took control of the Yab Yum brothel with partners from the Dutch Hells Angels. An unknown gunman killed Klepper at Amsterdam's Great Gelderlandplein mall on October 10, 2000. Mieremet survived a murder attempt in 2002, then was killed in Thailand on November 10, 2005.

Angelo Bruno

The so-called 'Gentle Don' of Philadelphia, Pennsylvania's ruling crime family was born in Villalba, Sicily, on May 21, 1910. Christened Angelo Annaloro, he emigrated to New York in the late 1920s, changing his surname to 'Bruno' on arrival. In Manhattan, he befriended up-and-coming members of the Mafia, including future boss Carlo Gambino. Bruno logged his first arrest in 1928, for reckless driving, and subsequently moved to Philadelphia, where the local Mafia was in turmoil.

Philly boss Salvatore Sabella was deported in 1927, then returned two years later to support New York mafioso Salvatore Maranzano in his war against Giuseppe 'Joe The Boss' Masseria. Both men were killed in 1931, while Philadelphia police jailed Sabella on charges of assault and battery with a motor vehicle. John Avena succeeded Sabella, ruling until he died from natural causes on October 22, 1946. Next came Joseph Ida, who named Bruno as his *consigliere* (counsel), while Antonio Pollina served as underboss. Avena fell under the influence of New York's Vito Genovese in 1957, after Genovese deposed Mafia 'Prime Minister' Frank Costello and conspired with others to assassinate rival Albert Anastasia. Philadelphia and southern New Jersey seemed on the verge of being annexed by the Genovese Family in 1959, when federal prosecutors sent Don Vito to prison for narcotics trafficking.

Avena retired that same year, naming Pollina as his successor, but Bruno soon learned of Pollina's plan to liquidate him as a potential rival. Huddling with Carlo Gambino, Bruno persuaded his friend – and the rest of the Mafia's ruling commission – to cancel the murder contract and depose Pollina, replacing him with Bruno. Magnanimous in victory, Bruno spared Pollina's life and thus established his 'gentle' reputation.

While avoiding bloodshed whenever feasible, Bruno was capable of enforcing family discipline. One unnamed

BELOW: A manacled Angelo Bruno arrives for questioning at FBI headquarters in Boston, Massachusetts, on December 13, 1963.

villain suffered Bruno's wrath when he robbed local bookmakers protected by the syndicate, continuing despite a warning to desist. The second time around, Bruno sent Nicodemo Scarfo to execute the offender, who was lured to a tavern, then stabbed and strangled to death. On Bruno's orders, Scarfo's crew then took the corpse into woodlands outside Philadelphia and placed it beside a grave dug by other family soldiers, leaving it uncovered. A second team arrived later, filling in the grave and planting the body elsewhere, to avert any 'squealing' in future by Scarfo, or his men.

By that time, in the 1960s, Scarfo was a problem for Bruno. First he insulted the daughter of *consigliere* Joe Rugnetta, who asked Bruno for permission to execute Scarfo. Bruno refused, out of respect for Scarfo's uncle, mafioso Nicholas 'Nicky Buck' Piccolo. Next, a friend of Scarfo's – Salvatore 'Chuckie' Merlino – breached Mafia protocol by seducing the niece of family members

ABOVE: The so-called 'Gentle Don' tried to avoid bloodshed wherever possible during his life of crime.

Alfonse and Guarino Marconi. Again Bruno balked at execution, probably relieved when Scarfo was jailed for manslaughter in 1963–64, after stabbing a Philadelphia longshoreman.

Bruno himself avoided indictments, although stubborn refusal to testify before grand juries in New Jersey jailed him twice, in 1970 and 1977–78. The first inquiry involved illegal gambling, while the second sought to probe Mafia infiltration of Atlantic City's newly legalized casinos. Bruno denied any involvement in either area, but he declined to say more despite grants of immunity from prosecution, thus earning citations for contempt. His desire to avoid entanglement with legal casinos may have been sincere, and paralleled a ban on drug dealing that rankled some of Bruno's younger subordinates. At the same time, however, he 'licensed' independent gangs to peddle drugs in Philadelphia and sometimes sanctioned execution of those – like dealer Mickey 'Coco' Cifelli in 1979 – who operated without permission. One favored crew was led by the 'Cherry Hill Gambinos' – brothers Giovanni, Giuseppe and Rosario – who operated out of Cherry Hill, New Jersey, paying tribute to the Bruno family.

Proximity fostered both cooperation and occasional uneasy competition between Philadelphia and New York City's Five Families. In the mid 1970s aging Alphonse 'Funzi' Tieri assumed command of the Genovese Family and launched incursions into the New Jersey gambling preserve of Bruno *consigliere* Antonio Caponigro, which earned the family $2 million per week. Rather than go to war, Bruno took his case to the Mafia commission, which chastised Tieri and ordered his troops to withdraw from Caponigro's turf.

Despite that outcome, Caponigro schemed to depose Bruno, plotting with Philadelphia loan-shark 'Barracuda Frank' Sindone and *caporegime* John Simone from Newark, New Jersey. Their plan also included the elimination of Bruno loyalists Nicky Scarfo, Philip 'Chicken Man' Testa and Frank 'Chickie' Narducci. On March 21, 1980, while Bruno sat in a car parked outside his South Philadelphia home, he was killed by a close-range shotgun blast. Family gossip

named Caponigro's brother-in-law, Alfred Salerno, as the triggerman.

Caponigro apparently believed that the Mafia commission would support his murder of Bruno. He was proved wrong on April 18, when soldiers led by Genovese Family member Vincent 'The Chin' Gigante tortured both Caponigro and Salerno to death, leaving their bodies in the trunks of separate cars parked in the Bronx. Police reported that both were beaten, stabbed, strangled and shot. Caponigro's corpse was found with $300 in 20-dollar bills stuffed into his mouth.

Philip Testa followed Bruno as boss of the Philadelphia family, but his reign was cut short by a nail bomb that shredded his body and shattered his home on March 15, 1981. Some observers suspected successor Nick Scarfo of murdering Testa, but he appeared to prove them wrong by hunting down the actual conspirators, Frank Narducci and Rocco Marinucci. Narducci died first, shot ten times at close range on January 7, 1982. Police found Marinucci on the anniversary of Testa's murder, shot multiple times in the face, neck and chest, with three large firecrackers stuffed into his mouth. Family warfare continued in Philadelphia through 1985 and ultimately led to Scarfo's imprisonment, while federal mob-watchers dubbed the late Angelo Bruno's former syndicate 'the most dysfunctional Mafia family in the United States.'

Lepke Buchalter

Louis Buchalter was born on New York City's Lower East Side in February 1897. His mother called him *Lepkeleh* ('Little Louis' in Yiddish), which friends soon shortened to 'Lepke.' His father died in 1910, then tuberculosis struck his mother, prompting a doctor's order that she move to Colorado. She left Lepke with a sister in 1913, but he fled that home the same day his mother departed New York, vanishing into Manhattan's underworld.

Between September 1915 and February 1920, police arrested Buchalter seven times for burglary and theft. One charge sent him to Connecticut's reformatory, while two others earned him four years in Sing Sing prison. Running mate Jacob 'Gurrah' Shapiro

boasted a similar record, but they were reunited by 1922 to cash in on Prohibition. More arrests followed during 1925–33 – seven each for Lepke and Gurrah – but each case in turn was dismissed as witnesses died, or changed their stories.

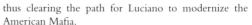

$25,000 REWARD
DEAD OR ALIVE

TWENTY-FIVE THOUSAND DOLLARS will be paid by the City of New York for information leading to the capture of "LEPKE" BUCHALTER, aliases LOUIS BUCHALTER, LOUIS BUCKHOUSE, LOUIS KAWAR, LOUIS KAUVAR, LOUIS COHEN, LOUIS SAFFER, LOUIS BRODSKY.

WANTED FOR CONSPIRACY AND EXTORTION

The Person or Persons who give Information Leading to the Arrest of "LEPKE" will be fully protected, his or her identity will never be revealed. The information will be received in absolute confidence.

RIGHT HAND

LEFT HAND

DESCRIPTION — Age, 42 years; white; Jewish; height, 5 feet, 5½ inches; weight, 170 pounds; build, medium; black hair; brown eyes; complexion dark; married, one son Harold, age about 18 years.

PECULARITIES—Eyes, piercing and shifting; nose, large, somewhat blunt at nostrils; ears, prominent and close to head; mouth, large, slight dimple left side; right-handed; suffering from kidney ailment.

Frequents baseball games.

Is wealthy; has connections with all important mobs in the United States. Involved in racketeering in Unions and Fur Industry, uses Strong-arm methods. Influential.

This Department holds indictment warrant charging Conspiracy and Extortion, issued by the Supreme Court, Extraordinary Special and Trial Terms, New York County.

Kindly search your Prison Records as this man may be serving a Prison sentence for some minor offense.

If located, arrest and hold as a fugitive and advise the THE DETECTIVE DIVISION, POLICE DEPARTMENT, NEW YORK CITY, by wire.

Information may be communicated in Person or by Telephone or Telegraph, Collect to the undersigned, or may be forwarded direct to the DETECTIVE DIVISION, POLICE DEPARTMENT, NEW YORK CITY.

thus clearing the path for Luciano to modernize the American Mafia.

As a reward for that and other contributions, Lepke was assigned to lead the new national crime syndicate's enforcement arm, nicknamed 'Murder Incorporated,' with mafioso Albert Anastasia as his second in command. The Brooklyn-based team of killers traveled nationwide, executing hundreds of contracts before gunman Abraham 'Kid Twist' Reles was arrested and turned state's evidence against his cohorts in 1940.

By then, Lepke was a fugitive from justice. Prosecutors indicted him for labor racketeering in November 1933, with Shapiro, and jurors convicted both defendants on November 12, 1936. They posted bail pending appeal, then vanished. Shapiro surrendered to serve his sentence on April 18, 1938, but a federal narcotics indictment encouraged Lepke to remain in hiding while his gunmen

LEFT: New York police offer $25,000 for the apprehension, dead or alive, of Lepke Buchalter.

BELOW: Under heavy guard, Buchalter shields his face during his 1941 murder trial for the shooting of Joseph Rosen.

While many gangsters focused on bootlegging, Lepke and Gurrah joined a gang of labor racketeers led by Jacob 'Little Augie' Orgen. When Orgen stalled their upward mobility, Buchalter and Shapiro killed him in a drive-by shooting on October 16, 1927, wounding bodyguard Jack 'Legs' Diamond at the same time. Now in charge of the gang, they branched out into collaborative efforts with allies Lucky Luciano, Meyer Lansky and Bugsy Siegel. On September 10, 1931, Lepke supplied a team of gunmen to eliminate mafioso Salvatore Maranzano,

ABOVE: An August 1939 mugshot of the Murder Inc. boss. His surrender to the FBI bought an end to a nationwide manhunt.

scrambled to eliminate potential witnesses. Pressured by lawmen and mobsters alike, Lepke surrendered in August 1939 and received a 30-year sentence in April 1940 – but his troubles weren't over.

New York prosecutor Thomas Dewey next charged Lepke with a murder he ordered in 1936. Elimination of Abe Reles in November 1941 came too late to save him, as jurors convicted Lepke and two triggermen a month later. All three were sentenced to death.

Ali Budesh

Mystery surrounds the early years of Indian mobster Ali Budesh, including the precise date of his 1957 birth in Bombay (now Mumbai). It seems he first drew the attention of police while living in the slums of suburban Vikhroli, near the Pankheshah Baba shrine, where he subsisted as a petty thief and pickpocket. Charged with assault on one victim, he apparently avoided spending time in jail. A chance encounter with cronies of local gangster and terrorist Dawood Ibrahim resulted in Budesh joining Ibrahim's syndicate, known as 'D-Company.'

Over time, dissatisfaction with Ibrahim's autocratic rule led Budesh to defect and create his own gang, backed by other D-Company dissidents including Dilawar Khan, bomber Ijaz Pathan and a pair of Pakistani operators, Irfan Goga and Shoaib Khan. Next came alliances with Ibrahim's sworn enemies, such as

Subhash Singh Thakur in suburban Virar. Finally, Budesh approached police with information on D-Company, resulting in the 1996 arrest of Ibrahim's brother Anees at Bahrain International Airport in Muharraq and the month-long detention of key Ibrahim aide Abu Salem in the United Arab Emirates. Such treachery would not go unrepaid, as Ibrahim himself fled underground, suspected of involvement with al-Qaeda in the Mumbai bombings that killed 257 victims and injured 713 during March 1993, but Budesh did his best to focus on business.

That business was extortion, mainly targeting Mumbai diamond merchants, construction firms and the 'Bollywood' film-making community. Builders paid Budesh to prevent fires, or other costly 'accidents,' while jewelers bought 'insurance' against robbery. Construction mogul Natwarlal Desai refused to pay, and was gunned down at Nariman Point on August 18, 1997. Nine months later, Budesh gunmen killed Keith Rodrigues, chief steward of the Copper Chimney restaurant at Saki Naka, to impress his uncooperative employer. In Bollywood, known victims of Budesh extortion included actor-producer Rakesh Roshan, director Mukesh Bhatt, producer Boney Kapoor and Ramesh Taurani, owner of the Tips Cassettes & Records production company.

Roshan paid up after a near-fatal shooting on January 21, 2000, by Budesh soldiers Sachin Kamble and Sunil Vithal Gaikwad.

By the time Natwarlal Desai was killed for refusing to purchase protection, Ali Budesh had fled from India to hide out in Bahrain. The change of scene did not prevent him from controlling operations of his syndicate, or from claiming credit for various crimes including Desai's murder. In fact, sporadic bulletins from fugitives at large appears to be an Indian tradition, followed by Dawood Ibrahim, longtime smuggler and mass-murderer Koose Muniswamy Veerappan Gounder and 'Bandit Queen' turned-politician Phoolan Devi, among others. In a similar vein, Budesh acknowledged that his soldiers battled police with guns and grenades in June 1998, leaving two officers and three gangsters dead at a hotel in Dahisar.

Budesh remains at large today, presumably still sheltered in Bahrain, but some of his associates are not so fortunate. Key aide Shamkishore Garigapatti was imprisoned in Mumbai, but used forged papers to escape from Kalyan Jail in 2002. Alleged defector Sachin Khambe was captured by Crime Branch officers on October 29, 2009, while trying to launch his own gang in Ghatkopar.

James Bulger

Future gang lord James Joseph Bulger Jr. was born in Dorchester, Massachusetts, on September 3, 1929, tagged 'Whitey' for his light blond hair. His family soon moved to South Boston, where James joined the Shamrocks street gang and logged his first arrest for larceny at 14. More charges, including forgery, assault and battery and armed robbery lodged him in a state reformatory from 1943 to April 1948. Upon release, he joined the Air Force, but continued misbehaving, serving time for assault and going AWOL. Nonetheless, he received an honorable discharge in August 1952 and returned to Boston.

Bulger resumed his criminal career by hijacking truckloads of liquor, then joined a gang that robbed banks in Indiana and Rhode Island during 1955. Indicted in January 1956 and captured two months later, he received a 25-year term in federal prison. While incarcerated in Atlanta, Georgia, Bulger volunteered for CIA-sponsored LSD experiments – part of the agency's 'MK-ULTRA' mind-control program – which left him plagued by nightmares and insomnia. Transferred to Alcatraz in 1959, Leavenworth in 1962 and Lewisburg

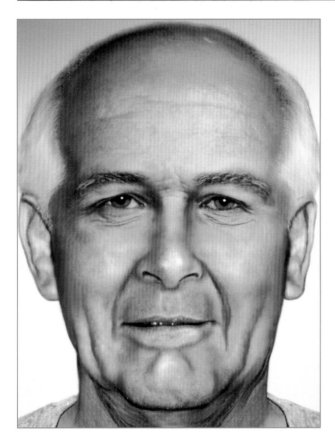

ABOVE: A police photo-fit of the notorious gangster James 'Whitey' Bulger. Despite being on the FBI's Ten Most Wanted list for 11 years, he remains at large.

local bookmaking from mobsters led by Joseph 'Indian Joe' Notarangeli. Bulger's gunmen murdered Notarangeli on April 18, 1973, and FBI agents soon marked Bulger as a rising gangland star. Instead of jailing him, however, they recruited him for the Bureau's 'Top Echelon Informant' program, an arrangement that granted Bulger virtual immunity from prosecution while he helped send his rivals to prison.

In 1979, Howie Winter and other ranking members of his gang were imprisoned for fixing horse races, but the indictment spared Bulger and chief enforcer Stephen 'The Rifleman' Flemmi. Bulger consolidated his power with a series of murders – later indictments placed the number at 18 – which FBI agents studiously ignored. On some occasions they went further still, directing Bulger to potential victims. One such, police informer, John Callahan, was slain in 1982 with cooperation from Agent John Connolly, sentenced to 40 years in prison for second-degree murder on January 15, 2009. Connolly's supervisor, ex-Agent John Morris, admitted taking bribes from Bulger and Flemmi, but escaped prosecution since the statute of limitations had expired.

With such friends behind him – and brother Michael serving as president of the Massachusetts State Senate – Bulger soon controlled the lion's share of rackets in New England, from gambling, loan-sharking and gun-running to drug trafficking in collaboration with Cuban mobsters in Florida. The FBI obstructed state and federal prosecutors, occasionally framing innocent men for Bulger's crimes, until agents from the Drug Enforcement Administration caught several of Bulger's cohorts red-handed. Even then, in December 1994, Agent Connolly tipped Bulger to impending charges, thus permitting him to flee the country with common-law wife Theresa Stanley.

in 1963, Bulger served a total of nine years.

Upon release, Bulger joined the South Boston gang led by Donald Killeen and participated in a war that rocked the local Irish underworld during 1971–72. Killeen's murder on May 13, 1972, left his gang in disarray, and Bulger gravitated to rival Howie Winter's Winter Hill Gang, spearheading a campaign to wrest control of

Despite his posting to the FBI's Ten Most Wanted list in 1999 (with a $2 million reward) and an Interpol 'red notice' issued in October 2007, Bulger remains at liberty. Alleged sightings in London, France, Italy, Spain and Uruguay have kept police hoping, but none has produced an arrest. He remains the classic 'one who got away.'

James Burke

Irish-American mobster James Burke, alias 'Jimmy the Gent,' was born in the Bronx, New York, to an unwed prostitute on July 5, 1931. His mother, Jane Conway, placed James in foster care, where he reportedly suffered abuse from successive unsavory families. At age 13, one of his foster fathers died in a car crash while turned at the steering wheel to strike James in the back seat. More beatings followed from his widowed foster mother, who blamed James for the accident. By the time he found the kind and caring Burke family in Queens, adopting their surname for life, James was well on the path to juvenile delinquency. In 1949, he received a five-year prison term for forgery, after passing a bad check for local mafioso Dominick Cersani.

Burke's refusal to 'squeal' impressed neighborhood mobsters, who adopted him as a kind of Mafia mascot. In later years, Burke's ties to the Italian mob were so extensive that friends dubbed him 'The Irish Guinea.' In his 1990 memoir *Wiseguy* (filmed as *Goodfellas*) associate Henry Hill said of Burke, 'He was a big guy and knew how to handle himself. He looked like a fighter. He had a broken nose and he had a lot of hands. If there was just the littlest amount of trouble, he'd be all over you in a second. He'd grab a guy's tie and slam his chin into the table before the guy knew he was in a war... Jimmy had a reputation for being wild. He'd whack you.'

Burke's crew specialized in hijacking truckloads of merchandise for sale on the black market, often tipping drivers $50 for the inconvenience of losing their loads. Such 'gentlemanly' behavior marked one side of Burke's reputation, but he was also known as a cold-blooded contract killer, hypothetically linked to dozens of still-unsolved murders. Hill said: 'Jimmy could plant you just as fast as shake your hand. It didn't matter to him. At dinner he could be the nicest guy in the world, but then he could blow you away for dessert.'

In 1972, Burke and Hill received ten-year prison terms in an extortion case, after beating victim Gaspar Ciaccio in Tampa, Florida, to collect a gambling debt. Burke served six years, emerging in time to carry out the largest-ever confirmed US robbery. Compulsive gambler Louis Werner, employed as a cargo supervisor for Lufthansa Airlines at New York's John F. Kennedy International Airport, owed Burke and company $20,000 in gambling debts. Unable to pay, he helped Burke and bookmaker Martin Krugman plan a heist at the cargo terminal. In the predawn hours of December 11, 1978, seven armed men struck Lufthansa, escaping with $5 million in cash and jewelry valued at $875,000. Lucchese crime family *caporegime* Paul Vario received $2 million, while Burke claimed the same amount (allegedly burying some at the home of his foster parents, without their knowledge) and distributed the rest among his soldiers.

Burke's greatest score had a tragic aftermath. Incensed that members of the holdup team had spent their loot too soon and too conspicuously, Burke began cleaning house with a vengeance, killing six associates and suspected informers between December 1978 and May 1979. Ironically, Burke himself became an FBI informer in 1980, to avoid a prison term for cocaine trafficking. Two years later, he received a 20-year sentence for fixing college basketball games, then drew a life sentence for one of his murders on February 19, 1985. Burke died in custody, from lung cancer, on April 13, 1996.

Tommaso Buscetta

Born in Palermo, Sicily, on July 13, 1928, the last of 17 children in an impoverished family, Tommaso Buscetta turned to crime as a youth. In 1946, he joined the Porta Nuova Mafia family led by Giuseppe 'Pippo' Calò, first smuggling untaxed cigarettes and later distinguishing himself as a contract killer. Buscetta was implicated in the Ciaculli massacre on June 30, 1963, wherein a bomb killed five policemen and two soldiers in a Palermo suburb. That atrocity prompted the arrest of 1,200 mafiosi nationwide, but Buscetta escaped the dragnet, fleeing to New York where he was sheltered by Carlo Gambino.

I n 1968, an Italian court convicted Buscetta *in absentia* on two counts of murder unrelated to the Ciaculli bombing, imposing a sentence of life imprisonment. Two more years elapsed before New York police identified and apprehended him, but Italian authorities strangely declined to seek extradition and Buscetta was released. To avoid further heat in the States, he decamped to Brazil and established a drug-smuggling network. Agents of Brazil's military junta arrested him in 1972, allegedly subjecting Buscetta to torture before deporting him to Italy. Although sentenced to life, he was nonetheless granted a day pass from prison in 1980 and promptly fled back to Brazil. In Buscetta's absence, Sicily's 'Second Mafia War' erupted between mafiosi from Corleone, led by Salvatore Riina, and Buscetta's longtime allies in Palermo. Between 1981 and 1983 that struggle claimed at least 800 lives, half of them lost in Palermo alone.

Brazilian police arrested and deported Buscetta for the second time in 1983. Upon arrival in Sicily, he first attempted suicide, and then joined the ranks of *pentiti* informers recruited by anti-Mafia magistrates Giovanni Falcone and Paolo Borsellino. With his inside knowledge of Mafia operations, Buscetta served as a star prosecution witness at the 'Maxi Trial' of 474 defendants (119 tried *in absentia*), held at Palermo's Ucciardone prison between February 10, 1986, and December 16, 1987. The defendants stood accused of 120 murders, plus multiple counts of extortion, drug trafficking and Mafia membership (banned by law in 1982). Buscetta's testimony described the Mafia as an international conspiracy, revealing the existence and inner workings of its Commission (or *Cupola*), created in 1975 'to settle

ABOVE: Tommaso Buscetta arrives in a fortified courtroom at Rebibbia jail in October 1984 for interrogation by Palermo magistrates.

disputes between members of the various families and their bosses,' later expanded to include 'the regulation of the activities of all families in a province.' Buscetta also named Michele 'The Cobra' Cavataio as the man behind the Ciaculli massacre. As a result of that testimony, the court convicted 360 defendants, handing down prison terms that totaled 2,665 years. Those sentences did not

include the life terms imposed on various bosses, among whom Giuseppe Lucchese, Bernardo Provenzano and Salvatore Riina were tried *in absentia*.

Buscetta also testified in the United States, in the record-breaking 'Pizza Connection' trial that lasted from October 24, 1985, to March 2, 1987. Charges in that case named 32 conspirators, but only 24 of those were found in the US, and several were killed before, or during trial. Conducted at a cost of $50 million to the prosecution, the trial convicted 18 mobsters on charges of drug trafficking and money laundering, with Sicilian native Gaetano Badalamenti sentenced to 47 years in prison. Badalamenti's son Vito was the only defendant acquitted – and promptly deported as an undesirable alien. At last report, he was still at large and subject to an international arrest warrant, believed to be hiding in Australia, or Brazil.

Buscetta's reward for sending so many fellow mafiosi to prison was freedom, with relocation in America under cover of the federal Witness Protection Program. At home in Sicily, meanwhile, the Mafia retaliated for the Maxi Trial with all-out war against the government. On May 23, 1992, a 320kg (700lb) bomb killed Giovanni Falcone and three bodyguards. A similar blast killed Paolo Borsellino and five policemen in Palermo, on July 19, 1992.

Buscetta resurfaced on November 16, 1992, appearing before the Italian Parliament's Antimafia Commission, chaired by Luciano Violante. There, he admitted concealing knowledge of the Mafia's political ties during the Maxi Trial, explaining that corrupt officials might have had him killed before his move to America. He specifically named Salvatore Lima – mayor of Palermo from 1958 to 1963 and 1965 to 1968, murdered on March 12, 1992 – as 'the politician to whom Cosa Nostra turned most often to resolve problems for the organization whose solution lay in Rome.'

Events in Sicily inspired the 1999 made-for-television film *Excellent Cadavers*, starring F. Murray Abraham as Tommaso Buscetta, opposite Chazz Palmentieri as Giovanni Falcone. Buscetta, back in the States and battling cancer, apparently enjoyed the small-screen portrayal of his exploits before the disease claimed his life on April 4, 2000. Several hundred *pentiti* continue the work he began, aiding authorities in their fight to dismantle the Mafia.

Martin Cahill

The son of a lighthouse keeper, born in a slum district of Dublin, Ireland, on May 23, 1949, Martin Cahill and his brother John began stealing food for their impoverished family before they were enrolled at school. In 1960, a slum clearance program shifted the Cahills to Crumlin, on Dublin's South Side, where Martin entered a Christian Brothers School, but seldom attended classes, preferring to run the streets and hone his skills at housebreaking. He tried to join the Royal Navy at 15, but was rejected after offering to serve as an official thief.

Convicted on two counts of burglary the following year, Cahill was sent to a trade school run by the Oblates of Mary Immaculate in County Offaly. Upon release, he found his family had been evicted for nonpayment of rent, relocated to the seedy Hollyfield Buildings tenement in Rathmines. Resuming burglaries with his brothers, Cahill soon graduated to armed robbery after stealing weapons from a Garda Síochána armory. Another four-year sentence followed, during which the Hollyfield Buildings were condemned and demolished in 1978. Upon his release, Cahill pitched a tent on the old site and stayed there until Lord Mayor of Dublin Ben Briscoe persuaded him to accept a new house in Rathmines.

Such tactics – and his skill at plotting robberies – earned Cahill his gangland nickname as 'The General.' One raid alone – on the posh O'Connor Jewelers in Dublin, on July 27, 1983 – netted a cache of gold and diamonds valued in excess of IR£2 million ($3.45 million). When some gold from that holdup went missing, Cahill reportedly nailed the miscreant mobster to a floor. Questioned about the incident later, he said, 'I've heard the story. I can only say there might be some truth in it, but I wasn't there at the time.'

Three years later, in May 1986, Cahill's gang stole 11 paintings valued at £30 million from Russborough House in County Wicklow. While trying to sell his loot, Cahill was nearly drawn into a trap by an Interpol agent posing as a Dutch art dealer, but Cahill's men escaped from the rural meeting site on motorcycles, eluding 50 officers and a spotter aircraft. As Garda Superintendent Dinny Mullens explained to reporters, 'You cannot surround a forest.' In August 1987, Cahill made matters worse for the police, burglarizing the Director of Public Prosecutions' office and stealing 145 files related to investigations of the gang.

Martin Cahill's luck ran out on August 18, 1994. While stopped at a street intersection near his Rathmines home, he was shot at point-blank range by a motorcyclist armed with a .357 Magnum revolver. Theories abound in his murder, including a claim that Cahill was killed by the Provisional Irish Republican Army for collaborating with loyalist paramilitaries of the Ulster Volunteer Force, or the rival Irish National Liberation Army. Another version, supported by certain Garda officers, suggests that Cahill was killed by two of his own gang members, John Gilligan and John Traynor, after demanding a share of their illicit drug revenue.

Gilligan was also suspected in the nearly-identical June 1996 murder of Irish journalist Veronica Guerin, but jurors acquitted him at trial in February 2000. The same panel convicted Gilligan of smuggling cannabis, resulting in a 28-year sentence, later reduced to 20 years on appeal. In February 2008, before the High Court, Gilligan named Traynor as the man responsible for Guerin's death.

Alaattin Çakici

Alaattin Çakici was born on January 20, 1953, in the Arsin district of Turkey's Trabzon Province, on the coast of the Black Sea. He quit school in eighth grade, around the time his family moved to Istanbul, where his father prospered with a hardware store and snack food kiosk. Despite growing prosperity, tragedy stalked the Çakici clan, with a nephew murdered in 1978 and Alaattin's father slain by leftist guerrillas two years later. As a result, Çakici joined the neo-fascist Grey Wolves and participated in Ahmet Kenan Evren's coup d'état of September 12, 1980. Evren then turned on the Grey Wolves, arrested 220 members on charges of committing 694 murders, but offered amnesty to those who joined his fight against the separatist Kurdistan Workers' Party.

Çakici declined that offer and was convicted of using the Grey Wolves to extort money from nightclubs, gambling houses and other businesses in Istanbul's Harbiye neighborhood. Released from prison on March 2, 1982, he opened a gambling casino, then started a collection agency under the name 'Hakettin Biber,' pursuing debtors in return for an illegal 50 per cent of the proceeds recovered. Yavuz Ataç, an officer of the Turkish National Intelligence Organization (MİT), recruited Çakici to manage the agency's security department in May 1987, despite admitting knowledge that 'Çakici has been a fugitive, sought for six or seven crimes at the time [Ataç] first met him.' To avoid embarrassment, Çakici was assigned to operations outside Turkey's borders, earning himself a place on the hit-list of Dev Sol – the Revolutionary People's Liberation Party – in 1995.

Throughout his service to the government, Çakici pursued a life of crime. In 1991, he wed a daughter of Dündar Kiliç, Turkey's 'Godfather of Godfathers,' then divorced her in November 1994 and paid henchman Nurullah Tevfik Ağansoy to kill her on Çakici's 42nd birthday. By then, Çakici was a fugitive traveling on false documents, sought in connection with 41 murders while he rambled through Belgium, France, Italy, South Africa, the United States, Singapore and Japan. When scandal related to drug trafficking and money laundering threatened the Turkish Commerce Bank in 1997, Çakici issued murder contracts on wealthy businessmen Cavit Çağlar and Mehmet Üstünkaya, but police disrupted those plots in the planning stage.

French police arrested Çakici in Nice, with bodyguard

BELOW: Turkish underworld boss Alaattin Çakici arrives in a Vienna courtroom in handcuffs escorted by members of the Austrian police on October 4, 2004.

Murat Güler and mistress-courier Aslı Fatos Ural, on August 17, 1998. Recordings of Çakici's conversations with MIT scandalized the Turkish government, forcing the resignation of Eyup Aık, Minister of State, who had tipped Çakici to impending indictments and thus enabled him to flee Turkey in 1992. Minister of the Interior, Meral Aksener, faced similar charges, but retained her office.

Çakici escaped from French custody after 16 months, then voluntarily returned to Turkey on December 14, 1999. Released from prison on December 1, 2002, but stripped of his passport, he decamped to Greece with more false documents, spent several months in France, then was captured near Graz, Austria, on July 14, 2004. Austria deported him on October 14, for trial on multiple charges in Turkey. Upon conviction, Çakici received 19 years and two months for his wife's murder; ten years and ten months for the attempted murder of speculator Adil Öngen; plus three years and four months each for attempted murder of a journalist and a March 2000 club shooting in Istanbul.

Al Capone

Alphonse Gabriel Capone was born in Brooklyn on January 17, 1899, six years after his parents left Naples for New York City. Expelled from school for punching a teacher at age 14, Capone fraternized with various street gangs before adopting mobster Johnny Torrio as his mentor. In 1917, while employed as a waiter by mafioso Frankie Yale, at the Harvard Club on Coney Island, Capone insulted another mobster's sister and received the knife wounds that produced his famous nickname: 'Scarface.' Capone himself preferred 'Snorky,' early gangland slang for 'elegant.'

Capone followed Johnny Torrio to Chicago in 1921, serving as Torrio's enforcer in the brawling city where multiple gangs vied for control of bootleg liquor traffic during Prohibition (1920–33). The combination of Torrio's brains and Capone's brute force imposed a measure of control until 1924, when full-scale warfare erupted with the rival North Side Gang led by Dean O'Banion. Capone eliminated O'Banion on November 10, 1924, but successors Hymie Weiss and George 'Bugs' Moran retaliated by ambushing Torrio in January 1925, prompting his retirement to New York.

Left in charge of the gang which insiders called 'The Outfit,' operating from headquarters in suburban Cicero, Capone unleashed his fury on rivals in every quarter. Aside from suppressing competitors, Capone also fought to control the Mafia, which barred him from membership since his parents were not Sicilian. Opponent Joe Aiello

RIGHT: American's most notorious gangster ruled Chicago with an iron fist during the Prohibition years.

ABOVE: Capone covers his head with a coat to avoid being photographed after his conviction for income tax evasion in October 1931.

Capone prevailed, decimating Aiello's gang and driving Aiello himself into hiding. On October 23, 1930, Capone machine-gunners surprised Aiello outside his lair on Kolmar Avenue and riddled him with 59 bullets – supposed to be a record for Chicago's liquor wars.

Despite such incidents, and Capone's alleged personal murder of Assistant State's Attorney William McSwiggin and two underworld companions on April 27, 1926, Capone's most famous battles were fought with the North Side Gang that drove Johnny Torrio from Chicago. A typical machine-gun ambush killed Hymie Weiss and a bodyguard, wounding three others, outside Holy Name Cathedral on October 11, 1926. Dozens more fell in the 'beer wars' before Capone staged an attempt to wipe out the North Side leadership in early 1929.

On February 14 – St. Valentine's Day – gunmen disguised as police cornered seven North Side gang members in a garage on North Clark Street. Mistakenly believing that boss Bugs Moran was among those present, the killers shot all seven with machine guns and sawn-off shotguns. That massacre, committed while Capone was on vacation in Miami, Florida, sparked public outrage across America and prompted President Herbert Hoover to order Capone's prosecution.

Meanwhile, Capone had more to fear from fellow mobsters who were put off by the fanfare of publicity contested Capone's bid to seize the Mafia throne through puppet nominees and hatched several plots to kill Capone, including one attempt to poison him with prussic acid.

surrounding his activities. Gang lords from throughout the eastern half of the United States gathered in Atlantic City, New Jersey, during May 1929 to resolve their territorial disputes, set limits on the future use of violence – and to deal with Al Capone. Capone was ordered to adopt a lower profile and submit to imprisonment on a minor charge to pacify America. Arrested by Philadelphia police on his way home to Chicago, he pled guilty to carrying a concealed weapon and received a one-year sentence, remaining in jail until March 1930.

The enforced 'vacation' did not save him. In April 1930, the Chicago Crime Commission published its first list of 'public enemies,' with Capone at Number 1. Bugs Moran, unnerved by his near-death experience in February 1929, and hoping to retire, was Number 12. Meanwhile, two teams of federal agents laid siege to Capone's bootleg empire. One unit – the famous 'Untouchables'

BELOW: Capone's nemesis, leader of the North Side Gang, George 'Bugs' Moran (left) with his lawyer.

led by Eliot Ness – raided illegal breweries and distilleries, while another investigated Capone's tax records. That team soon discovered that Al had never filed a tax return. On June 5, 1931, a federal grand jury indicted Capone on 22 charges involving tax evasion during the years 1925–27.

Capone's attorneys negotiated a deal with federal prosecutors that would have allowed Capone to pay his back taxes and serve less than three years in prison, but Judge James Wilkerson rejected the bargain, forcing Capone to trial in fall 1931. Jurors convicted him on October 17, and Wilkerson imposed sentence on

October 24: 11 years in prison, with a $50,000 fine and $30,000 in court costs.

Prisoner Capone entered the federal prison in Atlanta, Georgia, as its most famous inmate. Reports of favored treatment soon emerged, including revelations that Capone received more sheets, socks and underwear than any other prisoner, that he was graced with special food, and that he paid for such favors with a fat roll of bills concealed inside the hollow handle of a tennis racket. Stung by those reports, in August 1934, US Attorney General Homer Cummings ordered Capone's transfer from Atlanta to Alcatraz Island, in San Francisco Bay.

The move changed everything. Strict discipline at Alcatraz stripped Capone of all privileges and reduced him to menial labor, prompting some hostile inmates to dub him 'the wop with the mop.' No longer shielded

---

BELOW: A reenactment of the St. Valentine's Day Massacre during which seven members of the North Side gang were executed on Capone's orders.

by a syndicate, he suffered personal attacks while tertiary syphilis – contracted as a brothel bouncer in the early 1920s – reduced Capone to a state of near-idiocy.

Released from Alcatraz on January 6, 1939, Capone spent ten months in another federal lockup at Terminal Island, California, then was paroled to his family's estate on Palm Island, Florida. Frequently incoherent, raving against Communists and Bugs Moran, Capone suffered a stroke on January 21, 1947. While rallying from that blow, he caught pneumonia on January 24, then suffered a fatal heart attack the following day. Moran, the object of Capone's obsession, outlived his nemesis by a decade. Jailed for bank robbery in 1946, he died in prison, from cancer, on February 25, 1957.

RIGHT: Capone used Chicago's Lexington Hotel as The Outfit's headquarters during his legendary crime spree.

Vicente Carrillo Fuentes

Born on October 16, 1962, at Guamuchilito in the Mexican state of Sinaloa, Vicente Carrillo Fuentes was destined to inherit his family's drug-dealing business. Elder brother Amado initially worked for Chihuahua drug lord Pablo Acosta Villarreal, earning his nickname 'Lord of the Skies' for flying 53,000 kg (58 tons) of cocaine per year across the US-Mexican border, then he organized the Juárez Cartel after Mexican Federal Police killed Acosta in April 1987. Instantly, brothers Vincente, Alberto, Cipriano, José Cruz and Rodolfo came aboard as ranking cartel officers. An uncle, Ernesto Fonseca Carrillo, was imprisoned that same year for his role in the 1985 torture-slaying of American DEA agent Enrique Camarena.

With headquarters in Ciudad Juárez, directly opposite El Paso, Texas, on the Rio Grande River, the Juárez Cartel was ideally placed to move tons of cocaine, heroin, marijuana and methamphetamine into the United States. More than 300 local *maquiladoras* (duty-free assembly plants) provide cover for drug shipments, while nonstop cross-border tourist traffic affords more opportunities for smugglers. Ruthless competition has turned Ciudad Juárez into a slaughterhouse, with more than 1,400 drug-related murders during 2007 alone, and the general disregard for human life has claimed more than 400 female victims of sexually-motivated slayings since 1993, branding the border city as a 'serial killer's playground.'

In that setting, the Carrillo Fuentes brothers ruled like kings – and Vincente was dubbed 'Viceroy' – but they were not untouchable. An unknown gunman killed Cipriano in 1989, under circumstances still deemed mysterious. Amado died on July 3, 1997, during an eight-hour plastic surgery procedure at Santa Mónica Hospital in Mexico City, apparently from an overdose of anesthetic sedatives. Investigators from the Office of the

ABOVE: Another day, another deadly crime scene in the brutal city of Ciudad Juárez, the headquarters of Vincente Carrillo Fuentes' cartel.

BELOW: An undated police photo of Carrillo Fuentes, head of the Juárez Cartel, who remains at large.

General Prosecutor remain undecided as to whether his death was an accident, or homicide.

Before succeeding his brother, Vicente Carrillo Fuentes had to suppress a rebellion by upstart cartel member Rafael Munoz Talavera, finally riddled with bullets in Ciudad Juárez during September 1998. Another presumed contender, Juan José Esparragoza Moreno, joined the Carrillo brothers as a lieutenant on par with Amado's son, Vicente Carrillo Leyva. When rival drug lord Joaquín Guzmán Loera escaped from prison in January 2001, some Juárez syndicate members defected to join his Gulf Cartel based in Matamoros, Tamaulipas, and bloodshed proliferated.

On September 11, 2004, a band of gunmen, presumably dispatched by the Gulf Cartel, ambushed Rodolfo Carrillo Fuentes and wife Giovanna Quevedo Gastélum outside a movie theater in Culiacán, killing both. Vicente Carrillo retaliated by killing Joaquín Guzmán Loera's brother, a drug runner known as *El Pollo* ('The Chicken'). More mayhem ensued, with police tabulating 200 murders in the first three months of 2008 alone. On October 28 of that year, authorities discovered the partly-burned corpse of José Cruz Carrillo Fuentes outside Culiacán, then lost it again when gunmen snatched the body from the government forensics laboratory on October 29. Police in Mexico City captured Vicente Carrillo Leyva on April 2, 2009, as he exercised in a public park.

Vicente Carrillo Fuentes remained at large as this book went to press, with a $5 million reward offered for his capture by the US State Department. Despite various setbacks, the Juárez Cartel remains active in 21 of Mexico's 31 states, with principal bases of operation in Ciudad Juárez, Culiacán, Cancún, Cuernavaca, Guadalajara, Mexico City, Monterrey and Ojinaga. In the US, collaborators from the street gang Barrio Azteca operate in Austin, Dallas, and El Paso, Texas, with outposts in Arizona and New Mexico.

Alfonso Caruana

Third-generation mafioso Alfonso Caruana was born at Castelvetrano, in the Sicilian province of Trapani, on January 1, 1946. Italian prosecutors call his family, the Cuntrera-Caruana Mafia clan an 'international holding... a holding which secures certain services for the Sicilian Cosa Nostra as a whole: drug-trafficking routes and channels for money laundering.' The tribe, they say, is 'a very tight knit family group of men-of-honour, not only joined by Mafia bonds, but also by ties of blood.' Drug routes span the world, from Sicily to Venezuela and Canada, where Alfonso Caruana managed the family's interests.

He arrived in Montreal during 1968, allegedly with no more than $100 on his person, posing as an electrician. Ten years later, around the same time he was granted Canadian citizenship, Swiss Customs officers caught Caruana at Zurich Airport with a suitcase containing $600,000. He paid a fine for failure to declare the money on arrival, then was released, presumably to stash the money in a numbered bank account.

Caruana's storied rise from rags-to-riches did not occur without setbacks. In the mid-1970s, he clashed with predecessors Giuseppe and Vincenzo Cotroni, who had previously driven the Cuntrera brothers – Gaspare, Liborio, Paolo and Pasquale – from Montreal to Caracas, Venezuela, a decade earlier. Caruana and his own brothers, Gerlando and Pasquale, followed the same escape route as action heated up in Montreal, then returned after dissension split the Cotroni family and boss Paolo Violi was murdered on January 22, 1978. The last significant Cotroni holdout, Rocco Violi, was gunned down in October 1980.

By then, Alfonso Caruana was dividing his time between Montreal and Switzerland, lounging in a £450,000 villa outside Lugano, supervising heroin shipments from Thailand, through England to Canada. Mafioso Francesco Di Carlo handled the British side of Caruana's network from a mansion in Woking, Surrey, until officers of British Customs and Excise joined the Royal Canadian Mounted Police to seize a shipment of 58 kg (127 lb) in June 1983. Arrested with three others, Di Carlo received a 25-year sentence in March 1987, while a Canadian court convicted Gerlando Caruana in the same case. Brother Alfonso escaped indictment and returned to Montreal, operating behind the façade of a modest suburban pizzeria.

During 1991–94 Caruana's new drug network smuggled tons of Colombian cocaine to members of the 'Ndrangheta syndicate in Calabria, Italy. In March 1994, Italian police staged 'Operation Cartagine,' seizing 5,500 kg (6 tons) of coke in Turin. Indictments followed in 1995, with prosecutors calling the Cuntrera-Caruana family 'the fly-wheel of the drug trade and the indispensable link between suppliers and distributors.'

Tried *in absentia* on July 30, 1997, Alfonso Caruana received a sentence of 21 years and ten months for Mafia association, conspiracy to traffic narcotics and aggravated importing, possession and sale of narcotics in large quantities. The judge noted that Caruana had 'escaped every judicial initiative during the last decades and succeeded in reaching the top of the international drug trade, adjusting his criminal contacts and showing such skill that he is to be considered as one of the most important exponents in this sector.'

Canadian police arrested Caruana in Woodbridge, Ontario, during July 1998. He fought extradition to Italy, portraying himself as a lowly car wash attendant, but authorities dismissed the ploy. RCMP Chief Superintendent Ben Soave observed, 'If organized crime was a hockey game, Mr. Caruana would be [Wayne] Gretzky.' In February 2000, Caruana pled guilty to smuggling 1,500 kg (1.6 tons) of cocaine and received a 22-year sentence. Ontario's Court of Appeal ordered Caruana's extradition in June 2007, and he was sent back to Italy on January 29, 2008.

Paul Castellano

A Brooklyn native, born on June 26, 1915, Constantino Paul Castellano logged his first arrest in 1934, for armed robbery, and served three months in jail. He joined Vincenzo Mangano's Mafia family in the early 1940s, later rising to the rank of *caporegime* under boss Albert Anastasia. In November 1957, Castellano attended the notorious Mafia meeting at Apalachin, New York, with Anastasia successor Carlo Gambino. Nine years later, when Gambino 'retired' to Florida, he named Castellano as acting boss of the family. He assumed full control with Gambino's death in October 1976.

While pursuing most of the Mafia's usual rackets, Castellano banned drug trafficking and threatened death to any family members who defied him. The order was based on Castellano's fear of federal investigation as successive US presidents declared a national 'War on Drugs.' Equally ruthless in his private life, Castellano ordered the death of his daughter's boyfriend in 1975, over a perceived insult. Five years later he had son-in-law Frank Amato slain for abusing the same daughter.

Castellano's autocratic rule – and the narcotics ban in particular – caused dissension among young subordinates such as John Gotti and his brothers. He also angered prolific family hitman Salvatore 'Sammy the Bull' Gravano by executing Gravano's brother-in-law, Nicholas Scibetta, for perceived improprieties. A March

RIGHT: Paul Castellano's tenure as Mafia kingpin was characterized by a ban on narcotics activities, a stance that he ruthlessly imposed.

1984 racketeering indictment threatened Castellano's liberty, but trial was still pending on that case in February 1985, when federal prosecutors filed new charges against the bosses of New York's five Mafia families and six high-ranking subordinates. Castellano posted $3 million bail to remain at liberty, while Gotti spread rumors that the 70-year-old boss had turned informer to save himself.

On top of those rumblings, never confirmed, Castellano himself added insult to injury. Longtime family underboss Aniello 'The Tall Guy' Dellacroce – a close friend of Gotti, passed over in line of succession when Carlo Gambino retired on the basis of Dellacroce's illicit 1960 affair with another mafioso's wife – died from lung cancer on December 2, 1985. Castellano refused to attend Dellacroce's funeral and replaced him as underboss with Tommaso Bilotti, a Castellano protégé nicknamed 'The Wig' for his ill-fitting toupee.

On December 16, 1985, Gotti invited Castellano to Sparks Steak House in Manhattan, to settle their differences. Arriving on schedule with underboss Bilotti, Castellano walked into an ambush that left both men dead and cleared Gotti's path to control of the family. It proved to be a tainted victory, however, as Gotti's flamboyant lifestyle and ruthless violence turned once-loyal subordinates against him. New family underboss Salvatore Gravano joined the ranks of FBI informers in 1991 and later testified against Gotti at trial, resulting in Gotti's conviction on 13 counts of murder that included victims Castellano and Bilotti.

Mickey Cohen

Born in Brooklyn to Ukrainian-Jewish immigrant parents on September 4, 1913, Meyer Harris 'Mickey' Cohen began selling newspapers at age six, delivered bootleg liquor for his brother from age nine, then turned to prizefighting as a teenager, after his family moved to Los Angeles. The switch to professional boxing carried Cohen back to New York, then to Cleveland, Ohio, where he became a protégé of mobster Louis Rothkopf, a partner of Moe Dalitz. Abandoning the ring in 1933, Cohen turned to crime full-time, robbing Cleveland gamblers who believed they could ignore demands for tribute from the Dalitz-Rothkopf syndicate.

LEFT: A bored Mickey Cohen waits to explain his plush income to the Senate Crime Committee in November 1950.

ABOVE: Cohen en route to Alcatraz on May 14, 1962. He had been released on $100,000 bail pending an appeal.

In 1937, after Bugsy Siegel left New York to dominate racketeering in Los Angeles, Cleveland's kingpins sent Cohen west 'to cover their end of the action.' He became Siegel's right-hand man, then succeeded him as rackets boss of southern California after Siegel's assassination in June 1947. The presence of a Jewish overlord rankled LA mafiosi led by Jack Dragna, who made multiple attempts on Cohen's life. Mickey replied in kind, pursuing a vendetta that littered Los Angeles with corpses and bombed-out buildings.

The US Senate's Kefauver Committee gave Cohen unwelcome attention in 1950, prompting him to launch a public relations counterattack. First, Mickey recruited author Ben Hecht to write his memoirs, then dropped the project after selling shares in its future presumed royalties to various gullible investors. Next, Cohen huddled with agents of evangelist Billy Graham, reportedly pocketing some $20,000 in exchange for Mickey's promise (never fulfilled) to 'find Jesus' at a rally held in New York's Madison Square Garden. The publicity backfired in 1951, when prosecutors sent Cohen to prison for tax evasion.

A term in federal prison failed to educate Mickey, who emerged in 1957 to sit for a televised interview with reporter Mike Wallace. In the course of their chat, Cohen declared, 'I have killed no man that in the first place didn't deserve killing by the standards of our way of life.' That said, Cohen attacked LA's police. 'I have a police chief in Los Angeles,' he announced, 'who happens to be a sadistic degenerate.' Chief William Parker threatened litigation, but the case languished while federal prosecutors built another tax evasion case against Cohen, sending him back to prison in 1961.

This time confined at Alcatraz, he was assaulted by a fellow inmate with a metal pipe and left paralyzed below the waist. When Alcatraz closed in March 1963, Cohen was transferred to Atlanta, Georgia. Prison doctors there misdiagnosed his stomach cancer as an ulcer, prior to releasing him in 1972, but free-world surgeons granted him a few more years of life. After touring America as a spokesman for prison reform, Cohen died in Los Angeles on July 29, 1976.

Vincent Coll

New York City's 'mad dog' killer of the Prohibition era was born Uinseann Ó Colla on July 20, 1908, at Gweedore, in Ireland's County Donegal. His family sailed for the United States on April 3, 1909, and settled in the rowdy Bronx – the second emigration for his parents, who had tried and failed to find their fortune in New York, in 1892–93. Pneumonia killed Vincent's mother in February 1916, while his alcoholic father left his brood to be raised by relatives, or the state. Vincent struggled in school, largely from failure to attend, and was legally branded 'an ungovernable child' in August 1920. One month later an arrest for theft sent him to the New York Catholic Protectory, a juvenile, gulag rife with physical and sexual abuse.

While disease thinned the ranks of his siblings, and Vincent himself survived a bout with tuberculosis, his police record lengthened. Caught with a pistol in November 1924, he was sent to the New York House of Refuge. He escaped in July 1926, but was quickly recaptured and transferred to state prison at Elmira, New York. Released in 1927, Vincent encouraged older brother Pete to join the bootlegging mob led by Bronx beer baron Dutch Schultz. The volatile pair made a poor match, with tension between them exacerbated by economics. Schultz earned millions per month, but held his soldiers to flat salaries of $150 per week while frustration simmered.

A parole violation sent Coll back to prison in December 1928. Released in spring 1929, he resumed work for Schultz in the Bronx. Schultz posted $10,000 bond when police caught Coll with a pistol in March 1930, suggesting that their relationship had not soured beyond redemption, but a split soon followed when the Colls demanded a larger piece of Dutch's action. Vincent reportedly slapped Schultz, a lapse in etiquette that led to brother Pete's assassination on May 30, 1931.

Vincent retaliated within hours, staging the first in a series of raids and drive-by shootings that would kill at least seven Schultz mobsters. Some reports place the death toll in double digits, while failing to identify specific incidents, or victims. Barred from proper bootlegging and nightclub management, Coll fattened his war chest by hijacking liquor shipments and kidnapping gangsters for ransom. His best-known victim, George 'Big Frenchy' De Mange, was a partner with Owney Madden in the Cotton Club and other venues. Snatched on June 15, 1931, De Mange was freed upon payment of $35,000.

Coll staged his most infamous hit on July 28, 1931, while gunning for Schultz partner Joey Rao in Harlem. A rolling shotgun fusillade missed Rao, but wounded several children, killing five-year-old Michael Vengali. Branded a 'mad dog' and 'baby killer,' Coll fled into hiding with help from anti-Schultz ally Legs Diamond. Captured in October, he stood trial with two confederates for the bungled murder – and was acquitted in December when his lawyer caught a key witness lying under oath.

Outraged police now dogged Coll's steps, arresting him on any excuse while his war with Dutch Schultz sputtered on. Finally, on February 8, 1932, killers surprised Coll in a pharmacist's phone booth and hosed him with machine-gun fire. Rumors persist that Coll was talking to Owney Madden when he died, kept on the line deliberately for the shooter's convenience. Dutch Schultz sent a wreath to Coll's funeral, with a banner reading 'From the Boys.'

Coll's killers were never formally identified, but all those named as suspects in the press subsequently died violently – one murdered by Bugsy Siegel in a later feud, another shot with his girlfriend by persons unknown and a third executed in Sing Sing prison's electric chair. Meanwhile, Coll's widow continued on a life of crime without him. In June 1933, with two male cohorts, she tried to rob a Bronx loan shark, but accidentally killed a female bystander. She pled guilty to manslaughter on February 26, 1934, receiving a sentence of six to 12 years.

Joe Colombo Sr.

The son of a murdered Mafia soldier, Joseph Anthony Colombo Sr. was born in New York City on December 14, 1914. He followed in his father's footsteps, rising through the ranks of the Profaci crime family to become a *caporegime* in the early 1960s. His opportunity for swift advancement came in 1963, when boss Giuseppe Magliocco conspired with Joe Bonanno to kill the chiefs of New York's three remaining crime families – Carlo Gambino, Gaetano Lucchese and Stefano Magaddino. Magliocco assigned Colombo to orchestrate the slayings, but instead he warned the mobsters who were marked for death. The Mafia's ruling commission accepted Magliocco's plea for mercy, fining him $50,000 and forcing him into retirement while Joe Colombo seized the family's reins, supporting his fellow bosses as war ensued with Bonanno in exile.

Colombo generally kept a low profile through the remainder of the 1960s, when some observers described him as Carlo Gambino's puppet. While occasionally behaving in true Mafia style – as when he reportedly ordered the death of a thief who robbed a Brooklyn church – Colombo posed as a legitimate realtor. When a grand jury investigated his business in October 1966, Colombo initially refused to testify and was cited for contempt. He stonewalled a second grand jury in January 1970, then found himself indicted for perjury on March 6, over lies told on his application for a realtor's license.

On April 7, 1970, after FBI agents arrested Colombo's son Joe Jr. on a charge of illegally melting $500,000 in US coins to harvest their silver, Joe Sr. had a bright idea. He organized the Italian American Anti-Defamation

League (later renamed the Italian-American Civil Rights League) and led 30 pickets to march outside the local FBI office, protesting alleged ethnic discrimination. Two months later, on June 28, some 50,000 New Yorkers rallied at Columbus Circle in mid-town Manhattan to celebrate the league's first Italian Unity Day. Five congressmen addressed the crowd, but Joe Colombo's speech was the highlight. 'If the FBI and Justice Department want to make me boss of a Mafia family,' he proclaimed, 'that's what I'll be. And I'll use my position to help people of Italian-American heritage.'

The campaign rolled on. Frank Sinatra staged a benefit concert for the league at Madison Square Garden in November 1970, and Hollywood took notice, dropping mention of the Mafia from films, television series and even commercials. Macy's abandoned sale of 'The Godfather Game,' while Justice Department bulletins substituted 'traditional organized crime' for the terms 'Mafia' and 'Cosa Nostra.' Despite receiving a 2½-year sentence for perjury in March 1971, Colombo seemed pleased with his celebrity as he planned the league's second Italian Unity Day for June.

But others were not.

Carlo Gambino seethed at the publicity surrounding Colombo, while family rebel Joey Gallo emerged from prison to resume his bid for power. As Colombo, free on bail, stood to address his fans on

June 28, 1971, faux press photographer Jerome Johnson fired three close-range shots into his skull. Bodyguards killed Johnson on the spot, thereby preventing him from naming his employers. Colombo, comatose, remained in hospital until August 28, when he was released to the care of relatives. Effectively removed from Mafia affairs, he lingered in a vegetative state until May 22, 1978, when he finally died.

Successor Vincenzo Aloi essentially blamed Joey Gallo for the shooting, and retaliated by killing Gallo on April 7, 1972. A grand jury quizzed him on that slaying, and his answers earned Aloi a seven-year sentence for perjury in August 1973, leaving Carmine Persico in charge of the family. Joe Colombo Jr. was acquitted of melting down coins, after a key witness recanted his testimony in what prosecutors called 'sinister' circumstances, but he and brother Anthony faced charges of illegal gambling in December 1973. Neither was convicted in that case.

LEFT: Mafia head Joe Colombo was to all intents and purposes a legitimate real estate agent.

Frank Costello

America's 'Prime Minister of the Underworld' was born in Lauropoli, Italy, on January 26, 1891, and christened Francesco Castiglia. His father emigrated to East Harlem, New York, and opened a grocery before sending for his wife and two sons in 1900. Elder brother Edward soon joined a street gang, then recruited Frank – who logged arrests for assault and robbery in 1908, 1912 and 1917. Castiglia served ten months for carrying a concealed weapon in 1918, then legally changed his name to Costello and joined a gang led by Ciro 'The Artichoke King' Terranova, underboss of the Morello Mafia family. Outside of strictly-Mafia circles, Costello forged friendships with comrades Lucky Luciano, Meyer Lansky and Bugsy Siegel.

Prosecutions and conflict with the rival Camorra decimated the Morello family's leadership, leaving Giuseppe 'Joe The Boss' Masseria in charge by 1922. Prohibition enriched the syndicate, but conflict flared again in 1929, as Masseria waged war against competitor Salvatore Maranzano. Disgusted with the Mafia's old 'Mustache Petes' and their ban on working with Irish, or Jewish colleagues, Costello joined Luciano's plot to modernize the Italian underworld. Luciano loyalists assassinated Masseria on April 15, 1931, briefly permitting Maranzano to rule as 'Boss of Bosses' before he was slain on September 10.

Costello emerged from that war as *consiglieri* (counsel) to Luciano and underboss Vito Genovese. In 1934, after New York police raided syndicate gambling dens, Costello negotiated with Louisiana senator Huey Long

incarcerated, prosecutors filed tax-evasion charges that sent him back to prison in May 1956. Paroled in April 1957, Costello next faced deportation as an undesirable alien. While fighting that move, on May 2, 1957, Costello was shot in New York by Genovese gunman Vincent 'The Chin' Gigante. He survived a superficial head wound, but police found a slip of paper in his pocket detailing weekly winnings from the Tropicana casino in Las Vegas, Nevada.

After his near-death experience, Costello made peace with Genovese and retired from leadership of the family. In return, he was allowed to live in peace atop the posh Waldorf Astoria hotel, while immigration officers strangely forgot their efforts to deport him. A heart attack killed Costello on February 18, 1973. A year later, upstart mafioso Carmine Galante, bombed Costello's mausoleum as a gesture of contempt spawned by a personal grudge.

ABOVE: Frank Costello, the 'Prime Minister,' survived an assassination in 1957 and later died of natural causes.

RIGHT: Costello, looking every inch the gangster, in the witness chair in March 1951. He refused to testify before the Senate Crime Committee.

to place slot machines statewide, with Long receiving 10 per cent of the take. Luciano was imprisoned in 1936 and Genovese fled the US to escape prosecution for murder in 1937, leaving Costello in charge of the family. Parole and deportation removed Luciano for good in 1946, and while Genovese returned to beat his murder charge, Costello relegated him to the rank of *caporegime*.

Costello stormed out of a televised Kefauver Committee hearing in March 1951, earning himself a citation for contempt of Congress that left him jailed from August 1952 to October 1953. While he was

Raffaele Cutolo

A poor sharecropper's son, Raffaele Cutolo was born in Otavanio, Italy, 29 km (18 miles) east of Naples, on December 20, 1941. At an early age, he witnessed the power of the Camorra – mainland Italy's version of the Sicilian Mafia – when his family was threatened with eviction. Cutolo's father appealed to the local godfather, who intervened with the landlord and thus permitted the Cutolos to retain their home. A discontented and disruptive student, Raffaele left school at age 12 to join a gang of teenage burglars. On February 24, 1963, he quarreled with a girl and slapped her for insulting him, then shot her boyfriend when he tried to intervene. Convicted of murder, Cutolo received a life sentence, reduced to 24 years on appeal.

Inmates at Poggioreale prison welcomed Cutolo as a 'man of honor,' fueling his ambition to achieve high rank in the Camorra. Renowned fellow inmate and *camorrista* Antonio 'The Badman' Spavone belittled Cutolo's aspirations, then declined the obligatory challenge to a knife fight. Soon after his release, Spavone survived a shotgun ambush with disfiguring wounds and resigned his post as a Camorra officer, further enhancing Cutolo's reputation. Though still imprisoned, Cutolo gathered soldiers including Pasquale 'The Animal' Barra, Vincenzo 'Big Black' Casillo, Antonino 'The Cudgel' Cuomo, Pasquale 'The Cardboard Picker' D'Amico and Giuseppe 'Japanese' Puca, dubbing their clique the New Camorra Organization (NCO). Despite his own lack of formal education, Cutolo was called 'The Professor,' for his spectacles and 'scholarly' approach to crime.

Formally established on October 24, 1970 – the day assigned to Saint Raphael by the Roman Catholic Church – the NCO appealed primarily to members from Campania, the province surrounding Naples. Casting himself as gangland's deep thinker, Cutolo told recruits, 'The day when the people of Campania understand that it is better to eat a slice of bread as a free man than to eat a steak as a slave, is the day when Campania will win.' Another pearl of wisdom declared: 'The value of a life doesn't consist of its length, but in the use made of it; often people live a long time without living very much. Consider this, my friends, as long as you are on this earth, everything depends on your will-power, not on the number of years you have lived.'

In 1980, still incarcerated, Cutolo published a collection of his thoughts and poems designed to inspire young *camorristi*. While casting himself as a prison reformer, and actively recruiting convicts in the process, Cutolo declared, 'The new Camorra must have a statute, a structure, an oath, a complete ceremony, a ritual that must excite people to the point that they would risk their lives for this organization.' Favored with a private cell at Poggioreale, where the average cage holds 25 inmates, Cutolo welcomed acolytes to kneel and kiss his ring. According to reports from the US Department of Justice, he also received money orders totaling 55,962,000 lire ($55,000) between March 5, 1981, and April 18, 1982, to ease his life in jail. Approximately half that sum was spent on clothes and food, including lobster and champagne prepared by a personal chef. In 1986, a film, *Il Camorrista,* dramatized Cutolo's life, with American actor Ben Gazzara cast as '*Il Professore.*'

Meanwhile, Cutolo's elder sister Rosetta – nicknamed *Occh'egghiaccio* ('Ice Eyes') – handled NCO business outside prison walls, ruling from Castle Mediceo, a 365-room palace built in the 16th century. She negotiated terms with Colombian drug cartels and plotted to bomb police headquarters in Naples, though the plan fell through and drove her underground in 1983. She surrendered in February 1993 to face trial for Mafia association, but jurors absolved her while prosecutors complained that Rosetta was the real brains behind the NCO. From prison, Raffaele chimed in, 'Rosetta has never been a *camorrista*. She only listened to me and sent me a few suitcases of money to prisoners like I told her to.'

Still imprisoned at this writing, with little prospect of release, Cutolo enjoys his life behind bars while granting frequent media interviews. 'I don't regret anything about my life,' he told one reporter. 'Crime is always a wrong move. It's true. However, we live in a society that is worse than criminality. Better to be crazy than to be a dreamer. A crazy man can be returned to reason. For a dreamer, he can only lose his head. A *camorrista* must be humble, wise and always ready to bring joy where there is pain. Only thus will he become a good *camorrista* before God. I am far from being a saint. I've made people cry, and I've done harm to those who wanted to harm me, making me cry. A *camorrista* is one who declares himself by his lifestyle. He who errors dies.'

Moe Dalitz

Allegedly born on Christmas Day 1899 – though no records exist to prove it – Morris Barney Dalitz was the second son of Jewish immigrant parents who met and married in Boston. The family moved to Detroit in 1903, where Moe and brother Louis shared classes with future members of the notorious Purple Gang. When Michigan went 'dry' in May 1918, the Purples grew rich by smuggling liquor from Canada aboard trucks owned by the Dalitz family laundry. Sidelines in gambling and labor racketeering followed, with numerous murders, as the gang defended its turf from local mafiosi and various outsiders.

While maintaining a residence and many business interests in Detroit, Dalitz moved his base of operations to Ohio in 1926, joining established racketeers Morris Kleinman, Louis Rothkopf and Samuel Tucker to complete 'the Cleveland Four.' Partnership with the Mafia and Irish mobsters led by Thomas McGinty forged an untouchable combination that eradicated independent competitors, corrupted Cleveland's police and defied the best efforts of legendary gangbuster Eliot Ness during 1935–41. During the same years, Dalitz and his partners planted outposts from Kentucky to New York, Florida, Arizona, California and Cuba.

While pursuing both illicit and legitimate investments, Dalitz met young union activist James Riddle Hoffa in Detroit, through a mutual mistress. Dalitz introduced Hoffa to local mobsters and to others nationwide, greatly advancing Hoffa's rise to power within the International Brotherhood of Teamsters. Hoffa subsequently repaid the favor with multimillion-dollar low-interest loans to finance Moe's construction of casinos, country clubs and bits of pricey real estate in California and Nevada. In later years, Dalitz would describe Hoffa as a fellow high-school classmate in Detroit, but that story foundered on the 14-year gap between their ages – and the fact that Hoffa never attended high school.

Dalitz served as an officer in World War II, managing army laundries in New York, then returned to full-time criminal pursuits in early 1945. After the war, Dalitz and his partners bought a controlling interest in the Desert Inn hotel-casino, in Las Vegas, Nevada. Exposure by the Kefauver Committee proved embarrassing in 1951, but failed to prevent acquisition of the Stardust casino nine years later. Dalitz faced multiple indictments over time – for bootlegging in 1930, illegal gambling in 1936 and 1943, smuggling warplanes to Egypt in 1948 and tax evasion in 1966 – but he never went to trial, or spent a night in jail. His power in Nevada was unrivaled, earning him the title 'Godfather of Las Vegas,' but he balanced underworld activities with extreme generosity, winning awards from various national groups for his charitable contributions.

In 1975, Dalitz filed a record-breaking libel suit against *Penthouse* magazine over an article that described his Rancho La Costa resort, outside San Diego, California, as a mob hangout built with Mafia money. The case dragged on into 1981, when both sides cut their losses and exchanged conciliatory letters. Nevadans mourned Moe's passing, from cancer and kidney failure, on August 31, 1989.

LEFT: Moe Dalitz (left) and Jack Donnelly arrive at a Las Vegas courtroom on August 10, 1966, to answer charges of tax evasion.

Jack Diamond

John Diamond Jr. was born to Irish immigrant parents in Philadelphia, Pennsylvania, on July 10, 1897. Brother Eddie followed in 1899. Their mother died in December 1913, after which their father moved the family to Brooklyn. John – normally called 'Jack' – soon joined the Hudson Dusters street gang and logged his first arrest in February 1914, for burglarizing a jeweler's shop. Along the way, Diamond earned his famous nickname, 'Legs,' either for his dancing, or his speed in fleeing crime scenes.

Diamond joined the army during World War I, but punched a sergeant who caught him stealing and served two years of a five-year sentence at Fort Leavenworth. Released with Prohibition underway, he joined the labor-racketeering gang led by Jacob 'Little Augie' Orgen. When fellow gang members Lepke Buchalter and Jacob Shapiro murdered Orgen on October 16, 1927, Diamond survived the first of many gunshot wounds that earned him the nickname 'Clay Pigeon of Gangland.'

Having failed as Augie Orgen's bodyguard, Diamond moved on to fill the same position for Arnold 'The Brain' Rothstein, mentor to many of Manhattan's leading Prohibition-era gangsters. Sadly for Rothstein, Diamond fared no better in his new job and was nowhere to be found when an unknown gunman fatally wounded Rothstein at the Park Central Hotel on November 5, 1928. Police grilled Diamond himself, as a suspect in that case, claiming that friction between Legs and The Brain had claimed five lives before Rothstein's, but no charges were forthcoming.

Deprived of a leader, Diamond adopted the lifestyle of an underworld renegade, hijacking liquor shipments from established bootleggers to stock his own Hotsy Totsy Club, sometimes kidnapping gangsters for ransom. Those activities sparked conflict with rival Dutch Schultz in the Bronx, while Diamond allied himself with another lethal Irish rogue, Vincent 'Mad Dog' Coll. Indictment on narcotics charges sent Diamond on a globe-hopping junket, rebuffed in turn by Ireland, England and Germany, but he returned to beat the charges in September 1929.

And still his rivals tried in vain to kill him. On October 12, 1930, unknown gunmen shot Diamond five times at Manhattan's Monticello Hotel. The *New York Times* declared him near death, but Diamond pulled through to punish his assailants personally. Another ambush, at a resort in the Catskill Mountains on April 27, 1931, sent Diamond back to hospital while leaving his would-be assassins frustrated. The law fared no better, arresting him 22 times while failing to convict him on charges of murder, kidnapping and tax evasion in various trials. Diamond was celebrating victory in the latter case, on December 18, 1931, when assassins tracked him to a hideout in Albany, New York,

RIGHT: A Philadelphia police mugshot of Jack 'Legs' Diamond from September 1930. Despite being arrested multiple times, Legs was never convicted of any crime.

BELOW: Diamond (with the hat) during a court hearing in Catskill, New York, on April 21, 1931, eight months before he died.

and shot him three times in the head, finally ending his long lucky streak.

Nor did the course of violence end with Diamond himself. On June 30, 1933, police found his widow, Alice Kenny Diamond, shot dead in her Brooklyn apartment, reporting that she had been dead for two days. That case, like her husband's murder, remains officially unsolved.

Jack Dragna

The future Mafia boss of Los Angeles, California, was born in Corleone, Sicily, on April 19, 1891. Christened Ignazio Dragna, he sailed for America with elder siblings Gaetano and Giuseppa on November 18, 1898, settling in Brooklyn, New York, with the family of fellow Corleone resident Antonio Rizzotti. Ignazio – known as Jack Ignatius Dragna in the States – returned to Sicily in 1909, where he joined both the Mafia and the Italian army. Back in New York by 1914, he befriended Bronx mafioso Gaetano Reina, later a *caporegime* under Giuseppe 'Joe The Boss' Masseria, killed in February 1930 during Masseria's war with rival Salvatore Maranzano.

New York police suspected Dragna of killing poultry dealer Bernard Baff in 1914. He fled to Los Angeles with cohort Benjamin Rizzotto, and received a three-year prison sentence there in 1915 for making 'Black Hand' extortion threats against victims in Long Beach. Brother Gaetano, now called 'Tom,' followed Jack upon his release from prison, and together they joined the Mafia family led by Joseph 'Iron Man' Ardizzone. Prohibition enriched the Dragnas, and when Ardizzone disappeared without a trace, presumed murdered in October 1931, Jack succeeded him as ruler of the family, supported by brother Tom, nephew Louis Tom Dragna and John Rosselli.

By the time Ardizzone vanished in LA, Lucky Luciano and associates had purged the New York Mafia of its die-hard 'Mustache Petes' and pioneered creation of a multi-ethnic national crime syndicate. Dragna's family took its place within that new association, but suffered a loss of prestige in 1937, when Bugsy Siegel and Mickey Cohen arrived to monopolize illegal gambling for the national consortium. Dragna swallowed his pride for a time, but friction persisted and erupted in sporadic acts of violence. Author Donald Wolfe claims that Siegel committed the infamous 'Black Dahlia' murder of prostitute Elizabeth Short in January 1947, as some kind of warning to Dragna, thus prompting Dragna to murder Siegel six months later. Most sources disagree, contending that Siegel died for mismanaging syndicate funds in Las Vegas, Nevada, but even if Wolfe is correct the Siegel hit accomplished little, since Cohen replaced him as boss of LA.

Any pretense of cooperation vanished during 1948, as Dragna and Siegel waged nonstop guerrilla war against each other. Shootings and bombings made regular headlines over the next three years, until Cohen was imprisoned for tax evasion. Immigration officials ordered Dragna's deportation in 1953, and while he stalled that move in court, Los Angeles police harassed him constantly, even arresting him for lewd acts with a mistress in a trailer they had bugged with microphones. Distracted from his duties as a mafioso, Dragna suffered a fatal heart attack on February 23, 1956.

Brother Tom promptly retired as *consiglieri,* ceding command of the LA family to Frank DeSimone, a law school graduate whose leadership left much to be desired. Informers claimed that DeSimone had raped the wife of underboss Girolamo 'Momo' Adamo, prompting Adamo to shoot his wife and commit suicide. Such incidents – and the proximity of Disneyland – led mobsters outside California to brand LA's family 'the Mickey Mouse Mafia.'

Jack's nephew Louis Tom Dragna remained with the family, arrested for extortion in 1959 and subsequently convicted in May 1961. Between those events, he claimed dubious honors as one of 11 gangsters banned for life from Nevada casinos, when the state's Gaming Commission created its controversial 'Black Book.' The US Court of Appeals overturned Dragna's conviction on February 13, 1963, and he persevered with the syndicate, reportedly appointed as acting boss of LA in 1975, after Dominic Brooklier was sentenced to prison. In 1978, federal prosecutors charged Dragna and four codefendants with murder, racketeering and extortion. Turncoat Jimmy Fratianno testified for the state, resulting in convictions for all. Dragna entered prison on June 27, 1981, and was released on March 18, 1985, barred from further underworld activity by terms of his parole.

Du Yuesheng

Chinese mobster Du Yuesheng was born in the village of Pudong, across the Huangpu River from Shanghai, sometime in 1887. As a youth, he joined the Green Gang, a faction of the Chinese Triad societies. The Triads were initially founded by Fong Toh Tak of the Shaolin temple to defend **Han** Chinese from the hostile Qing dynasty and seek restoration of the Ming dynasty deposed in 1644. Triad members also controlled the Kuomingtang (or Chinese Nationalist Party) organized by gang member Sun Yat-sen in 1919, led from 1927 onward by successor Chiang Kai-Shek. Du Yuesheng – known as 'Big-Eared Du' for his most prominent feature – rose to command the Green Gang by the early 1920s, from headquarters in Shanghai's French Concession. He controlled the local opium trade, plus gambling, prostitution and protection rackets, in collaboration with Huang Jinrong, corrupt chief of Chinese detectives in the French Concession's Garde Municipale.

S pring 1927 brought mayhem to Shanghai, as Kuomingtang warriors launched a wave of 'white terror' against pro-communist rebels. Green Gang members did their part, operating as the Society for Common Progress to join in the slaughter of 5,000 leftists on April 12. Afterward, Chiang Kai-Shek appointed Du Yuesheng as a general in the nationalist army for his efforts, thus securing his iron-fisted control of local rackets. British authors W.H. Auden and Christopher Isherwood, in their 1939 volume *Journey to a War*, wrote of Du Yuesheng: 'Du himself was tall and thin, with a face that seemed hewn out of stone, a Chinese version of the Sphinx. Peculiarly and inexplicably terrifying were his feet, in their silk socks and smart pointed European boots, emerging from beneath the long silken gown. Perhaps the Sphinx, too, would be even more frightening if it wore a modern top-hat.'

In 1932, Du Yuesheng became a member of the French Concession's Municipal Council. The following year, Shanghai's edition of *Who's Who* listed his accomplishments as follows: 'Entered business at an early age. At present, most influential resident, French Concession, Shanghai. Well-known public welfare worker. 1932 councillor, French Municipal Council. President, Chung Wai Bank, and Tung Wai Bank, Shanghai. Founder and chairman, board of directors, Cheng Shih Middle School. President, Shanghai Emergency Hospital. Member, supervisory committee, General Chamber of Commerce. Managing director, Hua Feng Paper Mill, Hangchow. Director, Commercial Bank of China, Kiangsu and Chekiang Bank, Great China University, Chinese Cotton Goods Exchange, and China Merchants Steam Navigation Co., Shanghai, etc. President, Jen Chi Hospital, Ningpo.'

The Shanghai Massacre did not end China's civil war. Communist forces battled on against the Kuomingtang until 1937, then joined forces with nationalist troops to oppose Japanese invaders, but resumed their liberation struggle in 1945. Du Yuesheng fled from Shanghai to British Hong Kong in 1937, then returned to his native city in 1945, expecting a triumphal welcome. Instead, he found himself hated for leaving Shanghai's people to the Japanese. Despite that shock, he remained loyal to martial nationalist forces and resumed the fight against Mao Zedong's communists. Mao's troops captured Nanjing, the Kuomingtang capital, on April 21, 1949, whereupon Chiang Kai-Shek led the bulk of his forces into exile on Taiwan.

Already disillusioned with Chiang's leadership, Du returned to Hong Kong in 1949 and spent his last years there, dying from natural causes at age 64, in 1951. Four decades later, Hong Kong actor Ray Lui starred as gangster 'Luk Yu-San' in a fictionalized version of Du's life, titled *Lord Of The East China Sea*. A sequel, *Lord of the East China Sea II*, continued his romanticized adventures in May 1993.

Rayful Edmond III

Following the April 1968 assassination of Dr. Martin Luther King Jr. and ensuing race riots, author Ben Gilbert published *Ten Blocks from the White House*, describing the squalor of ghettoes existing within sight of the United States Capitol. Future drug lord Rayful Edmond III was a child of those slums, born on November 26, 1964. He managed to avoid convictions as a young street gang member, and by his late teens had organized the most successful drug-trafficking network active in Washington, DC.

E dmond owed much of his success to Colombian brothers Dixon Dario and Osvaldo 'Chiqui' Trujillo Blanco, sons of Griselda Blanco, the Medellín Cartel's ruthless 'godmother' based in Miami, Florida. Although Edmond never personally met the brothers until they were later imprisoned together, he purchased an average 1,000 to 2,000 kg (1.1–2.2 tons) of cocaine per week from their syndicate, refining it with baking soda into 'crack' or 'rock' form for smoking. Agents of the US Drug Enforcement Administration later credited Edmond with introducing crack to the nation's capital – and for helping double the city's murder rate between 1985 and 1988. Edmond himself was suspected of ordering 400 murders, plus the attempted slaying of Rev. William Bynum, shot 12 times after leading an anti-drug march through Northeast Washington.

Fabulously wealthy from his criminal pursuits – earning some $300 million per year by his personal estimate – Edmond enjoyed a lavish lifestyle. He spent $457,619 in one Georgetown clothing store alone, Linea Pitti, which closed in March 1991 following owner Charles Wynn's conviction for laundering drug profits for Edmond. In his leisure time, Edmond developed a near obsession for Georgetown University's basketball team, the Hoyas, which Edmond described as 'Black America's Team' and '12 angry black men,' idolized by inner-city gangsters. Edmond personally befriended several Hoyas players, a circumstance that angered Coach John Thompson and provoked a tense meeting, at which Thompson issued a strict hands-off order.

Federal agents arrested Edmond in 1989, confining him at the Marine Corps base in Quantico, Virginia, as a hedge against potential rescue attempts by his gang. Airlifted daily from the base to Washington's federal courthouse for his trial, in 1990, Edmond was convicted on charges that included conducting a criminal enterprise, conspiracy to possess and distribute cocaine, illegally employing persons under 18 years of age, interstate travel in aid of racketeering, and unlawful use of communications facilities. On September 17, 1990, he was sentenced to life imprisonment without parole. His mother and several sisters, convicted at the same trial, received sentences averaging 14 years each.

Imprisonment at Lewisburg, Pennsylvania, failed to halt Edmond's criminal activities. In October 1991, an informer tipped police that Edmond was running his network from behind bars. FBI agents tapped four prison phones between April and October 1992, recording Edmond's conversations. In July 1992, agents intercepted two of Edmond's cohorts with $470,000 earmarked for the Trujillo Blanco syndicate. In July 1994, officers jailed Edmond's girlfriend and five others in a drug sting, then followed up with raids in August 1996 that bagged 13 hirelings with 60 kg (130 lb) of cocaine and $200,000 in cash. Faced with a threat of being silenced by his Colombian partners, Edmond turned state's evidence and vanished into the Witness Protection Program.

Pablo Escobar

Colombian drug lord Pablo Escobar once described himself as 'a decent man who exports flowers.' Later, in a more expansive mood, he declared, 'Sometimes I am God. If I say a man dies, he dies that same day. There can only be one King. All empires are created of blood and fire.'

Born in poverty on December 1, 1949, Pablo Emilio Escobar Gaviria learned the value of education from his mother, a Medellín school teacher. He studied political science at the Universidad de Antioquia, but was forced to drop out by rising tuition fees. Reverting to crime, Escobar began stealing gravestones and grinding off their inscriptions for resale to new customers. His next step up the illicit ladder, was as an employee of contraband smuggler Alvaro Prieto, and made Escobar a millionaire by age 22. He compounded that fortune by smuggling cocaine to the United States, making connections with others involved in the growing traffic.

By 1975, Escobar had joined a select handful of allies – José Abello Silva, Carlos Lehder Rivas, the Ochoa brothers and José Rodríguez Gacha – to form the Medellín Cartel, one of four major drug-smuggling syndicates active in Colombia. Demand from the United States proved insatiable, boosting cartel profits to an estimated $60 million per day in the 1980s. By 1989, *Forbes* magazine would rank Escobar as the seventh-richest man on Earth.

That wealth allowed Escobar to flaunt his notoriety. His enormous personal estate, dubbed Hacienda Napoles, included a manmade lake and a private zoo. In 1982, despite his recognition as a cocaine baron – or because of it – Escobar won election to Colombia's Chamber of Representatives as a deputy/alternate member of the Liberal Party.

The Medellín Cartel's twin pillars of support were bribery and murder, embodied in the motto *plato o plomo* – 'silver or lead.' Police, public officials, journalists, or anyone else who refused cartel bribes would be killed, sometimes by Escobar himself. Mayhem increased after Colombia's government approved extradition of cartel leaders to the United States for trial, sparking a declaration of war against the state by Escobar and others who called themselves 'The Extraditables.'

On November 6, 1985, guerrillas from the revolutionary M-19 movement financed by Escobar stormed Bogotá's Palace of Justice, killing 11 of the nation's 25 Supreme Court justices and burning files related to extradition of cartel commanders. Before soldiers recaptured the building, a total of 120 persons were slain. On August 18, 1989,

ABOVE: Pablo Escobar's illegal smuggling activities made him a millionaire by the age of 22.

ABOVE: An undated photograph of Escobar alongside partner-in-crime Jorge Ochoa. As members of the Medellín Cartel, they bribed and murdered their way to great riches.

cartel gunmen murdered presidential candidate Luis Galán Sarmiento in Bogotá. On November 27, while trying to kill candidate César Gaviria Trujillo, cartel bombers destroyed Avianca Airlines Flight 203 with 107 persons aboard. (Gaviria missed the flight.) Nine days later, another cartel bomb exploded in Bogotá, outside headquarters of the Administrative Department of Security, claiming 52 lives, wounding more than 1,000 people and destroying 300 buildings.

Those crimes and others like them mobilized Colombia's government to arrest Escobar, but he remained at large until 1991, when a new constitution banned extradition to America. He then surrendered on condition that the government construct a special prison outside Medellín, dubbed La Catedral, where Escobar relaxed in luxury, conducting his business affairs and executing several rivals on the prison grounds. When authorities tried to relocate Escobar on July 22, 1992, he escaped from custody and fled once more into hiding.

Thus began the greatest manhunt in Colombian history, with members of the US Army's Delta Force and Navy SEALs assisting officers of a special Colombian strike force known as the Search Bloc. Aside from duly-authorized law enforcement personnel, Escobar was also hunted by a vigilante group called 'Los Pepes' – short for *Los Perseguidos por Pablo Escobar* ('People Persecuted by Pablo Escobar'). While ostensibly devoted to law and order, leaders of Los Pepes included members of the rival Cali drug cartel, sporadically at war with Escobar's Medellín syndicate since the mid-1980s. In pursuit of Escobar, Los Pepes killed more than 300 cartel associates and their relatives, while destroying property valued in millions of dollars.

Search Bloc technicians, using radio triangulation gear supplied by US military forces, finally traced Escobar to a middle-class Medellín neighborhood on December 2, 1993. After a brisk exchange of gunfire, Escobar fled his hideout with bodyguard Alvaro de Jesús Agudelo, leading police on a wild chase across the rooftops of adjoining homes. Pursuers killed both fugitives, with Escobar receiving bullet wounds to the head, torso

and leg. Rumors of suicide, or point-blank execution were refuted by an autopsy report showing that Escobar received his fatal head shot from more than arm's length away. Even then, controversy lingered, with conspiracy theorists suggesting that Escobar had escaped, leaving a look-alike dead in his place. Exhumed at the request of relatives on October 28, 2006, Escobar's corpse was subjected to DNA testing which confirmed his identity.

By then, the Medellín Cartel had crumbled, with Escobar's cofounding partners imprisoned, or dead. Carlos Lehder, extradited to America in 1987, received

BELOW: Members of the Colombia army raid the house of drugs king Pablo Escobar in fall 1989.

a 55-year prison term. José Rodríguez Gacha, his son, and four other cohorts died in a shootout with Colombian National Police near Tolú, on December 18, 1989. Jorge and Juan Ochoa surrendered in 1991, served five years each, and retired to live off their fortunes in peace, while brother Fabio drew a 30-year sentence in the United States.

Despite the greed and violence that surrounded him, Pablo Escobar remains a folk hero to some Colombians.

Brother Robert Escobar – the Medellín Cartel's 'minister of finance,' blinded by a letter bomb in prison during 1993 – maintains that Pablo 'said he felt like Robin Hood.' As recently as November 2007, journalist Alex Roland, raised in Colombia, reported that 'the regular people, many people, especially from Medellín, love him. He built towns and he gave money to the people. Half the city loves him; the other half hates him.'

Demetrius Flenory

African Americans have always played a role in organized crime. Traditionally, some served as hirelings for white mobsters, while others – like Ellsworth 'Bumpy' Johnson in New York City – dominated rackets in black urban ghettoes. Still, it required the 1960s civil rights movement and America's 'war on drugs' to produce black gangsters rivaling those from other ethnic backgrounds. The Black Mafia Family (BMF) is a case in point.

Brothers Demetrius and Terry Flenory, known respectively to fellow thugs as 'Big Meech' and 'Southwest T,' began their criminal careers peddling crack cocaine on the streets of Ecorse, Michigan, and South Detroit. Demetrius was older, born in 1969, and led the way in creating the BMF's network of smugglers and dealers that ultimately spanned the continent, headquartered in Atlanta, Georgia, with cocaine distribution hubs in Alabama, California, Florida, Kentucky, Missouri, North Carolina, Tennessee and Texas. Investigators say that BMF membership exceeded 500 by 2001, when a falling out between the brothers sent Terry Flenory off to Los Angeles, bent on creating his own syndicate.

Part of the problem was Demetrius's free-wheeling lifestyle. Both brothers loved to party, but Terry, two years younger, worried that Demetrius was overdoing it. DEA wiretaps recorded Terry's complaints to relatives about Demetrius, protesting that his elder brother's wild life was distracting him from business and attracting the attention of authorities. Specific items on the gripe list: a $100,000 birthday party thrown by Demetrius for himself, complete with live exotic animals, at Atlanta's Compound

nightclub; accumulation of $5 million in debt at Atlanta's Ritz-Carlton Hotel, paid off one afternoon in cash; and a penchant for ever-shifting residences, including a rental home in Miami, Florida.

By the time Terry logged those complaints, federal agents had been tracking BMF activities for nearly a decade. Between October 1996 and October 2005, authorities in eight states seized 470 kg (1,032 lb) of cocaine and $9,309,125 in cash from Flenory couriers. Some of those arrested in the raids turned state's evidence to spare themselves from prison, including trusted BMF members Eric Bivens, Arnold Boyd, Daniel Corral, Benjamin Johnson, William 'Doc' Marshall, Charles Parson, Ralph Simms, Damon Thomas, Marc Whaley and Harold Wilcox. All furnished damning testimony against the Flenory brothers, buttressed by 900 pages of wiretap transcripts.

DEA agents arrested the brothers and 30 more BMF members in October 2005. Both Flenorys and 47 cohorts were indicted for drug trafficking and money laundering on June 15, 2006, with further charges added on July 25–26, 2007. The brothers pled guilty in November 2007 and received matching 30-year sentences in September

2008. They are eligible for parole in December 2031, when Demetrius will be 62 years old and Terry age 60. BMF lieutenant Fleming Daniels was sentenced to 20 years, while Barima 'Bleu DaVinci' McKnight got five years and four months. Trial is pending for other BMF defendants, including Vernon Marcus Coleman, captured on July 17, 2009.

Rolando Florián Féliz

Born in 1965, Rolando Florián Féliz rose from a childhood life of poverty to rule the Dominican Republic's largest drug-trafficking network by age 31. During those years, he fathered 15 children, collected a small harem of mistresses and spent millions of dollars maintaining a lavish lifestyle. Through it all, despite his crimes, many Dominicans revered him as 'a saint.' The reason for that attitude may lie in the results of a World Bank survey conducted in 2008, revealing that 81 per cent of all Dominican natives view their government as corrupt, with 38 per cent calling it 'very corrupt.' Reports of Florián's activities in newspapers such as *Diario* routinely challenge the veracity of statements from police.

At the height of his power, Florián proved elusive enough that Dominican authorities tried him *in absentia* during 1994, convicting him of importing 900 kg (1 ton) of cocaine. The charge carried a 20-year sentence and a $500,000 fine, but arresting Florián was problematical. Agents of the Dirección Nacional de Control de Drogas finally caught him by chance, on June 10, 1996, after Florián was spotted at the luxurious Cannes Villa Resort in Guayacanes. The officers declined a $2 million bribe, and Florián subsequently received an additional six years for killing Víctor Augusto Féliz, son of ex-senator and social reformer, Augusto Féliz Matos.

Prison life was hardly arduous for Florián. His wealth and corruption of officials ensured Florián a deluxe cell with ready access to books, television and call girls. Even so, he longed for freedom, attempting escape on at least five occasions. In December 2005, during construction work at Najayo Penitentiary in Monte Plata, officers found an incomplete tunnel intended for Florián's premature exit. A judge in San Cristóbal Province then ordered Florián's transfer to a cellblock for common prisoners, presumably restricting his privacy and privileges. The move prompted Florián to press for early parole, ironically describing himself as a 'model prisoner.'

While that fruitless campaign was underway, in April 2006, US authorities petitioned for extradition of Florián's brother, Juan Danilo Florián Féliz, on charges of drug trafficking with defendant Euleterio Guante and a third subject still at large, known only as 'El Flaco.' Guante had been arrested three years earlier, after transporting 1,360 kg (1.5 tons) of cocaine from the Dominican Republic to Puerto Rico, a US possession.

Rolando Florián would not survive to see the outcome of his brother's case. On May 16, 2009, he hosted a party for fellow inmates and two female visitors. Police Captain Lino Oscar Jimenez arrived to halt the festivities at 8:00 p.m. and later claimed that Florián attacked him with a knife, slicing his cheek before Jimenez shot Florián eight times. Even then, Florián survived another 13 hours in hospital, dying in the early hours of May 17. Relatives and admirers termed the shooting a summary execution, sending Florián off on May 18 with a lavish funeral ceremony, calling for the death of Captain Jimenez. Inquiries at the prison revealed Florián's special treatment in custody, but failed to remove the warden responsible.

Frankie Fraser

Born in Lambeth, London, on December 13, 1923, Frank Davidson Fraser began stealing at an early age and described his pursuit of crime as 'inevitable,' claiming that 'every other family [in Lambeth] was into crime.' Drafted into military service during World War II, he repeatedly deserted and served two prison terms for burglary. Despite those setbacks, he recalled the war years as 'wonderful, for thieving wise, gangster wise and everything,' once saying, 'I'll never forgive Hitler for surrendering. They were great days.'

Back in civilian life, Fraser drew another two-year sentence for looting a jeweler's shop, was certified insane in prison – hence his 'Mad Frankie' nickname – and emerged in 1949 to serve as bodyguard for London gangster Billy Hill. A sideline in bank robbery sent Fraser back to prison, where he was certified insane a second time and packed off to Broadmoor Hospital pending release in 1955. The following year, Fraser led a gang that attacked mobster Jack 'Spot' Comer and his wife, earning Mad Frankie another seven-year sentence.

Released in the early 1960s, Fraser allied himself with South London gangsters Charlie and Eddie Richardson, who waged sporadic warfare against rivals Reginald and Ronald Kray. Despite that feud – and Fraser's near-miss acquittal in the 1966 murder of Kray loyalist Richard Hart – he later described the Kray twins as 'absolute gentlemen.' In 1967, jurors convicted Fraser once again, this time on charges of torturing gang victims whose teeth he extracted with pliers.

In all, Fraser spent 42 years in various British prisons, frequently attacking guards and joining in cellblock riots. Authorities named him as a ringleader of the 1969 Parkhurst prison melee, which left him hospitalized for six weeks. Finally released in 1985, as something of a gangland celebrity, Fraser survived a 1991 shooting in Clerkenwell, London, and blamed rogue police for the attack. Authorities preferred to lay the blame on members of a London crime syndicate known as 'The A-Team,' led by violent brothers Patrick, Terry and Tommy Adams.

Today, Frankie has become a media commodity. An Internet website hails him as 'gangland's elder statesman, one of the great continuing professional criminal links of the last century.' He has appeared in two feature films and half a dozen television programs, produced five books

with co-author James Morton, led tours of London's one-time gangster haunts and, in 1999, appeared at London's Jermyn Street Theatre in a one man show titled *An Evening with Frankie Fraser.*

BELOW: Frankie Fraser earned notoriety in the 1960s as a henchman for the Richardson twins, before becoming a gangland celebrity in later life.

Jimmy Fratianno

Born in Naples on November 14, 1913, Aladena Fratianno emigrated to Cleveland, Ohio, with his parents when he was four months old. Despising his given name as too feminine, Fratianno called himself 'Jimmy' while running with street gangs in Little Italy. In his teens, Fratianno drove a limousine for gamblers patronizing casinos owned by Moe Dalitz and his partners, establishing contacts with the local Mafia.

From Ohio, Fratianno gravitated to Los Angeles and joined the crime family run by Jack Dragna, embroiled in sporadic conflict with Jewish mobster Mickey Cohen. Shuttling between LA and Las Vegas, Nevada, Fratianno later claimed involvement in 11 contract murders ordered by Dragna and successor Dominic Brooklier. His best-known victims were the 'Two Tonys' – Anthony Brancato and Anthony Trombino – shot in Los Angeles on August 6, 1951 after robbing the

BELOW: Jimmy Fratianno (far right) alongside mobster associates and singer Frank Sinatra in September 1976.

ABOVE: Fratianno photographed during an interview in March 1981. The gangster claimed involvement with 11 murders during the 1950s.

RIGHT: Jimmy 'the Weasel' Fratianno in a Los Angeles court in relation to the murder of Sam Rummell, in December 1950.

claimed Licata's life in October 1974, clearing the throne for Dominic Brooklier.

Brooklier's ascendancy spelled trouble for Fratianno, who soon got wind of a contract placed on his life and turned state's evidence against the Mafia, sending Brooklier and others to prison. He also collaborated with different authors on two memoirs, *The Last Mafioso* (1980) and *Vengeance is Mine* (1987). Some of

Flamingo hotel-casino in Las Vegas. Other acknowledged victims include ex-bootlegger Frank Borgia, strangled with 'the Italian rope trick' in 1951; another 1951 target, Mickey Cohen loyalist Frank Niccoli; and gambler Louis 'Russian Louie' Strauss, killed and secretly buried in April 1953 for attempting to blackmail Las Vegas casino owner Benny 'The Cowboy' Binion.

Convicted of extortion in 1954, Fratianno received a 6½-year sentence, but emerged from prison unreformed. Instead, the LA family had changed with Jack Dragna's death in February 1956 and Frank DeSimone's ascension to command, frustrating the ambitions of contender and Fratianno ally John Rosselli. Some mafiosi accused DeSimone of tarnishing the family's reputation, to the extent that Eastern mobsters dubbed LA's clique 'The Mickey Mouse Mafia.' Stricken with a fatal heart attack in August 1967, DeSimone was succeeded by Sicilian-born Nicolo 'Old Man' Licata, who had furnished Fratianno's alibi on the night he killed the Two Tonys. Age and illness his memories were unreliable – such as the 'murder' of a Nevada gambler who actually died from leukemia – while others simply served to inflate his reputation, as in scenes where Fratianno allegedly beat up Las Vegas mogul Morris Kleinman, a longtime syndicate VIP and partner of Moe Dalitz. When called as a witness for Dalitz's Rancho La Costa resort, in Moe's libel action against *Penthouse* magazine, Fratianno admitted lying frequently to FBI agents and his biographers alike. Some of those lapses may have been explained when Fratianno died on June 30, 1993. An autopsy report attributed his death to Alzheimer's Disease.

Carmine Galante

The son of Sicilian immigrants, born in East Harlem, New York, on February 21, 1910, Carmine Galante formed his own street gang at age 11 and logged his first arrest three years later for shoplifting. Sent to reform school as an 'incorrigible' youth, he emerged unrepentant and continued racking up arrests for petty larceny, grand larceny, assault and robbery. In 1926, he served a prison term for second-degree assault and robbery. Four years later, on Christmas Day 1930, he and two companions wounded a policeman and a six-year-old bystander during an attempted hijacking. Caught when he slipped and fell on ice, Galante endured jailhouse beatings without naming his accomplices and received a 12½ -year prison term.

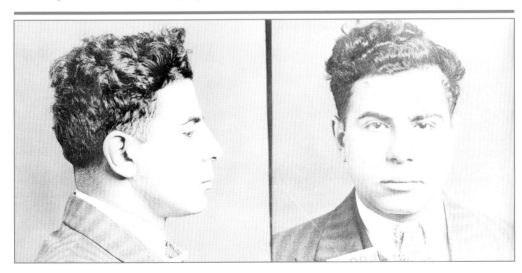

ABOVE: A police mugshot of Carmine Galante following his arrest in 1943 in relation to the murder of Carlo Tresca.

Paroled in May 1939, Galante resumed his duties with the New York Mafia and built his reputation as a merciless contract killer. Police detained him as

ABOVE: Head bowed, Galante is escorted into court by federal officers on June 3, 1953, on suspicion of narcotics offenses.

the presumed triggerman in journalist Carlo Tresca's murder on January 11, 1943, ordered by Vito Genovese from exile as a favor to Italian dictator Benito Mussolini, but they ultimately filed no charges. When not stalking victims, Galante served as chauffeur and bodyguard for boss Joe Bonanno, later advancing to *caporegime,* then to underboss. Federal prosecutors interrupted his ascendancy in July 1956, with an indictment for drug trafficking. Galante dodged arrest until June 3, 1959, when he was captured in New Jersey and held without bail. His first trial closed without a verdict, when the jury foreman fell downstairs

in an abandoned building and snapped his spine. Convicted at his second trial in 1962, Galante received a 20-year sentence.

For reasons still unclear, Galante blamed deceased mafioso Frank Costello for his incarceration. Within two days of his parole, on January 25, 1974, a bomb shattered the bronze doors of Costello's mausoleum at Greenwood Cemetery. Installed as acting boss of the Bonanno Family in early 1975, when boss Phillip 'Rusty' Rastelli was jailed for extortion and violation of federal anti-trust statutes, Galante also threatened powerful godfather Carlo Gambino, whom he blamed for Joe Bonanno's dismissal in the mid-1960s. Police suspected Galante's soldiers of killing eight Gambino Family members, but as usual, the crimes remain officially unsolved.

Operating from headquarters at L & T Cleaners on

Mulberry Street, in Manhattan's Little Italy, Galante schemed to expand his power within New York's underworld. While using daughter Nina as his personal chauffeur, Galante considered enlisting her as the Mafia's first 'made' woman, then tried another tack and arranged her marriage to Alphonse Persico, son of Colombo Family boss Carmine 'The Snake' Persico.

Galante's plans hit a snag on October 11, 1977, when federal agents arrested him for violating his parole through association with known criminals. His parole was formally revoked on March 3, 1978, but then Galante won a legal ruling that restricted his imprisonment to 60 days. Prosecutors contested that judgment and wrangling continued in court for 11 more months; the feds lost their case on March 23, 1979, after failing to meet Judge T.F. Gilroy's deadline for a formal revocation hearing.

By the time he was released from custody, Galante's fate was sealed. On July 12, 1979, he ate lunch at Joe and Mary's Italian-American Restaurant in Bushwick, Brooklyn, with bodyguard Leonard Coppola and cousin Giuseppe Turano, the restaurant's owner. As the men finished their meal, a firing squad appeared at their outdoor table and killed all three with close-range shotgun blasts. Galante died with a cigar clenched in his teeth, while the assassins fled in a stolen car, soon found abandoned nearby.

Gangland talk named the shooters as Anthony 'Bruno' Indelicato, Phillip 'The Priest' Giaccone and Dominick 'Big Trin' Trinchera, acting under orders from Indelicato's father, Bonanno Family *caporegime* Alphonse 'Sonny Red' Indelicato. Those rumors were supported by surveillance camera footage shot at a Manhattan social club on July 12, which revealed Anthony Indelicato receiving congratulations from uncle J.B. Carnone. Since the club doubled as headquarters for Gambino Family underboss Aniello Dellacroce, authorities concluded that Galante's murder had been sanctioned by the Mafia's ruling commission.

Such murders commonly remain unsolved, but Anthony Indelicato was convicted of Galante's slaying at the 'Mafia Commission Trial' held in New York City's federal court between February 25, 1985 and November 19, 1986, receiving a 13-year sentence. Paroled in 2000, he was arrested for parole violation in 2002 and served eight more months. In February 2004, another parole violation sent him back to prison for two years. Alleged gunmen Giaccone and Trinchera were murdered with Alphonse Indelicato on May 5, 1981, while attending peace talks with dissident Bonanno Family members at the 20/20 Night Club in Clinton Hill, Brooklyn. Gambino Family *caporegime* John Gotti arranged burial of the corpses on a vacant lot in Lindenwood, Queens, where FBI agents recovered them in December 2004.

Joey Gallo

Born in Brooklyn's Red Hook district on April 7, 1929, Joseph Gallo followed the usual path of juvenile crime that produces most mafiosi. The film *Kiss of Death* (1947) so impressed 18-year-old Gallo that he consciously mimicked actor Richard Widmark's gangster mannerisms and learned to recite long passages of the movie's dialogue from memory. In real life, with brothers Albert and Larry, he sought affiliation with the Mafia family run by Giuseppe 'Joe' Profaci. The brothers specialized in violence, earning Joseph the nickname 'Crazy Joe,' while Albert was dubbed 'Kid Blast.' Some reporters name the Gallos as the executioners of Albert Anastasia in October 1957.

True or not, the brothers felt themselves badly treated by Profaci – who, in turn, resented their frequent rule breaking and their unauthorized alliances with black gangsters in Brooklyn. Profaci's soldiers bungled an attempt to kill Joey in May 1961, then succeeded with Gallo loyalist Joseph Gioelli, dumping his body at sea while returning his clothes stuffed with fish. Police foiled an attempt to strangle Larry Gallo at a Brooklyn supper club, in August 1961. (Both incidents were later fictionalized in *The Godfather*.) An extortion conviction

removed Joey from the battlefront before year's end, while cancer killed Profaci in June 1962, thus apparently ending the war.

Crazy Joe rediscovered himself while imprisoned in Attica, New York, immersed in classic literature and friendship with radical black inmates. Released in February 1971, Gallo found himself a celebrity of sorts,

BELOW: Joey (front left) and brother Larry (front right) outside Kings County Court, New York, on October 10, 1961.

thanks to novelist Jimmy Breslin's pastiche of the Gallo–Profaci war, published in 1969 as *The Gang That Couldn't Shoot Straight*. Director James Goldstone filmed the dark comedy in 1971, starring Jerry Orbach as lead character 'Kid Sally,' and Gallo fell into the actor's orbit for a whirl of parties and receptions prior to the film's premiere on December 22. Suddenly in demand, a figure to be coddled and quoted, Gallo appeared to be a changed man.

But appearances may be deceiving.

In Joey's absence, control of the Profaci family had fallen to Joseph Colombo, no friend to the Gallo brothers. Joey revived his bid for power and was widely deemed responsible for the shooting that left Colombo

RIGHT: Mobster Joey Gallo, pictured in 1961. 'Crazy Joe' and his brothers fought a bloody battle for control of the Brooklyn underworld.

BELOW: The crime scene outside Umberto's Clam House following Joey Gallo's murder on April 7, 1972.

comatose on June 28, 1971. Retaliation came on April 7, 1972, as Gallo celebrated his 43rd birthday at Umberto's Clam House in Manhattan's Little Italy. Two gunmen crashed the party, killing Gallo with five shots and wounding bodyguard Peter 'Pete the Greek' Diapoulas in the buttocks. At Gallo's funeral, his sister predicted

ABOVE: Joey Gallo's funeral took place in Brooklyn three days after his execution. His widow, Sina (wearing dark glasses) follows the casket.

that 'the streets will run red with blood,' but no war was forthcoming.

Carlo Gambino

A native of Caccamo, Sicily, born on August 24, 1902, Carlo Gambino was raised in a Mafia family and reportedly committed his first murders as a teenager. He reached New York City in 1921, as a stowaway, and soon immersed himself in bootlegging, gambling and drug trafficking. While allied with Giuseppe 'Joe the Boss' Masseria during his war with rival Salvatore Maranzano in 1929–31, Gambino joined underboss Lucky Luciano in a plot to remove the American Mafia's 'Mustache Petes.'

With the elimination of Masseria in April 1931 and Maranzano five months later, Gambino found himself assigned to a new family led by Vincenzo Mangano.

Unwilling to give up bootlegging when Prohibition ended in 1933, Gambino continued selling untaxed liquor. Federal prosecutors convicted him in May 1939, resulting in a 22-month prison sentence, but that conviction was quashed on appeal eight months later. Between 1942 and 1945 Gambino earned millions from stealing and selling government gasoline ration stamps. Vincenzo Mangano's disappearance in April 1951 placed Albert Anastasia in charge of the family, with Gambino promoted to second in command.

By 1957, Anastasia's enemies far outnumbered his allies. Gambino saw an opportunity, working with Vito Genovese and Meyer Lansky to arrange Anastasia's murder that October. Gambino succeeded to the family throne, but suffered embarrassment on November 14, when police arrested him with 62 other mafiosi at Apalachin, New York. No convictions resulted from that raid, but J. Edgar Hoover created the FBI's 'Top Hoodlum Program,' which mounted

RIGHT: Carlo Gambino in March 1970, following his arrest for plotting to rob an armored car containing $6 million.

THE CARLO GAMBINO FAMILY

BOSS

CARLO GAMBINO
ALIAS
"DON CARLO"
FBI #934-450
N.Y.C.P.D - B#125760
(1A, 2, 3, 4, 4A, 5, 6, 8)

Successor to:

ALBERT ANASTASIA
DECEASED
N.Y.C.P.D.*B2300
MURDERED
(2, 6, 8)

VINCENT MANGANO
ALIAS
N.Y.C.P.D - B#7381
PRESUMED MURDERED

PHILIP MANGANO
N.Y.C.P.D - B#35867
MURDERED

KEY TO ACTIVITY CODE
1A. CURRENTLY IN JAIL FOR NARCOTICS
1B. AWAITING TRIAL FOR NARCOTICS
1C. PREVIOUS CONVICTION FOR NARCOTICS
1D. SUSPECTED OF BEING ACTIVE IN NARCOTICS
2. GAMBLING
3. SHYLOCKING
4. LABOR RACKETEERING
5. VENDING MACHINES AND/OR JUKE BOXES
6. EXTORTION, STRONG ARM AND MURDER
7. COUNTERFEITING
8. CRIMINALLY RECEIVING
9. ALCOHOL TAX VIOLATIONS
* IDENTIFIED BY JOSEPH VALACHI

UNDERBOSS

JOSEPH BIONDO
"JOE BANDY" "JOE SANTI" "CUNNIGLIEDDU"
FBI *709692, N.Y.C.P.D -B#55092
(1A, 3, 4, 6)

Successor to:
FRANK SCALICE
"DON CHEECH"
N.Y.C.P.D - #1805
MURDERED
(1A, 3, 6, 8)

CONSIGLIERE

JOSEPH RICCOBONO
ALIAS
"STATEN ISLAND JOE"
FBI *557933, N.Y.C.P.D -#729580
APPREHENDED WITHOUT GENESE SHARING STRONG ATTEMPT
(1B, 3, 4, 6)

CAPOREGIME

PRESENT

PAUL CASTELLANO
ALIAS
"CONSTANTINE"
FBI *862467, N.Y.C.P.D -B#92685
(2, 3, 4, 6)

PAOLO GAMBINO
ALIAS
"DON PAOLO"
FBI *112277, N.Y.C.P.D -E#70407
(2, 3, 4)

ARTHUR LEO
ALIAS
"CHINK"
FBI *103293, N.Y.C.P.D -E#80145
(3, 4, 6)

ROCCO MAZZIE
ALIAS
"ROGIE"
FBI *39185, N.Y.C.P.D -E#79185
(3A, 4)

ANTHONY BEDOITO
ALIAS
"TONY THE CREEP"
FBI *135598, N.Y.C.P.D -E#88085
(3, 4, 6)

ANTHONY ZANGARRA
ALIAS
"CHARLIE BRUSH"

JOSEPH COLAZZO
ALIAS
"GUS"
N.Y.C.P.D -B#92685

ANIELLO DELLACROCE
ALIAS
"O'NEIL"
FBI *793280, N.Y.C.P.D -E#76385
(1A, 3, 6)

CHARLES DONGARRO
ALIAS
"ROSARIO"
FBI *59180, N.Y.C.P.D -E#78186
(3, 6)

PETER FERRARA
ALIAS
"PETEY PUMPS"
FBI *112080, N.Y.C.P.D -E#80870
(3, 6)

CARMINE LOMBARDOZZI
ALIAS
"THE DOCTOR"
FBI *300908, N.Y.C.P.D -E#90894
(2, 3, 4, 6)

ETTORE ZAPPI

FORMER

JOHN ROBILOTTO
ALIAS
"JOHNNY ROBERTS"
DECEASED
(6)

VINCENT SQUILLANTE
ALIAS
"JIMMY JEROME"
MISSING
(6)

ANTHONY ANASTASIA
ALIAS
"TOUGH TONY"
FBI *179681, N.Y.C.P.D -E#95085
(4, 6)

FRANK CASTELLANO
DECEASED
(3, 6)

STEVEN ARMONE
N.Y.C.P.D -B#45687, FBI *94380
DECEASED
(1C)

ARMAND RAVA
ALIAS
"TOMMY RAVA"
MISSING - PRESUMED MURDERED
(1A, 6)

GIUSEPPE TRAINA
FBI *109893, N.Y.C.P.D -E#70093
(3, 6)

SOLDIERS - BUTTONS

ANDREW ALBERTI
FBI *709893
N.Y.C.P.D -E#70693

GERMAIO ANACLERIO
ALIAS
"JERRY"
N.Y.C.P.D -B#70493
FBI *709893
(3A, 6)

JOSEPH ARMONE
N.Y.C.P.D -B#45687
FBI *94380
(1C, 6)

EDUARDO ARONICA
ALIAS

PETER BARATTA
ALIAS
"BULL" "PETE BARATO"
FBI *709593, N.Y.C.P.D -E#79893

CHARLES BARCELLONA
ALIAS
"CHARLIE THE WOP" "SLEEPY"
FBI *79893, N.Y.C.P.D -E#79693

FRANK BARRANCA
N.Y.C.P.D -B#79893
FBI *79693

ERNESTO BARESE
ALIAS
"FRANK MARTIN"
FBI *79593

SEBASTIANO BELLANCA
ALIAS
"BALD HEAD" "BENNY THE BUM"
N.Y.C.P.D -B#79893, FBI *79693
ARRESTED GAMBLING, BELIEVED ASSAULT
(3A, 6)

SALVATORE BONFRISCO
ALIAS
FBI *79593, N.Y.C.P.D -B#79693

MICHAEL BOVE
ALIAS
"MICKEY BONE"
FBI *79593

ANTHONY CARMINATI
ALIAS
"LITTLE TONY"
FBI *79593
(3A, 6)

JAMES CASABLANCA
ALIAS
"VINCENT CASABLANCA" "JAMES COSSA"
FBI *79593
(1C)

MATTHEW CUOMO
ALIAS
"JOE CUOMO"
FBI *79593

ALEX D'ALESSIO
ALIAS
"POPE"
(3A, 6)

JOHN D'ALESSIO
ALIAS
"JOHNNY DEE"
(3A, 6)

MIKE D'ALESSIO
ALIAS
"MIKEY DEE"
FBI *79593
(3A, 6)

CHARLES De LUTRO
ALIAS
"CHARLIE WEST"
FBI *79593
(3A, 6)

NICHOLAS DiBENE
ALIAS
"BENNY"
(3A, 6)

ALEX DeBRIZZI
(1A, 3A, 6)

CHARLES GAGLIOCOTTO

FRANK GAGLIARDI
ALIAS
"FRANK THE WOP"

MICHAEL GALGANO
ALIAS
"BLACKIE" "BLACK MIKE"
FBI *79593

PASQUALE GENESE
ALIAS
"PATSY JEROME"
(3A, 6)

ANTHONY GRANZA
ALIAS
"ORANGE"
FBI *79593
(3A, 6)

FRANK GUGLIEIMINI

SALLY GUGLIEIMINI

JOSEPH INDELICATO
ALIAS
"JOE SCOOTCH"
FBI *79593

GIUSEPPE LoPICCOLO
ALIAS
"JOSEPH"
(1B, 3A, 6)

FRANK LUCIANO
ALIAS
"FRANK MILLER"
FBI *79593

ANIELLO MANCUSO
ALIAS
"WAHOO"

JERRY MANCUSO

JOSEPH MANFREDI
ALIAS
"JOJO"
FBI *79593

JAMES MASSI
ALIAS
"JIMMY WARD"
FBI *79593
(1A, 6)

FRANK MOCCARDI
ALIAS
"FRANK THE BOSS"
FBI *79593
(3A, 6)

SABATO MURO
ALIAS
"SAMMY MINTZ"
FBI *79593

FRANK PASQUA
ALIAS
"BIG FRANK"
FBI *79593
(3A, 6)

MICHAEL PECORARO
ALIAS
"SKINNY MIKE"
FBI *79593
(1A, 6)

DOMINICK PETITO
ALIAS
"JOE PITTS"
FBI *79593

LARRY PISTONE
FBI *79593
(3A, 6)

HUGO ROSSI
FBI *79593

ANTHONY PLATE
ALIAS
"TONY PLATE"
FBI *79593
(3A, 6)

GIACOMO (JOHN) SCALICI
FBI *79593, N.Y.C.P.D -B#79693

JOSEPH SCALICI
FBI *79593

SALVATORE SCALICI
FBI *79593

GIACOMO SCARPULLA
ALIAS
"JACK"
FBI *79593

MIKE SCANDIFIA
ALIAS
"MIKE SCANDY"
(3A, 6)

AL SERU
N.Y.C.P.D -B#79693
FBI *79593

JAMES STASSI
(6)

JOSEPH STASSI
ALIAS
"JOE RODGERS" "HOBOKEN JOE"
(6)

FELICE TETI
FBI *79593
(6)

ARTHUR TORTORELLA
FBI *79593

PETER TORTORELLA

PAUL ZACCARIA
N.Y.C.P.D -B#79693
FBI *79593

LEFT: A chart showing the hierarchy of the Gambino Family, used as evidence during a Senate crime inquiry in October 1963.

ABOVE: Cars line the street for Don Carlo's funeral, the event was attended by close to 2,000 mourners.

---

surveillance on Gambino for the rest of his life.

It did not seem to cramp Gambino's style. His family earned an estimated $500 million per year from various rackets, while other New York bosses went to prison, died, or fled the city. Tagged as New York's unofficial 'Boss of Bosses' in media reports, Gambino endured, dodging indictments to fraternize with singer Frank Sinatra in Las Vegas and to hear the lilting melody of 'Speak Softly Love' – theme music from *The Godfather* – played upon his entrance to stylish New York restaurants.

In 1972, the local Mafia suffered a string of kidnappings engineered by Irish mobster James McBratney. Lucchese family member Frank Manzo was released on payment of $100,000 ransom, followed on December 28 by Don Carlo's nephew, Emanuel Gambino. One of the kidnap team forgot to blindfold Gambino, whereupon he was killed to ensure his silence. Orders came down for McBratney's capture and death by torture, a favor which *caporegime* John Gotti was anxious to perform. Instead, however, soldier Ralph Galione shot McBratney on sight, prompting Gotti's murder of Galione against orders issued by underboss Paul Castellano. Gambino excused Gotti's lapse, but bad blood remained between Gotti and Castellano.

A heart attack killed Gambino on October 15, 1976, leaving Castellano in charge of the family while Gotti and his brothers simmered in dissatisfaction. Two thousand mourners – including police, judges and politicians – thronged Don Carlo's funeral at Saint John's Cemetery in Queens, New York.

LEFT: Gambino took to crime from an early age and logged his first conviction in May 1939.

Juan García Abrego

It might be said that Juan García Abrego inherited criminal genes. By the time he was born on a ranch outside Matamoros, Mexico, in 1944, his uncle – Juan Nepomuceno Guerra – was a renowned smuggler who learned his trade in Prohibition, shipping illegal liquor across the US border into nearby Brownsville, Texas. When Repeal slashed profit margins for rum-runners, Nepomuceno switched to marijuana, later adding heroin and cocaine to his inventory. His Gulf Cartel is generally recognized as the first of Mexico's major drug-trafficking syndicates, and nephew Juan García Abrego learned from the master, taking full advantage of his uncle's political connections.

Nepomuceno seemed to lead a charmed life, ignored by law enforcement except for a tax evasion charge that jailed him for several weeks in 1991. Another arrest, for killing his wife in a jealous rage, was resolved with a ruling of 'self-defense.' Describing himself as 'a newspaper reporter' in his declining years, Nepomuceno remained 'a legend' among smugglers to Brownsville mayor Ramon Sampayo. When asked about his nephew in 1996, Nepomuceno told a *New York Times* reporter, 'He's one coyote, and I'm a different coyote. He took his road, and I took mine.'

García's road led to violence, as when Mexican policeman-turned-trafficker Tomas Morlet confronted García on January 27, 1987, at the Piedras Negras

Restaurant in Matamoros. Guns blazed during a quarrel, killing Morlet and one of García's soldiers – and, by all accounts, leaving García in charge of the local drug trade. By 1990 he was shipping an average 300,000 kg (330 tons) of cocaine per year across the Tex-Mex border, bound for distribution cells in Dallas, Houston, San Antonio, New Orleans, Oklahoma City, Chicago, Los Angeles and New York. One of García's refinements involved corrupt Federal Express employees who delivered drugs nationwide, laundering at least $53 million in illicit profits between 1989 and 1993.

García earned a spot on the FBI's Ten Most Wanted list in March 1995 and was captured at a ranch outside Monterrey, Nuevo León, on January 14, 1996. A ledger seized at his arrest detailed bribes of $1 million to the head of Mexico's Federal Judicial Police, $500,000 to the FJP's operations chief and $100,000 to its Matamoros commander. Another $100,000 went to FBI Agent 'Claude de la O,' whose exposure forced retirement without prosecution. Embarrassed Mexican officials extradited García to the US, where his trial began in Houston, Texas, on September 16, 1996. Jurors convicted him on October 17, and García received 11 life sentences on January 31, 1997, plus a fine of $350 million which his lawyer called 'a symbolic grab at nothing.'

Three weeks later, García's brother Humberto escaped from custody in Mexico City, while under interrogation at the downtown federal building. Mexico's attorney general called his disappearance 'inexplicable.' By then, the Gulf Cartel had demonstrated its ongoing power, slaughtering a family of four in Mexico City on December 5, 1996. One of the adult victims, Yolanda Figueroa, had published a book on Juan García Abrego titled *The Capo of the Gulf.*

Vito Genovese

A native of Naples, born on November 27, 1897, Vito Genovese emigrated to the United States with his parents in 1912. The family settled first in Queens, New York, then moved to lower Manhattan, where police arrested Vito with a concealed pistol in 1917. He served 60 days on that charge, but failed to reform, enlisting during Prohibition as an enforcer for Giuseppe Masseria's Mafia family. Underboss Lucky Luciano became a close friend and Genovese followed his lead when Luciano conspired to revolutionize American organized crime in 1931. On April 15 of that year, Genovese joined Joe Adonis, Albert Anastasia and Bugsy Siegel to kill Masseria at a restaurant on Coney Island. Following elimination of rival boss Salvatore Maranzano five months later, Genovese served as underboss of Luciano's new family.

In May 1937, police pulled the corpse of mobster Ferdinand 'The Shadow' Boccia from New York's Hudson River, asserting that he was killed in 1934 on orders from Genovese. Upon indictment for that slaying, Genovese fled to Italy and befriended dictator Benito Mussolini despite Mussolini's outspoken hatred of the Mafia. From exile, Genovese arranged the January 1943 murder of Carlo Tresca, publisher of an anti-fascist newspaper in New York, and thereafter received Italy's highest medal available to civilians. When Allied forces captured Italy in 1944, Genovese shed his fascist façade and volunteered as a US Army interpreter, using his trusted position to profit from black-market sales. Military police arrested him in August 1944 and soon identified him as a fugitive from murder charges in America.

By the time Genovese returned for trial in June 1946, the prosecution's witnesses were dead, or missing. New family boss Frank Costello demoted Genovese to *caporegime,* and Genovese spent the next decade plotting a comeback, finally forcing Costello into retirement after a near-miss murder attempt in May 1957. Five months

later, he collaborated with Meyer Lansky to eliminate rival boss Albert Anastasia. His arrest in November at Apalachin, New York, was embarrassing, but failed to produce a conviction.

Two years later, Don Vito's luck ran out, as federal prosecutors indicted him for heroin trafficking. Some reports claim Genovese was 'framed' by ambitious underboss Carlo Gambino, or other gangland rivals who despised him, but jurors convicted him on April 17, 1959, resulting in a 15-year sentence and a $20,000 fine. Transferred to the US Medical Center for Federal Prisoners at Springfield, Missouri, in 1968, Genovese died there from a heart attack on February 14, 1969.

LEFT: Vito Genovese in police custody in June 1945 on suspicion of the murder of Ferdinand Boccia 11 years earlier.

BELOW: A police mugshot of the notorious Don Vito from December 1937. Genovese fled to Italy shortly afterward.

RIGHT: The coffin of Vito Genovese at a New York cemetery on February 18, 1969, four days after his death.

Sam Giancana

The son of a Sicilian pushcart operator, Salvatore Giangana was born in Chicago's Little Italy on May 24, 1908. As a teenager, with Prohibition underway, he joined the Forty-Two Gang, renowned as a recruiting ground for The Outfit led by Al Capone. While altering his name, he impressed mobsters Frank Nitti and Tony Accardo with his skill as a getaway driver and gunman. Explosive violence earned him the nickname 'Mooney' – slang for 'crazy' – which Giancana himself reportedly shortened to 'Momo.'

Convicted of burglary in March 1929, Giancana received a three-year prison term, served two, and was released in 1931. Like New York's Carlo Gambino, Giancana continued bootlegging beyond the repeal of Prohibition – and with similar results. Federal agents raided his still in January 1939, filing charges that brought Giancana a four-year sentence. Paroled in 1942, he faced the prospect of military service in World War II, but dodged conscription by freely admitting his criminal ties to the draft board. At liberty for the duration, Giancana expanded his horizons through black-market trading and hostile takeover of the numbers racket in Chicago's ghetto.

Giancana's earnings for The Outfit impressed boss Tony Accardo, who named Sam as his successor in 1957. Most reports claim Giancana attended the Mafia gathering at Apalachin, New York, on November 14, 1957, but he was not among the 63 mobsters detained by state police. Despite avoiding that embarrassment, he soon became a target of the FBI's new 'Top Hoodlum Program.'

At the same time, Giancana

LEFT: Sam Giancana handcuffed to a chair in a Chicago detective bureau in April 1957. He was questioned in connection with the murder of banker Leon Marcus.

was involved in national – and international – politics. In September 1960, the Central Intelligence Agency asked Giancana and other mafiosi to kill Cuban leader Fidel Castro, a fruitless effort that continued into 1963. Meanwhile, Giancana was recruited by ex-bootlegger Joseph Kennedy to help his son win the presidency. Today, historians acknowledge Giancana's role in carrying Illinois votes for candidate John F. Kennedy – and some name him as a suspect in JFK's assassination three years later.

By 1966, Giancana's high profile moved Accardo to depose him and 'suggest' a long exile in Mexico, beyond reach of federal prosecutors. Giancana languished in

RIGHT: A file photo of Giancana from 1974, a year before he was executed in his home.

BELOW: Chicago police undertake surveillance on the home of mobster Sam Giancana during the summer of 1963.

luxury south of the border until 1973, when Mexican authorities belatedly noticed and deported him. In 1975, the US Senate opened hearings on CIA misconduct, and Giancana was summoned to testify. On June 19, before his scheduled appearance, an unknown gunman executed Giancana in the basement of his home, shooting him once in the back of the head, then six times around the mouth.

Detlef Gloutsbach

In 1995, Germany's Federal Criminal Police Office informed officials of the European Union that a year-long study revealed no organized crime groups active within the nation's borders. That same year, Klaus von Lampe, an assistant professor at John Jay College of Criminal Justice in Manhattan, presented a paper to the Academy of Criminal Justice Sciences in Boston, titled *Understanding Organized Crime in Germany*. While acknowledging that 'in recent years organized crime has come to be considered one of Germany's major problems,' von Lampe concluded that the country 'certainly has no Mafia, Cosa Nostra, or Yakuza of its own.'

Police and journalists in other nations disagree. On October 23, 1998, police arrested two German nationals, Detlef Gloutsbach and Jocmen Hartel, in the Jomtien district of Pattaya, Thailand. Officers captured the pair – described in press reports as members of 'the German Mafia' – during a raid at Jomtien's Condo Villa Germania, staged in response to informers' reports of gun-running. The raiders confiscated a .357 Magnum pistol with 50 rounds of ammunition, another 25 cartridges for some unspecified automatic weapon, a loaded magazine for a Czech-manufactured CZ 75 pistol and a gun barrel whose serial number traced it to Police Sergeant Suwan Sukhsuwan in Chonburi Province.

Police Colonel Phirom Pariyakon of the Foreign Crimes Division told the *Pattaya Mail* that 'two German Mafia organizations were preparing for a war' in Thailand, presumably using arms supplied by Gloutsbach and Hartel. While stating that the two suspects were involved in other criminal activity in Pattaya and Chiang Mai, Colonel Pariyakon painted the 'war' as a local matter – specifically, provoked by 'a disagreement over who was to be the head of the board of directors of the condominium.' That limited goal notwithstanding, the *Mail* claimed that 'Thailand has experienced many wars between rival German Mafia factions, as well as numerous murders.'

While details of those crimes were not forthcoming, and new reports have surfaced concerning the trial of Gloutsbach and Hartel, later news items suggest that German criminals view Thailand as both a haven and a hunting ground. On January 25, 2006, Bangkok newspapers announced the arrest of Becker Hans Dieter, sought in his native Germany on charges of bribery and tax evasion. On November 29, 2000, officers in Pattaya arrested Helmut Knut Goffringman, described as 'an element in the German Mafia,' on charges of murdering a Frankfurt arms dealer in 1992. On October 19, 2007, the *Pattaya Mail* announced that three foreign syndicates controlled Koh Samui island, a tourist Mecca in Thailand's Kra Isthmus. Calling Koh Samui 'a bustling mafia hub,' the paper reported that German gangsters run the island's restaurants, while British and Scandinavian immigrants focus on real estate. Most recently, in August 2009, German national Uwe Keienburt was killed in Chonburi by a bomb strapped to his body, in a crime which Police Major General Bandid Kunachak blamed on a 'foreign mafia gang.' Kunachak speculated that the bomb 'had been attached to Mr. Keienburt's stomach apparently to force him to negotiate, or to reveal certain information.'

Waxey Gordon

The son of Polish-Jewish immigrants, born on Manhattan's Lower East Side in 1889, Irving Wexler earned his 'Waxey' nickname for his skill as a youthful pickpocket, later adopting the 'Gordon' surname in a bid to conceal his ethnic roots.

Police caught him 'dipping tobacco' in 1905 and sent him to Elmira Reformatory, hauling him back in 1908 for parole violations. That year also saw him arrested on the same charge in Boston, where he served four months in jail. A purse-snatching in Philadelphia earned him another 19-month sentence in 1909.

Finally convinced to change his trade, Gordon joined a New York gang of labor sluggers led by Benjamin 'Dopey Benny' Fein, logging his next arrest for murder in 1914. Jurors acquitted him on that charge, but a $465 robbery sent him to Sing Sing prison before year's end. Paroled in 1916, Gordon earned his keep as a thug of all trades until 1920, when Prohibition offered boundless opportunities. Teamed with Detroit racketeer Max Greenberg, Gordon secured advice and a loan from Arnold 'The Brain' Rothstein, establishing a bootleg syndicate that made him rich, peddling liquor from Philadelphia to New Jersey. Federal agents indicted Gordon for rum-running in October 1925, but key witness Hans Fuhrmann 'committed suicide' in January 1926, scuttling the prosecution's case.

After Rothstein's murder in November 1928, Gordon collaborated with Meyer Lansky and Bugsy Siegel, but suffered from a clash of personalities. Hijackings and murders resulted, while Gordon carried on a simultaneous feud with Dutch Schultz in the Bronx. That underworld 'War of the Jews' continued until April 27, 1933, when a federal grand jury indicted Gordon for tax evasion. Four witnesses were slain over the next two months, but the prosecution forged ahead – aided, some historians believe, by tips from Lansky. Jurors convicted Gordon on December 1, 1933, resulting in a ten-year sentence and an $80,000 fine.

Paroled on October 22, 1940, Gordon told reporters at the gates of Leavenworth prison, 'Waxey Gordon is

ABOVE: Waxey Gordon nonchalantly lights a cigar shortly after being handed a ten-year sentence for tax evasion in December 1933.

ABOVE: New York racketeer, Waxey Gordon, on his way to a Senate hearing in September 1944.

dead. From now on, it's Irving Wexler salesman.' As to what he might be selling, it remained a mystery. Gordon moved to San Francisco, but found himself unwelcome there, ordered to leave town on November 7. Nine days later, police in New York jailed Gordon for vagrancy, followed by another banishment order from NYPD Commissioner Lewis Valentine on November 21. On December 30, 1941, Justice Department attorneys secured a $320,382 judgment against Gordon, on an estimated tax bill of $2.5 million, but the government had no hope of collecting the money. Drifting back to California as World War II monopolized headlines, Gordon faced a new federal indictment in October 1942 for illegally stockpiling 4,500 kg (10,000 lb) of coupon-rationed sugar for sale to illicit liquor distilleries. Convicted of that offense on December 31, 1942, he entered prison with a one-year sentence two weeks later.

The war's end brought no respite from trouble for Waxey. On November 5, 1947, he was arrested in New York with four other suspects on charges of fencing stolen goods. That case was dismissed nine days later, freeing Gordon for another trip to California with visions of founding a heroin empire. Agents from the Federal Bureau of Narcotics tracked his progress, employing ex-convict Morris Lipsius to approach Gordon in December 1950, posing as a potential buyer. Arrested for drug trafficking on August 2, 1951, and convicted by a New York jury on November 21, Gordon found himself at risk of life imprisonment under the Baumes Law, which stated perpetual confinement for four-time convicted felons. Judge Francis Valente counted Gordon's 1909 purse-snatching case as his first strike, imposing a sentence of 25 years to life on December 13, 1951.

In his final ruling, Judge Valente said, 'Since his first act of lawlessness 46 years ago, his contempt for authority manifested by progressively more serious criminality, has been like a malignant cancer, weakening the dignity and good order of the community.' Addressing Waxey directly, Valente added, 'You have demonstrated repeatedly that there is no crime, or racket, to which you would not resort in order to make a dollar. Your latest and most dastardly offense is typical of your hostility, and it should bring down the curtain on your parasitical and lawless life.'

Initially confined in New York on state narcotics charges, Gordon was slapped with a federal drug indictment on April 10, 1952, transferred to California for charging on May 2. Confined at Alcatraz with his trial scheduled to start on August 18, Gordon suffered a fatal heart attack on June 24, 1952. Assistant US Attorney Joseph Karesh announced Waxey's death, surprising nine codefendants

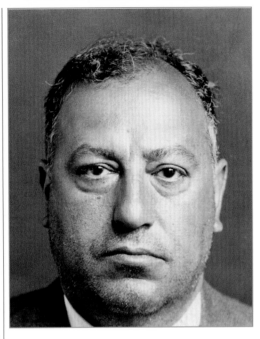

ABOVE: Gordon was arrested in April 1933, after a 25-day search, and indicted on tax evasion charges.

with news that Gordon had turned state's evidence against them, planning to testify for the prosecution. Despite his death, two cohorts were convicted on August 22, 1953.

John Gotti

John Joseph Gotti Jr. was born and raised in New York City's tough South Bronx district. One of 11 children sired by a 'rolling stone' father, of whom Gotti said, 'He never worked a... day in his life. He never provided for the family. He never did nothin'. He never earned nothin'. And we never had nothin'.' Determined to do better for himself, Gotti Jr. turned to crime as an adolescent with mixed results, spending most of his 14th summer in hospital with injuries suffered during a robbery. He logged five arrests between 1957 and 1961, but the charges were dismissed, or 'punished' with probation.

Affiliation with the Gambino Mafia family improved Gotti's prospects in the 1960s. With two of his brothers, he hijacked trucks and staged robberies at New York airports. FBI agents arrested Gotti twice in 1968, resulting in a guilty plea and a three-year sentence to federal prison. Upon release in January 1972, Gotti was promoted to the rank of *caporegime* of his own 'crew' in Queens, New York. An October 1973 murder indictment sent him into hiding, but FBI agents found him in June 1974 and Gotti pled guilty to a reduced charge of attempted manslaughter in August 1975, receiving a four-year sentence. Paroled again in July 1977, he found the Gambino Family changed.

Boss Carlo Gambino died of natural causes in October 1976, elevating Paul Castellano to the family throne.

Gotti despised Castellano, chafing at his ban on drug sales, but personal tragedy distracted him in March 1980, when a neighbor struck and killed Gotti's 12-year-old son with a car. Police ruled the death accidental, but the driver, John Favara, was kidnapped four months later and vanished forever, declared legally dead in 1983.

Getting back to business, Gotti engineered the public murder of Paul Castellano in December 1985, thereafter seizing control of the family. That action put a bull's-eye on his back, as prosecutors focused on deposing him. In March 1986, Gotti and a cohort were acquitted on charges of assault and theft, when alleged victim Romual

---

BELOW: John Gotti appears relaxed in court during his trial for assault and conspiracy in January 1990.

Piecyk recanted his accusations at trial. A month later, Gotti, his brother and five associates faced trial in federal court for racketeering. Jurors stunned the prosecution in February 1987, by acquitting all seven defendants.

In January 1989, local police charged Gotti and a cohort with assault and conspiracy in the nonfatal 1986 shooting of union official John O'Connor. Trial convened in January 1990, and jurors acquitted both defendants on February 9. Newspapers then labeled Gotti the 'Teflon Don,' to whom no charge would stick. Brother Gene Gotti was less fortunate: convicted of heroin trafficking in May 1989, he received a 50-year prison term and a $75,000 fine.

By that time, FBI agents had bugged Gotti's headquarters, collecting hours of tape that included discussions of multiple murders and various other crimes. On December 11, 1990, G-men and New York police stormed Gotti's office, arresting Gotti, family underboss Salvatore 'Sammy the Bull' Gravano and two other associates on charges that included Paul Castellano's murder and 12 more, plus conspiracy to commit murder, loan-sharking, racketeering, obstruction of justice, illegal gambling and tax evasion. Confronted with tape recordings in which Gotti debated his execution, Gravano turned state's evidence, confessed to 19 slayings, and

ABOVE: The Teflon Don arrives at the New York State Supreme Court on February 9, 1990, to learn that, once again, charges did not stick.

received a token five-year racketeering sentence in return for testifying against Gotti.

It was the last straw for Gotti. Between Gravano's gruesome testimony and Gotti's own voice on tape, condemning his victims to death, conviction was inevitable. On June 23, 1992, Gotti received a prison term of life without parole. Confined at the federal 'supermax' prison in Marion, Illinois, Gotti became a target for inmates who wanted to build a reputation. Black inmate Walter Johnson bloodied Gotti's face in an August 1996 racial altercation,

ABOVE: Gotti's defense attorney Albert Krieger addresses the press following his client's conviction for racketeering and murder in June 1992.

BELOW: Mourners at the funeral of John Gotti on June 15, 2002, following the gangster's death from cancer.

RIGHT: As one of criminal history's most notorious gangsters, Gotti's 1992 conviction made big news.

prompting Gotti's offer of $100,000 for the Aryan Brotherhood to kill Johnson. Prison officials learned of the contract and transferred Johnson to another prison.

In September 1998, a cancer diagnosis sent Gotti to the United States Medical Center for Federal Prisoners in Springfield, Missouri, where surgeons removed a tumor from his throat. Despite an optimistic prognosis, the cancer persisted, undeterred by removal of Gotti's lower jaw, and claimed his life on June 10, 2002.

In the free world, trouble persisted for Gotti's kinfolk. Son, John Gotti III, and 39 others were indicted on multiple racketeering counts in January 1998. 'Junior' Gotti pled guilty to extortion, loan-sharking, gambling, mortgage fraud and tax evasion in April 1999 and received a 77-month sentence, while forfeiting $1.5 million in cash and property.

In June 2002, shortly before his brother's death, Peter Gotti was indicted for money laundering, labor racketeering and attempting to extort money from actor Steven Seagal. Convicted in 2003, he received a 20-year sentence. A second conviction in April 2004, for extortion and plotting to kill Sammy Gravano, added another 9½ years to his jail time.

Junior Gotti, paroled in 2005, was re-arrested three years later in Florida, on racketeering and murder conspiracy charges. Jurors failed to reach a verdict, resulting in a mistrial on December 1, 2009, and

prosecutors dropped the case. In January 2010, John III announced a career change, casting himself as an author of children's books.

Turncoat Sammy Gravano left the federal witness protection program in 1995 and moved to Arizona,

ABOVE: Mafia boss John Gotti's residence in Howard Beach, New York, photographed in April 1992.

subsequently resuming his criminal lifestyle. Convicted with his son on drug-trafficking charges in October 2002, Gravano received a 19-year term in state prison.

New Jersey prosecutors charged him with conspiracy to kill a policeman in 1980, then dropped that charge after key witness Richard 'The Ice Man' Kuklinsky died in prison. Today Gravano suffers from Graves' disease, a thyroid disorder that has left him – in the words of fellow inmate Anthony 'Gaspipe' Casso – resembling 'a dying AIDS patient.'

Danny Greene

Daniel Patrick Greene was born in Cleveland, Ohio, on November 9, 1933, to young Irish immigrant parents who married five days before his arrival. His mother died in childbirth, whereupon his father started drinking, lost his job and soon placed Danny in a Catholic orphanage. Rescued from church care when his father remarried in 1940, Danny disliked his stepmother and ran away from home repeatedly, until he was sent to live with an aunt. Expelled from St. Ignatius High School for fighting, he excelled as an athlete in public school, but was soon expelled again, in 1951, for bullying classmates. Greene then joined the Marine Corps, and despite various conduct infractions, was honorably discharged in 1953.

Back in Cleveland, he worked on the Lake Erie docks and witnessed underworld corruption in the Mafia-dominated International Longshoremen's Association. Casting himself as a 'Celtic warrior' against Italian mobsters, Greene joined the union to reform it, but instead drew attention from the FBI for threatening to kill one corporate leader's children. An embezzlement conviction (overturned on appeal) drove Greene from the ILA, and he dodged a retrial by pleading guilty and paying a $10,000 fine. Thereafter, Danny turned to full-time labor racketeering on the waterfront, in league with Louis 'Babe' Triscaro of the Teamsters union.

Curiously, he was chosen to lead the local ILA in 1961, immediately raising dues and pushing laborers to 'volunteer' service toward a vague 'building fund.' Fifty who refused were fired. By 1964, with workers ready to revolt, Greene joined the FBI's 'Top Echelon Informant' program while continuing his criminal activities. New investigations produced a second conviction for embezzlement and falsifying union records, reversed on appeal. Once again, Greene pled guilty to reduced charges and escaped with a $10,000 fine.

Moving on to another union, the Cleveland Solid Waste Trade Guild, Greene moonlighted as an enforcer for local racketeers. In May 1968, he nearly killed himself while preparing to lob a bomb at one of his targets, leaving him deafened in one ear. Bad luck continued in 1971, when Greene went to war with established mafiosi for control of Cleveland's underworld, as designated hitman Art Sneperger lost his life while planting an October car bomb. Greene tried more traditional methods the following month, killing his intended target – 'Big Mike' Frato – with gunfire. Mayhem ensued on both sides, worsening as Greene cut ties with Jewish mobster Alex 'Shondor' Birns, himself killed by a car bomb in March 1975. Meanwhile, enemies fired at Greene while he was jogging and bombed his apartment, nearly killing his mistress. Operating from the Celtic Club, Greene surrounded himself with Irish-American thugs and fought back. Dozens of bombings followed – 36 in 1976 alone – before Greene's luck ran out.

On October 6, 1977, a remote-control car bomb killed Greene outside his dentist's office. While mafiosi celebrated, FBI agents built a case against the killers. Jimmy Fratianno pled guilty to Greene's murder in February 1978 and helped convict two accomplices, Kenneth Ciarcia and Thomas Lanci.

Joaquín Guzmán Loera

Born on April 4, 1957, in the Mexican state of Sinaloa, Joaquín Guzmán Loera – alias *El Chapo* ('Shorty') – grew up watching members of the Sinaloa Cartel get wealthy from smuggling drugs across the US border. Organized by Guzmán's uncle, Pedro Avilés Pérez, in the late 1960s, the cartel first specialized in marijuana, then fed America's growing appetite for cocaine and heroin over successive decades. Some narcotics officers credit Avilés with pioneering use of private planes to smuggle drugs, and he taught nephew Joaquín to carry on the business. Mexican police killed Avilés on September 15, 1978, leaving Guzmán in charge and ably supported by lieutenants including Rafael Caro Quintero, Ernesto Fonseca Carrillo and Miguel Ángel Félix Gallardo (who later defected to form the rival Guadalajara Cartel).

Under Guzmán's leadership, the Sinaloa Cartel expanded to operate in the states of Baja California, Chihuahuah, Durango and Sonora. The Baja incursion subsequently led to bloody conflict with the locally-based Tijuana Cartel, founded and led by nephews of Miguel Ángel Félix Gallardo (by then imprisoned for a 1989 conviction). Gunmen dispatched by the Tijuana Cartel tried to kill Guzmán

ABOVE: Joaquín 'Shorty' Guzmán Loera in high security jail, on June 10, 2000. He was later smuggled to freedom in a laundry van.

shooters killed Roman Catholic Cardinal Juan Jesús Posadas Ocampo and six other innocent victims. While no arrests resulted in that case, authorities named Tijuana Cartel members Juan Francisco Murillo Díaz and Édgar Nicolás Villegas, as the massacre's instigators.

Police in Guatemala arrested Guzmán on June 9, 1993, prosecuting him for bribery, criminal association and crimes against health. Upon conviction, he received a 20-year sentence at La Palma prison (now Altiplano). On November 22, 1995, Guzmán was transferred to Puente Grande prison in Jalisco, Mexico, pending extradition to the United States for trial on drug trafficking charges that carried a sentence of life imprisonment without parole. Despite being lodged in 'maximum security,' Guzmán led a pampered life at Puente Grande and escaped on January 19, 2001, days before his scheduled flight to America. Subsequent investigation, implicating 78 accomplices, revealed that Guzmán was smuggled out of prison in a laundry van.

In November 2004, half an hour after recognizing Guzmán's voice on a telephone tap, 300 Mexican paratroopers stormed a hideout in the Sierra Madre Mountains, but Guzmán eluded the soldiers. Guzmán's son was arrested in Guadalajara on February 15, 2005, sentenced to five years in prison, then released in April 2008 by a judge's order. On March 17, 2007, authorities in Mexico City seized $205.6 million from a mansion owned by alleged Guzmán partner Zhenli Ye Gon. Two participants in the raid were murdered on August 2, 2007. In March 2008, Guatemalan officials linked Guzmán to a shootout that

on May 24, 1993, in the parking lot of Guadalajara International Airport, but the ambush resulted from a tragic case of mistaken identity. Instead of Guzmán, the most powerful people. The US Drug Enforcement Administration's $5 million reward for Guzmán's capture seems almost paltry by comparison, and thus far has brought no takers.

Although in hiding, Guzmán retains control of the Sinaloa Cartel, also named in various official reports as the Guzmán-Loera Cartel, the Pacific Cartel and The Federation. While no precise calculation is possible – and narcotics officers admit intercepting a bare 10 per cent of the illicit drugs imported to America each year – the DEA claims that Guzmán's cartel smuggled at least 200,000 kg (220 tons) of cocaine into the US between 1990 and 2008, plus untold amounts of heroin, marijuana and methamphetamine.

New trouble arose for the Sinaloa Cartel following

ABOVE: Mexican police arrest Mario Gonzalez Martinez (second from left), a key member of Guzmᗩn's cartel, in May 2009.

claimed ten lives. A year later, on April 18, 2009, police found two Mexican soldiers executed near a home owned by Guzmán in Durango.

Shorty Guzmán Loera remains at large today, ranked as Mexico's top narcotics trafficker since Osiel Cárdenas Guillén of the rival Gulf Cartel was arrested on May 1, 2008, later sentenced to 25 years in prison. Ten months after Cárdenas Guillén's arrest, in March 2009, *Forbes* magazine ranked Guzmán at Number 701 on its list of the world's richest people, with an estimated net worth of $1 billion. His presumed fortune remains at $1 billion today, but expansion in the ranks of the super-rich dropped Guzmán to Number 937 in March 2010. In November 2009, *Forbes* ranked Guzmán 41st among the world's 67

BELOW: Alfredo Beltrᗩn Leyva, head of money laundering operations for the Sinaloa Cartel, is arrested in January 2008.

the January 2008 arrest of Alfredo Beltrán Leyva, who supervised the syndicate's money laundering operations. Worse yet, Beltrán Leyva's brothers blamed Guzmán for Alfredo's incarceration, retaliating with the murder of Guzmán's son, Édgar Guzmán Moreno, by 15 gunmen at a Culiacán shopping mall. The remaining Beltrán Leyvas then aligned themselves with the Juárez Cartel led by Vicente Carrillo Fuentes and further mayhem ensued. That struggle continues, claiming scores of lives each year, while Guzmán remains Mexico's most-wanted fugitive.

George Enrique Herbert

A native of Belize, born in 1973, George Enrique Herbert graduated from petty juvenile crime to become his nation's most powerful drug trafficker in his 20s. His syndicate, the violent George Street Crew based in Belize City, battled competitors while carving out a lucrative territory and forging international alliances, making Herbert a multi-millionaire in the process.

In March 2001, a corrupt Belizean official recruited Herbert for a smuggling operation conducted in collaboration with Mexico's Juárez Cartel led by Vicente Carrillo Fuentes. Between that date and August 2002, members of the George Street Crew received at least 14, 900kg (1ton) shipments of cocaine from Medellín Cartel supplier Mauricio Ruda-Alvarez, transporting the drugs from pickup points on Colombia's Atlantic coast to Calderita, Mexico. There, Juárez Cartel members received the drugs and shipped them into the United States with aid from paid-off Mexican police. The US Coast Guard captured two shipments in spring 2002, but at least a dozen others made it to distributors and addicts in the States.

The operation began to unravel in October 2001, when Hurricane Iris forced Juárez Cartel lieutenants Victor Manuel Adan Carrasco and Jorge Manuel Torres Teyer to land a plane with 1,500 kg (1.65 tons) of cocaine aboard near Belize City. Both were extradited in August 2002, for trial in the US, and pled guilty to drug trafficking in spring 2003. In May 2004, Torres received a 38-year sentence, while Adan was sentenced to 22 years. Meanwhile, Mauricio Ruda-Alvarez was murdered in Medellín during October 2002.

Based on testimony from Adan and Torres, federal prosecutors indicted George Herbert in early 2003, charging him with smuggling more than 10,000 kg (11 tons) of cocaine into the United States. On April 25, police raided Herbert's home in Belize City, removing him 'for questioning,' then placed him on a plane bound for America. Held for trial in New York City, Herbert was convicted on December 14, 2004, with the list of charges including four counts of drug trafficking and one count of using firearms in narcotics crimes. On June 2, 2005, Herbert received a sentence of 33 years and four months in prison, which left him eligible for release on May 9, 2032, at age 59. As this book went to press, Herbert was confined at the medium-security federal prison located in Coleman, Florida.

In Herbert's absence, the Supreme Court of Belize ruled his kidnapping illegal and awarded his family $25,000 in damages, but thus far no officials have been punished for the unorthodox extradition. Former Police Commissioner Carmen Zetina conceded in an affidavit that he authorized Hebert's delivery to US agents without proper legal documentation, acting solely on the statement of a DEA agent – later proved false – that Herbert had waived his rights and volunteered for trial in New York. Two associates of Herbert's snatched on the same day, Brian Brown and Liston McCord, avoided trial by turning state's evidence and testifying against their ex-friend. The George Street Crew remains active in Belize City without its old boss.

Dawood Ibrahim

India's most notorious fugitive was born Dawood Sheikh Ibrahim Kaskar on December 26, 1955, at Mumka village in the state of Maharashtra. The son of a police constable, he was raised in Dongri, an impoverished district of Central Bombay (now Mumbai), inhabited chiefly by Muslims. After dropping out of Ahmed Sailor High School, Dawood briefly worked as a mechanic, then turned to supporting himself with con games, scamming bargain hunters at Mumbai's Crawford Market. It was a short step from there to smuggling and executing contract murders for 'Don of Mumbai' Karim Lala, before Ibrahim organized his own gang, known as 'D-Company.'

In the years between 1983 and 1988, Ibrahim rose to dominate Mumbai's underworld. His ascendancy was due in equal parts to Dawood's ruthless violence and his collaboration with agents of Pakistan's Inter Services Intelligence agency. Constantly at odds with India, the ISI sought agitators who could generate mayhem on demand, and Dawood fit the bill. The deal was doubly beneficial for Dawood, since he received payment from the ISI for services rendered, plus official protection while smuggling gold and other contraband in Pakistani coastal waters.

Flush with cash, D-Company expanded from traditional gangland pursuits into real estate and 'Bollywood' film production, stepping on rival toes in the process. Rival mobster Samad Khan wounded Dawood's brother, Iqbal Kaskar, on May 10, 1984, whereupon

BELOW: Activists burn an effigy of Dawood Ibrahim during May 2000 protests in Calcutta.

Dawood retaliated by killing both Khan and his father in 1986. Sometime ally Ramabhai Naik fell in a shootout with police in 1988, the same year that Mumbai godfather Varadarajan Muniswami Mudaliar died from natural causes. Dawood, headquartered in Dubai since 1986 and hobnobbing with royalty, next moved against rival Chotta Rajan in 1992, when Ibrahim hireling Subhash Thakur killed three of Rajan's followers. By 1997, D-Company's war with Rajan would claim more than 100 lives, including hotelier Ramanath Payyade (who paid Rajan for 'protection'), Rajan-allied film producer Mukesh Duggal and builder O.P. Kukreja (a friend of Rajan). Rajan's most prominent victim was Mirza Dilshad Beg, a Nepali parliamentarian linked to D-Company, assassinated on June 29, 1995.

In the midst of that mayhem, Dawood carried out his most notorious act of terrorism for the Pakistani ISI, orchestrating a series of 13 bomb blasts that rocked Mumbai on March 12, 1993. When the smoke cleared, 257 persons were dead, with another 1,400 injured. Another blast in Calcutta killed 60 on March 17, while two more bombings in Mumbai on August 25, 2003, claimed a further 52 lives. Police arrested 129 suspects, finally convicting 100 at trial in 2006, but alleged instigators Dawood Ibrahim and Mushtaq Abdul 'Tiger' Memon remained at large. Memon's brother Yakub was sentenced to death, while three other kinsman received life prison terms. Chotta Rajan later blamed the Mumbai bombings for his conflict with D-Company, although violence between the two gangs actually began a year earlier.

In permanent exile, shielded from arrest and extradition by royal friends in Dubai, Dawood Ibrahim remains India's most-wanted fugitive, maintaining control of his various rackets. Shortly after the 1993 bombings, Mumbai Commissioner of Police Amarjit Singh Samra said of Dawood, 'In ten years, this ordinary-looking son of a police head constable had become, virtually, omnipresent in any crime.' Ibrahim allegedly controls drug trafficking in Mumbai, as well as the pervasive *hawala* system exchanging money without resort to banks, or other official agencies.

While Ibrahim is seemingly untouchable, the same is not true of his relatives, however. Brother Anees Ibrahim Kaskar was arrested in Dubai in December 1993, but reports conflict as to whether he was freed on bond, or deported to Pakistan. Brother Iqbal Kaskar was deported from Dubai to India in 2003 for trial on murder and land-grabbing charges, acquitted for lack of evidence on June 14, 2007. Nephew Danish Parkar

died in a 2005 auto crash which relatives describe as a 'planned operation.' Another nephew, Sameer Wagle, was arrested for extortion in Byculla, in February 2006. That same year, Dawood's sister Haseena Parkar faced charges of extortion, reduced to 'cheating' in a plea bargain. Nephew Sajid Wagle went to jail in July 2008 for running a protection racket among cable television operators in Mumbai.

Ibrahim's agents struck again on November 28–29, 2008, when a rash of terrorist bombings and shootings killed 166 Mumbai residents and injured 308. Police killed nine of the raiders, while only one – Pakistani national Mohammed Ajmal Amīr Kasāb – was caught alive. He claimed credit for the militant *Lashkar-e-Taiba* ('Army of the Pure'), then admitted to police that D-Company provided weapons and explosives for the attacks. Coincidentally, or otherwise, ten members of Ibrahim's gang were arrested in Dubai and deported to India seven days before the latest Mumbai atrocities.

Pappu Kalani

Gangster-politician Suresh Budharmal 'Pappu' Kalani was born in Ulhasnagar, on the western coast of India, sometime in 1951. Four years later, some 100,000 refugees from newly created West Pakistan settled in Ulhasnagar, imparting a wide-open atmosphere to the town. By the 1960s, Ulhasnagar was notorious for bootleg 'duplicates' of various consumer items, widespread illegal construction and related corruption with thriving 'protection' rackets. Pappu's uncle, Dunichand Kalani, served as president for the local unit of the Indian National Congress Party, while his family owned several hotels and liquor distilleries. Another uncle, Keemat Kalani, ran a criminal gang that handled dirty work for the Congress Party.

In 1983, Pappu Kalani joined mobster Gopal Rajwani to murder A.V. Narayam, a writer for *Blitz* magazine who exposed local crimes. Rajwani was charged with the stabbing, then acquitted when witnesses proved scarce. Kalani and Rajwani squabbled over spoils from their protection racket in 1985, with the argument settled by Rajwani's arrest in April. Rajwani blamed Kalani for his arrest, and for an ambush that nearly killed him en route to jail. Retaliating, Rajwani's men killed Pappu's uncle

Dudhichand Kalani in April 1989, touching off a gang war that claimed 22 lives in the next five months.

Meanwhile, in 1986, Kalani was elected to the Maharashtra Legislative Assembly as a Congress Party member, doubling as president of the Ulhasnagar Municipal Council. Voters did not seem to mind when he was accused of four murders in 1990, with all four victims named as members, or associates, of Gopal Rajwani's crime syndicate. Two victims – mortally wounded

Rajwani bodyguard Maruti Jadhav and an injured bystander – named Kalani as their assailant, whereupon he was held without bail. Those charges forced his expulsion from the Congress Party, but voters re-elected him as an independent in 1995 and 1999. Jailed for nine years without trial under India's repressive Terrorist and Disruptive Activities Prevention Act, Kalani was finally released on bond in 2002. He subsequently joined the Republican Party of India, winning yet another term in the Maharashtra Legislative Assembly in 2004.

While still under bond, theoretically facing trial on 19 felony charges – including eight counts of murder (Gopal Rajwani's January 2000 courthouse ambush slaying among them) – Kalani set about repaying his grassroots supporters. In 2005, when the Bombay High Court condemned 855 illegal structures in Ulhasnagar and ordered their demolition, Kalani passed a law legitimizing them and spared the occupants from eviction.

Meanwhile, legal problems dogged Kalani and his family. He placed various corporations in his wife's name, only to see her indicted on charges of forgery, tax evasion and illegal liquor distilling. Kalani himself faced new accusations of intimidation involving families whose land was stolen for construction projects. Brother Narayan was arrested in 2004, on three counts of murder dating from the 1990s. A year later, Pappu's son was charged with assault and extortion. Kalani felt the cumulative weight of scandal in 2007, when wife Jyoti lost her bid for municipal office and Kalani's party carried only 15 of 76 seats in the Maharashtra Legislative Assembly.

Harry Kalasho

According to FBI spokesmen, 'The Chaldean Mafia, composed predominantly of Iraqi nationals, operated a narcotics distribution network, moving drugs from Phoenix and San Diego to Detroit. Involved in violent crimes, such as homicide, assault, kidnapping, armed robbery and arson, the gang used intimidation and brutal force to move the narcotics and collect drug proceeds.' And the driving force behind that syndicate was Khairi 'Harry' Kalasho.

The youngest of four brothers who emigrated with their parents to Detroit, Michigan, sometime in the early 1970s, Kalasho lost his father in a 1974 auto crash, which also left brother Tahrir brain-damaged and the family without means to support themselves. Their salvation lay with an uncle, Louis Akrawi, who owned a successful restaurant and a party-supply shop – and whom other Iranian immigrants recognized as the boss of their neighborhood's 'Mafia.' Loving and brutal by turns, once slamming his own head through a tavern wall in a fit of rage, uncle Akrawi took charge of the boys, molding them in his own image. The brothers took to crime without a backward glance, forming a gang that peddled drugs and practiced strong-arm robbery.

Despite his relative youth, Harry emerged as the dominant and more successful brother. Bahaa was imprisoned for life in 1984, after an elderly victim died during one of his home invasions, and Harry followed in 1985, with a sentence of 8½ to 20 years for drug trafficking. Brother Dhia and cousin Ray Akrawi kept the business running with connections to the Medellín Cartel. Harry hit the streets again in 1988, just as a federal sting operation snared Medellín contacts Joseph Frontiera and Anthony Montello in Florida. He found a new supplier in New York, but clashed with rivals Salaam 'Sam' Gaggo and Munthir 'Mark' Salem. Hired killers Kevin Minley and Edward Stevenson executed Gaggo on November 17, 1988. A month later, Minley and Stevenson killed Salem but foolishly used their own car, which was identified by witnesses. Arrested and facing life terms, they named Harry Kalasho as their employer.

Prosecution was not on the cards, however. On February 3, 1989, a gunman fatally wounded Harry Kalasho in Detroit. He died on February 20, while witnesses identified the shooter as Raed Jihad, a friend of Munthir Salem. Police questioned the identification, while Kalasho's family blamed authorities for the murder, noting that Jihad had met with Detroit's prosecutor several times before the shooting, casting himself as a

Salem family spokesman. In any case, Jihad never faced trial. Gunned down outside a Detroit coffee house, he took unanswered questions to the grave. Friends suspected Ray Akrawi of Jihad's murder, but police could only tag him with a firearms violation in August 1990. While serving that 18-month sentence, Akrawi was indicted and later convicted of trafficking in drugs.

Thus far, state and federal prosecutors have convicted 111 members of the Chaldean Mafia, while seizing 6,500 kg (7.1 tons) of marijuana, 25 kg (55 lb) of cocaine, 2 kg (5 lb) of crystal methamphetamine, 78 firearms and $5.3 million in cash.

Khun Sa

Asia's premier drug lord of the 20th century was born on February 17, 1933, in Norng Leng village, in Shan State, eastern Burma (now Myanmar), to an ethnic Chinese father and Shan mother. Named Chang Chi-fu at birth, he later adopted the pseudonym Khun Sa ('Prince Prosperous'). In 1949, when Mao Zedong's communist forces defeated the Kuomintang (Chinese Nationalist Party), many soldiers of the losing side fled into Burma from neighboring China's Yunnan province. Khun Sa soon joined their number, rising through the ranks until he tired of taking orders and formed his own Ka Kwe Ye ('home guard') militia loyal to Burmese Prime Minister Ne Win. In return for battling Shan rebels, Khun Sa received money, weapons and other equipment for his private army. Later, as his force topped 800 men, Khun Sa stopped serving Ne Win and shifted into opium production. Defeated in a 1967 campaign against his former Kuomintang allies, Khun Sa was arrested two years later and sentenced to prison.

Freedom came in 1973, when Khun Sa's second in command kidnapped two Russian physicians, holding them hostage until his chief was liberated. Khun Sa decamped to Thailand, establishing a new opium network headquartered at Ban Hin Taek, defended by an ever-growing Shan United Army ostensibly pledged to winning autonomy for his mother's people. Expelled from Thailand in January 1982, Khun Sa built new bases along Burma's side of the border and formally joined forces with Mong Heng's Thai Revolutionary Council on March 25, 1985. Following Mong's death in July 1991, Khun Sa became chairman of the TRC and renamed it Shan State Restoration Council.

In the midst of those apparent political events, on March 15, 1990, a federal grand jury in New York

indicted Khun Sa on charges of importing more than 1,600 kg (3,500 lb) of heroin into the United States between September 1986 and February 1988. Prosecutors called the indictment 'a significant step forward in the government's drug war,' while admitting there was 'no indication that Khun Sa will be brought to trial in the United States anytime soon, if at all.'

The charge did have some effect, however. Apparently troubled by the possibility of extradition, Khun Sa struck a bargain with Burmese officials and surrendered in January 1996. His army disbanded without a shot fired, simultaneously dissolving Khun Sa's heroin network and eliminating the largest single Shan insurgent group still active against Myanmar's military junta. Nicholas Burns, speaking for the US State Department, described

the aging 'Opium King's' surrender 'the result of a successfully concluded peace agreement between the Burmese government and the representatives of Khun Sa.' He added: 'Given the criminal notoriety of Khun Sa and his organization's extensive involvement in the international heroin trade, we are concerned that this apparent political agreement could facilitate the continued drug trafficking operations.' Addressing Khun Sa directly, Burns said, 'He should know that there is a very high degree of importance placed upon his eventual arrest, his eventual trial and his eventual conviction in the United States on drug charges.'

Myanmar declined to cooperate, replying that Khun Sa's case would be handled under Burmese law. Placed under 'house arrest' in Yangon (formerly Rangoon), the retired warlord lived comfortably from 'significant investments' in that city, Mandalay and Taunggyi, until his death from natural causes on October 26, 2007. Unable to punish the man who, by some estimates, smuggled 60

ABOVE: Drug baron Khun Sa, known as the 'Heroin King', accompanied by armed bodyguards.

BELOW: Boy soldiers in Khun Sa's army practice with rifles. His army disbanded in 1996, after Khun Sa's surrender to Burmese officials.

per cent of all heroin consumed in the United States, prosecutors pursued any available subordinates.

On February 8, 2001, federal agents seized 57 kg (126 lb) of heroin, valued at $7.3 million, concealed in bales of cotton towels aboard a ship docked at Elizabeth, New Jersey. Announcing the seizure, spokesmen for the Drug Enforcement Administration reported that one of Khun Sa's 'minor wives' and three accomplices had been arrested in Bangkok, Thailand, charged with conspiracy and importing heroin. Felix Jimenez, the DEA's agent in charge for Manhattan, told the *New York Times*, 'Definitely the organization is crumbling, but we feel they are still very powerful in Burma, where he is still operating.'

Agent Jimenez deemed the new arrests significant, since Khun Sa's 1996 surrender had changed the nature of New York's heroin trade. Between 1997 and 2001, supplies shifted away from 'China white' heroin produced in the so-called Golden Triangle of Laos, Myanmar and Thailand, to 'brown' heroin from Mexico and Colombia. Following the US invasion of Afghanistan in 2001, that nation rose to dominate the world's heroin traffic, tripling its exports within a year and reaping drug profits of $124.4 billion by 2010. Nine years after their arrest, no progress had been made toward extradition of the smugglers detained in Bangkok.

LEFT: Khun Sa addresses his comrades in his rebel jungle state in Myanmar some time in the 1990s.

Reginald and Ronald Kray

Born in Hoxton, East London, on October 24, 1933, the Kray twins completed a family of four. An older sister had died in infancy, in 1929, and the twins seemed destined to follow when diphtheria struck both of them in 1936. Surviving that, they had another close scrape in 1942, when a scuffle between them left Ron with a near-fatal head injury. Meanwhile, their father was called up for military service at the start of World War II, but fled into hiding for the duration.

At school, the twins surprised their teachers, being described by one as 'salt of the earth, never the slightest trouble to anyone who knew how to handle them.' Another recalled, 'If there was anything to be done in school, they'd be utterly cooperative. They'd always be the first to help. Nothing was too much trouble.' Still,

schoolwork was not their forte. Influenced by maternal grandfather Jimmy 'Cannonball' Lee, the boys turned to amateur boxing in 1948. Before year's end Reg was declared Schoolboy Champion of Hackney, won the London Schoolboy Boxing Championships and was a finalist for the Great Britain Schoolboys Championship. In 1949, he held titles as the South Eastern Divisional Youth Club Champion and the London ATC Champion, while Ron became Schoolboy Champion of Hackney and won the London Junior Championships.

LEFT: The infamous Kray twins with their mother, Violet, outside the family home in 1965.

BELOW: Ronnie and Reggie enjoy a cup of tea at home after being questioned about the murder of George Cornell in 1966.

ABOVE: A handcuffed Reggie on temporary release from prison to attend his brother's funeral in March 1995.

prison, where they set fires, repeatedly assaulted guards and other inmates, and staged one abortive escape. A matched set of dishonorable discharges finally released the twins, while ending any hope for a professional boxing career. Imprisonment also evoked the first symptoms of mental illness in Ronnie, revealed in eccentric behavior and savage mood swings.

In Bethnal Green, the Krays leased a rundown snooker hall – The Regal – cleaned out its rowdy clientele, and launched their own careers as hijackers, extortionists and gambling proprietors. When Maltese gangsters tried to muscle in, the twins defended their turf with fists and bayonets. In 1957, police charged both twins with assaulting victim Terry Martin in Stepney. Reggie was acquitted, while Ronnie received a three-year sentence. In his absence, Reg acquired another club, The Double R, with financing from brother Charlie. The empire soon expanded, adding more nightspots, while those whose owners balked at selling out were prone to firebombings. Ronnie's erratic behavior continued in prison, resulting in a diagnosis of paranoid schizophrenia.

Alarmed by Ron's decline in custody, Reg switched places with him during a jailhouse visit, granting his brother five months at liberty before he was recaptured. Released in May 1959, his mood swings were barely controlled by medication, and his condition worsened when Reg was arrested soon after, sentenced to 18 months in prison for extortion.

Reunited at the onset of the Swinging Sixties, the Krays presided over a syndicate known as 'The Firm,' competing for control of London's underworld. As Ron later recalled, the decade was '… the best years of our lives. The Beatles and the Rolling Stones were the rulers of pop music, Carnaby Street ruled the fashion world, and me and my brother ruled London. We were… untouchable.' Seeming to prove that point, their 1965 arrest for threatening a rival club owner sparked angry questions in the House of Commons and they beat the charge in court. At liberty, the brothers fraternized with celebrities including Judy Garland and Mafia-connected singer Frank Sinatra. *The Sunday Mirror* settled out of court on libel charges, after hinting that Ron had enjoyed a homosexual affair with Lord Boothby, a Conservative MP, and Scotland Yard received orders to bury that case.

Victories in the ring paralleled multiple arrests in London, but the twins avoided prison until they were called up for military service with the Royal Fusiliers in 1952. Following their father's example, they deserted several times, once assaulting a policeman who tried to arrest them. A court-martial verdict sent them to military

ABOVE: The Krays mixed in London high society during their criminal reign. Here, Ronnie is pictured with Christine Keeler.

On March 9, 1966, Ron shot and killed George Cornell, a rival mobster who had slain one of their men the previous day. On December 12, 1966, the Krays helped gangster Frank 'The Mad Axeman' Mitchell escape from Dartmoor Prison, then allegedly killed him when he proved uncontrollable, dumping his body at sea. The gang's last known murder occurred in October 1967, when the twins killed renegade gang member Jack 'The Hat' McVitie, Ron clutching him in a bear hug while Reg stabbed McVitie repeatedly.

Scotland Yard arrested the Krays and nine associates on May 8, 1968, charging them with three murder counts and various related offenses. At trial in early 1969, both twins were convicted of the Cornell and McVitie slayings, sentenced to life terms with a minimum of 30 years. Five other Firm members were also convicted in McVitie's death, and one in Cornell's, receiving minimum sentences of 15 to 20 years. Charlie Kray and Freddie Foreman, convicted as accessories to McVitie's murder, drew ten-year prison terms. Cornelius Whitehead received a seven-year term for complicity in McVitie's death, plus two years for carrying a gun. In a separate trial, Reg Kray received another five years for aiding Frank Mitchell's prison break, but was acquitted of his murder.

So the Kray Firm was dismantled. Charlie was paroled in 1975, then arrested once more in 1997 for conspiracy to smuggle cocaine valued at £39 million, receiving a 12-year prison sentence. Hospitalized for a severe chest infection in July 1999, he subsequently returned to Franklin Prison and died there from heart failure on April 4, 2000.

Soon after his 1969 conviction, prison psychiatrists certified Ron Kray insane and dispatched him to

Broadmoor Hospital, where he remained until a heart attack claimed his life on March 17, 1995. Brother Reg, a self-proclaimed born-again Christian, was released on compassionate leave with inoperable cancer in August 2000. He died in his sleep five weeks later, on October 1.

Vladimir Kumarin

The man known as 'Russia's Al Capone' and 'last Mafia boss' was born on February 15, 1956, in a poor village in Central Russia's Tambov Oblast. After a stint in the army, he moved to Leningrad (now St. Petersburg) and enrolled at the Leningrad Institute of Mechanics and Optics, then dropped out in the early 1980s to work as a bouncer in local sporting clubs. In that setting, he met gangsters and public officials alike, including one Vladimir Putin, deputy-mayor of St. Petersburg in 1991–96 and later president of Russia.

Kumarin's rise through criminal ranks was interrupted in 1985 by a three-year prison term for forgery, hooliganism and illegal possession of weapons. Released in 1988, he founded the Tambov Gang with Valery Ledovskikh and resumed traditional protection rackets, earning Kumarin another three-year sentence in 1990. Determined to remake himself upon release in 1993, Kumarin changed his surname to 'Barsukov' and pursued a range of legitimate investments, without abandoning his gangland ties. Dissent within the Tambov Gang sparked warfare, climaxed with an ambush on June 1, 1994, that cost Kumarin his right arm, while leaving bullet fragments in his heart. While recovering in Germany and Switzerland, the wounded mobster purged his enemies, regaining control of the gang by mid-1995.

In 1994, Vladimir Putin chose the Petersburg Fuel Company (PTK) as sole supplier of the city's gasoline. Four years later Kumarin/Barsukov emerged as the firm's deputy president, linked in media reports to majority stockholder Vladimir Smirnov. Viktor Novosyolov, speaker of St. Petersburg's legislature, happily supported Kumarin's appointment, thereby deepening suspicions that PTK was controlled by the Tambov Gang. Novosyolov had lost both legs in a 1993 gangland bombing, and another claimed his life on October 20, 1999. That blast sparked rumors of another war within the Tambov Gang, and Kumarin resigned from the PTK.

In June 2003, the German magazine *Der Spiegel* published government accusations that a Darmstadt-based real estate firm, St. Petersburg Immobilien und Beteiligungs AG (SPAG), laundered money for Kumarin's syndicate. German police raided SPAG that spring, declaring that Vladimir Putin had served as an advisor to the firm since 1996. On August 24, 2007, police arrested Kumarin on charges of banditry, fraud, money laundering, organizing a gang and ordering a 2006 ambush that wounded St. Petersburg oilman Sergei Vasiliev and killed one of his bodyguards. Convicted of fraud and money laundering on November 12, 2009, Kumarin received a 14-year sentence.

While Prosecutor General Yury Chaika declared that Kumarin's syndicate 'has been exposed,' with 40 members indicted, the Tambov Gang survives without its founder. Spanish police arrested 20 members of the organization on June 13, 2008, announcing ties between the gang and Vladislav Matusovich Reznik, chairman of the Rus Insurance Company and Chairman of the State Duma Committee on Finances. One jailed gang member, Gennady Petrov, lived next door to a sister of King Juan Carlos I. Simultaneous raids in Berlin netted Michael Rebo, one of the gang's money-launderers, while bank accounts totaling $19 million were frozen pending further legal action.

Meyer Lansky

Underworld financial genius Meyer Lansky was born Maier Suchowljansky in Grodno, Poland (now Belarus), sometime in 1902. When his family arrived in New York City nine years later, immigration officials assigned young Maier a birthdate of July 4 – America's Independence Day. As a youth on Manhattan's Lower East Side, he soon met Benjamin 'Bugsy' Siegel and forged a lifelong friendship. With the onset of Prohibition in 1920, they and others followed the lead of older racketeer Arnold Rothstein into wholesale bootlegging and smuggling. With partner Lucky Luciano, Lansky and Siegel became wealthy liquor entrepreneurs and casino proprietors.

In 1931, mafioso Giuseppe 'Joe The Boss' Masseria ordered Luciano to eliminate his Jewish partners. **Lucky killed Masseria instead,** and joined Lansky to create a multi-ethnic crime syndicate spanning America from coast-to-coast. Smuggling connections in Cuba paved the way for offshore gambling casinos easily accessible from Florida, where Lansky first built the Nacional, then ceded it to Moe Dalitz and erected the larger Riviera. Enemies who trespassed on his turf and threatened earnings for the syndicate at large were either killed, like Albert Anastasia, or imprisoned on convenient charges, like Vito Genovese.

After Bugsy Siegel 'discovered' Nevada's legalized gambling in 1945, Lansky persuaded his allies to finance construction of lavish resorts on the future Las Vegas Strip, while claiming a piece of the action for himself. 'Skimming' of untaxed profits was the rule, banking millions each year for mob bosses nationwide. Fidel Castro's Cuban revolution closed Havana's casinos in 1960, but when efforts to kill 'The Beard' failed, Lansky shifted his attention to the neighboring Bahamas and built a new gambling empire on Paradise Island.

Thus far, Lansky had been fortunate. His only conviction – for illegal gambling at Saratoga Springs, New York, in 1952 – resulted in a minor three-month jail term. In 1972, however, Lansky partners, Sam Cohen and Morris Lansburgh, were charged with skimming from the Flamingo hotel in Vegas. Both pled guilty and went to prison, while Lansky was indicted for tax evasion. He fled to Israel, claiming sanctuary as a 'returning' Jew, but authorities there refused to shelter him. Arrested upon his return to Miami in November 1972, Lansky was subsequently convicted of contempt for ducking a

ABOVE: Meyer Lanksy, pictured in 1951, made a fortune skimming the untaxed profits from his string of casinos.

federal subpoena on March 1, 1973, and received a one-year suspended sentence, pending further legal action. Jurors acquitted him of tax evasion on July 25, 1973, and

ABOVE: Family members mourn the passing of underworld boss Meyer Lansky in Miami, Florida, in January 1983.

another year passed before federal prosecutors announced that his outstanding charges would 'lie dormant' due to Lansky's failing health.

Skeptics questioned that decision as Lansky lived on, identified by *Forbes* magazine in September 1982, as one of America's 400 richest people, with an estimated fortune of $100 million. Strangely, after lung cancer finally killed him on January 15, 1983, a tabulation of Lansky's estate revealed only $2 million and change.

Luciano Leggio

Born in Corleone, Sicily, on January 6, 1925, Luciano Leggio served his first jail term at age 18 for stealing corn to feed his family. Released after six months, he murdered his accuser and embarked upon a full-time life of crime. Corleone's new Mafia boss, Dr. Michele Navarra, recruited Leggio in 1945 to carry out a purge of rivals that claimed 57 lives over the next three years. One prominent victim, trade union leader Placido Rizzotto, was shot by Leggio and hurled from a cliff wrapped in chains. Police arrested Leggio in that case, jailing him for nearly two years on suspicion of murder, then released him after his two alleged accomplices were slain. Subsequently, Leggio was twice tried *in absentia* for Rizzotto's murder, cleared both times for lack of evidence.

While incarcerated, Leggio met mafioso Salvatore Riina, serving six years for manslaughter. When both were released, they joined forces with another upstart mobster, Bernard Provenzano, to generate rebellion against Michele Navarra. Full-blown war erupted in 1953, producing another 153 murders around Corleone over five years. In June 1958, Navarra invited Leggio to a peace conference, then sent 15 gunmen in his place. Leggio escaped from that trap with a minor wound to one hand and retaliated on August 2 with a rural ambush that killed Navarra and an innocent companion. While Leggio assumed leadership of Corleone's crime family and took a seat on the ruling Mafia Commission,

reciprocal murders sputtered on into 1963.

Police in Corleone arrested Leggio in May 1964, surprising him at the home of a woman once engaged to murder victim Placido Rizzotto. Despite complaints of ill health and 'old age,' Leggio faced trial for the murders of Michele Navarra and a fellow doctor, winning acquittal on grounds of insufficient evidence. He was detained thereafter, pending trial in 1968 with 113 codefendants on charges arising from Sicily's 'First Mafia War' and the deadly Ciaculli bombing of June 1963. Leggio was

BELOW: Sicilian police officers escort mafioso Luciano Leggio from a Palermo courtroom on May 8, 1983.

ABOVE: The town of Corleoni, Sicily, where Luciano Leggio ruled the local mafia from 1958.

uphold Leggio's 1969 acquittal. Police jailed 114 mafiosi after the shootings, but Leggio slipped through the net.

After the Scaglione assassination, Leggio settled in Milan, orchestrating a series of profitable ransom kidnappings. Early in 1973, he happened to meet Damiano Caruso, a gangster whom Leggio blamed for killing one of his comrades during the 1960s. According to later testimony from syndicate informers, Leggio killed Caruso and disposed of his corpse, then raped and strangled Caruso's girlfriend and her 15-year-old daughter when they started asking inconvenient questions. Police wiretaps led to Leggio's capture in Milan on May 16, 1974, whereupon he was packed off to serve his life sentence. Most observers agree that Leggio retained control of the Corleonesi Mafia from prison, through lieutenant Salvatore Riina. Tried on new charges in 1977, based on statements from informer Leonardo Vitale, Leggio and his codefendants were acquitted after revelation of Vitale's self-mutilation and other eccentric behavior cast doubts on his sanity.

acquitted in that case as well, with 102 others, but still remained in prison as prosecutors prepared their third case against him. In 1969, he faced trial with Salvatore Riina and 60 other mafiosi, charged with killing nine of Michele Navarra's soldiers. That case collapsed amid charges of perjury and evidence tampering, ending with acquittal of all defendants.

Released on bond while prosecutors appealed his acquittal, Leggio checked into a private clinic in Rome during July 1969, for treatment of Pott's disease (a form of tuberculosis affecting the spine). When his acquittal was reversed in January 1970, Leggio fled the clinic and vanished into hiding as a fugitive. A Sicilian court convicted him of murder *in absentia* during December 1970, imposing a life sentence, while media reports scandalized Leggio's supposed allies in government. One of those was Pietro Scaglione, chief prosecutor of Palermo, killed with his chauffeur on May 5, 1971, while visiting his wife's grave at Cappuccini Cemetery. Mafia informers named Leggio as the triggerman, claiming that he killed Scaglione over the prosecutor's failure to

Leggio's next round in court was the Mafia 'Maxi Trial' held at Palermo's Ucciardone prison between February 10, 1986, and December 16, 1987. Indicted with 473 other defendants – 119 of them tried *in absentia* – Leggio faced more charges of murder, extortion, drug trafficking and Mafia association (banned by law in 1982). His specific charges included the slaying of magistrate Cesare Terranova, killed with a police bodyguard in Palermo on September 25, 1979. Leggio served as his own attorney, questioning Tommaso Buscetta and other mobsters-turned-informer while branding his indictment an act of political persecution. The final verdict cleared Leggio and 113 codefendants on all charges, due to insufficient evidence. Leggio suffered a fatal heart attack on November 16, 1993.

Carlos Enrique Lehder Rivas

The son of a German father and Colombian mother, Carlos Lehder was born in 1950 at Armenia, Colombia, 290 km (180 miles) west of Bogotá. As a young man, he moved to the United States, settling in Michigan as a low-level drug dealer and car thief. Convicted of transporting stolen cars across state lines, Lehder was sent to a federal prison in Connecticut, where he met marijuana smuggler George Jung. By the time they were paroled together in summer 1976, America was awash in Colombian cocaine, much of it supplied by the Medellín Cartel. Bankrolling their initial operation with small-scale smuggling runs, the partners next purchased an airplane and began smuggling larger shipments into the US through the Bahamas, bribing local officials and cementing relations with Medellín drug lord Pablo Escobar in the process.

In 1978, Lehder began buying land on Norman's Cay, a small island in the Exumas, southeast of Nassau, that consisted of 100 homes, a yacht club and marina and an airstrip. After purchasing a house and a hotel, Lehder began harassing other residents and buying out their property until he had the island to himself. One couple that refused to leave were killed aboard their yacht, found drifting at sea in July 1980. Meanwhile, Lehder built a 1,000 meter (3,300 ft) runway for drug planes, receiving and shipping an average 300 kg (660 lb) of cocaine per day at the peak of Norman Cay's illicit operations. Pocketing 25 per cent of the proceeds, Lehder shipped coke to dealers in Florida, Georgia and the Carolinas. Some of his millions were invested in a posh Colombian estate, noteworthy for its life-sized statue of a nude John Lennon scarred by bullet wounds.

While Lehder's high-profile activities on Norman's Cay drew unhealthy attention from law enforcement agencies, Pablo Escobar ordered the slaying of Colombian Minister for Justice, Rodrigo Lara Bonilla on April 30, 1984. That crime ended President Belisario Betancur's opposition to extradition of drug cartel leaders, just as Lehder's name topped the US Drug Enforcement Administration's most-wanted list. One of Lehder's pilots, Jack Carlton Reed, narrowly evaded federal agents in Starkville, Mississippi, but left behind sufficient evidence to produce an indictment of Lehder (and later result in his own life sentence, reduced on appeal to 23 years). Still

RIGHT: A Tampa police mugshot of Colombian drug smuggler Carlos Lehder Rivas, shortly after his arrest on February 4, 1987.

trusting in the power of corruption, Lehder was surprised when Colombian police raided his estate on February 4, 1987, arresting him with 14 of his bodyguards. One day later he was placed aboard a flight to Jacksonville, Florida, where jurors convicted him on ten counts of drug trafficking and one count of running a criminal enterprise. One of the prosecution's key witnesses was George Jung, avoiding prison in exchange for damning testimony, while his ex-partner received a sentence of life plus 135 years on July 20, 1988.

Disinclined to die in jail, Lehder put out feelers to his captors. After Panamanian dictator Manuel Noriega was arrested for narcotics trafficking in January 1990, Lehder volunteered to testify for the prosecution. Appearing at Noriega's trial in April 1992, Lehder shared responsibility for the resulting guilty verdict and 40-year sentence (reduced to 30 years on appeal). That service reduced Lehder's own prison term to 55 years, but he still felt cheated, penning a letter to his trial judge that complained of Washington reneging on a promise to let him finish his time in a German prison. Federal agents claimed to view that letter as a threat against the judge's life, whisking

Lehder off to the US Bureau of Prisons' Mesa Unit in Arizona during fall 1995, where he was housed with other informers in protective custody.

Following that transfer, false tales circulated claiming that Lehder had been released from custody. Journalist Tamara Inscoe-Johnson debunked those rumors, suggesting that 'witnesses' to Lehder's freedom may have been misled by sightings of look-alike brother Federico Guillermo Lehder Rivas, still at large in Colombia. That said, it is worth noting that the Federal Bureau of Prisons' website lists no inmates named 'Carlos Lehder' among prisoners received since 1982. It *does* list nine named 'Carlos Rivas,' eight of them released from custody between 1982 and 2006. Of the two still incarcerated, one – a 36-year-old inmate scheduled for parole in February 2013 – is confined at Lompoc, California. The other, 'in transit' as of March 26, 2010, is 42-year-old Carlos Urias Rivas. We know that Lehder was still in prison in May 2007, when he petitioned Colombia's Supreme Court for aid in securing parole, and in May 2008, when his attorney filed a writ of habeas corpus demanding a response from the Justice Department within 30 days.

Salvatore Lo Piccolo

'The Baron' of Sicily's Mafia was born on July 20, 1942, in the Palermo suburb of Partanna Mondello. No record of Salvatore Lo Piccolo's early criminal career remains, but at some point, he joined Palermo's Mafia, led by Rosario Riccobono, advancing to serve as Riccobono's personal bodyguard and chauffeur. He had a front-row seat for bloody action in April 1981, when mafiosi from Corleone launched Sicily's so-called 'Second Mafia War' against Palermo's urban syndicate, beginning with the assassination of Stefano Bontade. Riccobono secretly sided with the Corleonesi rebels, luring several of his presumed allies into fatal traps, but his treachery backfired on November 30, 1982, when he vanished without a trace. Informers later described Riccobono's murder by hitman Giuseppe 'Pino' Greco, but his body has never been found.

Twenty more mobsters associated with Riccobono fell during the final weeks of 1982, but Lo Piccolo saved himself by swearing allegiance to the Corleonesi victors, convincing bosses Giuseppe 'Pippo' Calò and Antonio Rotolo that he was more valuable alive than dead. Two decades later, Rotolo would rue that

decision, being overheard on wiretapped lines describing Lo Piccolo as 'one who should have died' in 1982. Seeking to remedy his oversight, Rotolo planned to kill Lo Piccolo and his son, Sandro, even procuring barrels of acid with which to dissolve their corpses. Police disrupted that plan – and may have averted another

ABOVE: An undated photo of Salvatore Lo Piccolo. Salvatore was groomed by Rosario Riccobono, leader of Palermo's Mafia.

Mafia war – when they arrested Rotolo in June 2006.

Long before that threat emerged, as a survivor of the early 1980s carnage, Salvatore Lo Piccolo secured his base in Partanna Mondello, then expanded into the towns of Capaci, Carini, Gangi, Isola delle Femmine, Passo di Rigano, San Lorenzo, Sferracavallo and Villagrazia di Carini. By the early 1990s, he controlled Cefalù on the Tyrrhenian Sea, together with the Messina suburbs of Mistretta and Tortorici. While immersed in all traditional

Mafia rackets, Lo Piccolo earned the lion's share of his income from narcotics trafficking and skimming from padded government contracts. In Palermo's low-income San Felippo Neri district, residents of crowded housing projects paid Lo Piccolo a special 'tax' to keep lights burning in their corridors.

Such arrogance inevitably drew attention from police. In March 2005, a special operation dubbed 'Notte di San Lorenzo' produced 84 arrest warrants naming members of Lo Piccolo's clan, but Salvatore evaded the manhunt with sons Sandro and Calogero. Following the capture of fugitive Bernardo Provenzano on April 11, 2006, notes found at Provenzano's hideout identified Lo Piccolo and Antonio Rotolo of Pagliarelli as the Mafia's highest-ranking bosses still at large. Rotolo sought to kill his rival, as described above, until his arrest with 44 associates in June 2006. Prosecutor Antonio Ingroia of Palermo's Antimafia Directorate then named Lo Piccolo as Sicily's reigning mafiosi. 'He's from Palermo,' Ingroia said, 'and that's still the most powerful Mafia stronghold.' Only Matteo 'Diabolik' Denaro from Castelvetrano seemed fit to challenge Lo Piccolo's rule, but neither was inclined to fire the first shot.

While newspapers delighted over the latest 'Pax Mafia,' Salvatore Lo Piccolo cleaned house in Palermo, settling old scores and eliminating potential rivals. On August 22, 2006, two gunmen killed 63-year-old mafioso Giuseppe D'Angelo in the town of Tommaso Natale. One month later, on September 21, Tommaso Natale boss Bartolomeo Spatola vanished amid media reports that he had supported Antonio Rotolo's plot to kill Lo Piccolo. On March 29, 2007, a large cache of weapons was found in the countryside near Palermo. Provincial Police Chief Giuseppe Caruso told reporters that the guns 'were ready to be used,' stating that the recent lull in bloodshed 'did not signify that the danger of a new Mafia war had been averted.'

As if to validate that statement, hitmen killed another Rotolo ally, Nicola Ingarao, on June 13, 2007. Prosecutor Maurizio de Lucia described that slaying as 'a sign of reorganization, stabilization, or potential war among gangs.' Antonio Manganelli, director of Italian State Police, addressed the upper house of Parliament

ABOVE: Sicilian police arrest Salvatore Lo Piccolo in November 2007. The mafia don had been on the run since 1993.

RIGHT: Sandro Lo Piccolo was apprehended in Giardinello, near Palermo, along with his father and two other mafiosi.

in July 2007, suggesting that recent murders heralded Lo Piccolo's advance work for the return of fugitive Inzerillo family members to Palermo. Recognized as allies of Rosario Riccobono in the Second Mafia War, the Inzerillos had been hounded to near-extinction by Corleonesi gunmen. 'If they are back,' Manganelli told troubled senators, 'it means that someone has authorized their return. This is not appreciated by the other side.'

On November 5, 2007, police cornered Lo Piccolo, son Sandro and two top lieutenants – Andrea Adamo and

Gaspare Pulizzi – at a villa in Giardinello. Seized in the raid was a list of ten rules described as a 'guide to being a good mafioso.' The list read:

1. No one can present himself directly to another of our friends. There must be a third person to do it.
2. Never look at the wives of friends.
3. Never be seen with cops.
4. Don't go to pubs and clubs.
5. Always be available for Cosa Nostra, even if your wife's about to give birth.
6. Appointments must be respected.
7. Wives must be treated with respect.
8. When asked for any information, the answer must be the truth.
9. Money cannot be appropriated if it belongs to others, or to other families.
10. People who can't be part of Cosa Nostra are anyone with a close relative in the police, with a two-timing relative in the family, anyone who behaves badly and doesn't hold to moral values.

Journalists mocked the Mafia's 'Ten Commandments,' noting the absence of rules against murder and theft, while police speculated on Lo Piccolo's probable successor. Matteo Denaro seemed the most likely candidate. A new anti-Mafia drive, christened 'Operation Addio Pizzo' climaxed with the arrest of Calogero Lo Piccolo on January 16, 2008.

BELOW: Police search for evidence at the hideout of Lo Piccolo, following his eventual arrest in November 2007.

Frank Lucas

African-American mobster Frank Lucas was born in La Grange, North Carolina, on September 9, 1930, and raised in Greensboro, a hotbed of activity by the white-supremacist, Ku Klux Klan. As a child, he witnessed the Klan murder of a 12-year-old cousin for 'reckless eyeballing' – defined as a black male staring at Caucasian women. Disenchanted with his home state's racial segregation and brutal police, Lucas pursued a life of minor rebellion until a fight with his white boss endangered his life in 1946, prompting flight to New York City. There, in Harlem's ghetto, he fell under the influence of racketeer Ellsworth 'Bumpy' Johnson, reportedly doubling as Johnson's chauffeur and enforcer.

LEFT: Frank Lucas (left) and Richard Roberts (who prosecuted Lucas in the 1970s) in a New Jersey courtroom in 2006.

Johnson received a 15-year sentence for narcotics trafficking in June 1953 and served ten years, emerging from prison to a hero's welcome in 1963. Johnson was facing new federal charges when a heart attack killed him on July 7, 1968, leaving a power vacuum in Harlem's underworld. Frank Lucas recognized that his success depended on breaking the Mafia's grip on the ghetto drug trade. To that end, with the Vietnam war in full swing, he recruited a relative by marriage – US Army Sergeant Leslie 'Ike' Atkinson – to arrange heroin shipments from Southeast Asia bypassing syndicate middlemen. Atkinson's success would prompt agents of the Drug Enforcement Administration to dub him 'Sergeant Smack.'

The means of smuggling heroin from Vietnam remains in dispute. While Lucas later claimed that special false-bottomed caskets were constructed, permitting drugs to be shipped home with the corpses of soldiers, Atkinson maintains that the heroin was concealed in imported furniture. In either case, the flow of 'China white' made Lucas fabulously wealthy, earning an estimated $1 million per day from addicts in Harlem. Special narcotics prosecutor Sterling Johnson, now a federal judge, called Lucas's syndicate 'one of the most outrageous international dope-smuggling gangs ever,' led by 'an innovator who got his own connections outside the US and then sold the narcotics himself in the street.'

Part of that success hinged on Lucas running a true family operation, recruiting blood relatives and close friends whom he trusted implicitly. Quality also mattered, with Lucas billing his 'Blue Magic' heroin as 98 to 100 per cent pure when shipped from Asia to the States. His profits bankrolled purchases of high-end real estate, including office blocks in Chicago and Detroit, apartment buildings in Miami and Los Angeles and a North Carolina ranch called 'Paradise Valley' where Lucas kept 300 cattle, with one bull valued at $125,000. Along the way, he bribed police, socialized with celebrities and banked a nest egg of $52 million in the Cayman Islands. 'I wanted to be rich,' he later told one interviewer. 'I wanted to be Donald Trump rich, and so help me God, I made it.'

In 1971, New Jersey authorities formed a Special Narcotics Task Force to investigate Lucas, led by detective-turned-prosecutor Richard Roberts. Agents raided Lucas's home in Teaneck on January 28, 1975, seizing $584,000 and other evidence, leading to ten arrests. One of those detained, a Lucas nephew, turned state's evidence and thus produced another 43 arrests, finally including Lucas. Convicted at state and federal trials, with sentences totaling 70 years, Lucas himself became a prosecution witness, providing information used in 150 separate multi-defendant cases. Those convicted thanks to Lucas's testimony included Mafia members, ex-friend Ike Atkinson, several DEA agents and 30 relatives of Lucas.

As a reward for his cooperation, Lucas saw his prison term reduced to 15 years and was released in 1981, after serving only five years, with a stipulation for lifelong supervised parole. He lasted three years on the street before his next arrest, in 1984, for trying to purchase a kilo (2.2 lb) of cocaine for $13,000 and an ounce (28 g) of heroin. At trial in August 1984, defended by ex-prosecutor Richard Roberts, Lucas was convicted and received a seven-year sentence.

Freed in 1991 and finally retired from drug trafficking, Lucas lived on to see himself portrayed by Denzel Washington in the 2007 film *American Gangster,* with Russell Crowe cast as Richard Roberts. Meanwhile,

RIGHT: In 2007, Lucas's notorious exploits were the subject of the movie *American Gangster*, starring Denzel Washington.

Bumpy Johnson's widow published a memoir disputing Lucas's claims of his service with Harlem's godfather. Her version of events contends that Bumpy never trusted Lucas and therefore restricted him to 'flunky' work. Lucas's tales of serving as Johnson's right-hand man, she said, were mostly lifted from the exploits of another gang member, Zach Walker, who lived with Johnson's family and later betrayed him to authorities.

Lucas, in retirement, offers advice to prospective gangsters: 'My lawyer told me they couldn't take the money in the offshore accounts, and I had all my money stored in the Cayman Islands. But that's bullshit; they can take it. Take my word for it. If you got something, hide it, 'cause they can go to any bank and take it.'

Tommy Lucchese

Gaetano Lucchese was born in Palermo, Sicily, on December 1, 1899, emigrating to New York with his family in 1911. At age 15, he lost the index finger of his right hand in an industrial accident, prompting comparisons with Chicago Cubs pitcher Mordecai 'Three Finger' Brown. The nickname stuck, but was never used in Lucchese's presence by friends, who called him 'Tommy.'

At age 18, Lucchese launched a window-washing company with Samuel Magliocco, brother of future Mafia boss Giuseppe Magliocco. The partners soon turned from cleaning windows to smashing them, if clients refused to purchase 'protection.' Lucchese thus entered the Mafia orbit, serving as a lieutenant of boss Gaetano Reina in the Bronx and upper Manhattan, simultaneously leading his own gang – the 107th Street Crew – in East Harlem. Prohibition's liquid gold rush brought untold wealth for urban gangsters, and while Lucchese compiled a long list of arrests on various charges, his only conviction – in 1921 – earned him a three-year prison term for auto theft.

Lucchese was back in circulation when Gaetano Reina secretly pledged allegiance to Salvatore Maranzano in his war against rival Giuseppe 'Joe the Boss' Masseria. Masseria had Reina killed on February 26, 1930, replacing him with ally Joseph Pinzolo. Lucchese and Gaetano Gagliano then conspired to eliminate Pinzolo, who was slain in an office he shared with Lucchese on September 5, 1930, by triggerman Girolamo 'Bobby Doyle' Santucci. Maranzano ally Lucky Luciano soon persuaded Lucchese and Gagliano to openly join Maranzano, resulting in the double-murder of Masseria lieutenants, Steve Ferrigno and Alfred Manfredi, on November 5, 1930. Luciano ended the war on April 15, 1931, with Masseria's murder at a Coney Island restaurant.

Salvatore Maranzano then proclaimed himself 'Boss of All Bosses,' while scheming to eliminate Luciano and others he viewed as potential rivals. Lucchese learned of those plans and warned Luciano, then visited Maranzano's office on September 10, 1931, to identify him for killers dispatched by Luciano ally Lepke Buchalter. When Luciano reorganized New York's Mafia into five equal families, Gagliano emerged as a boss, with Lucchese as his underboss. Temporarily content, Lucchese became a naturalized US citizen on January 25, 1943, but never gained the right to vote (stripped from convicted felons in those days) despite a 'good conduct' certificate issued by his parole board in 1950.

Confusion surrounds the date of Lucchese's ascension to lead the former Gagliano Family. In testimony before the US Senate, Lucchese claimed that Gagliano died on February 16, 1951. Other reports date his death from 1953, while a story in the *New York Times,* published on March 19, 1959, reports the deportation of 'Gaetano Gagliano, described as a leading figure in the Mafia crime syndicate.' In any case, Lucchese was in charge by 1962, when his daughter married the eldest son of mafioso Carlo Gambino. One thousand guests attended the ceremony, where Gambino gave Lucchese $30,000 as a 'welcome to the family.' Together, Lucchese and Gambino

ABOVE: Tommy Lucchese (and his famous three fingers) at a Senate Labor Rackets Committee hearing in July 1958.

dominated New York's Mafia and the brotherhood's national commission. Lucchese's territory included Idlewild Airport (now John F. Kennedy International) with countless opportunities for plunder, and his 107th Street Crew was immersed in 'French Connection' heroin traffic.

Such lucrative business – and the 'Banana War' sparked by rival boss Joe Bonanno in the mid-1960s – distracted Lucchese from his operations in New Jersey, where family *caporegimes* Stefano Badami and Anthony 'Ham' Delasco waged sporadic warfare. Badami's murder prompted successor Filippo Amari to create his own upstart family in Elizabeth, New Jersey, later led by Simone 'Sam the Plumber' DeCavalcante. Meanwhile, turncoat mafioso

Joe Valachi exposed the New York syndicate's inner workings to the US Senate in 1963, naming Lucchese as one of the city's five bosses. Questioned by prosecutors, Lucchese replied, 'Valachi's crazy. I know nothing about any Cosa Nostra. The only thing I belong to is the Knights of Columbus.'

Lucchese's luck ran out in 1967. Diagnosed with an inoperable brain tumor, he retired to his Long Island home in April and died there on July 13. Aging successor Carmine Tramunti marked time until heir Anthony 'Tony Ducks' Corallo left prison in 1970, ruling until his next conviction and 100-year sentence, imposed on January 13, 1987. New boss Vittorio Amuso and underboss Anthony 'Gaspipe' Casso led the Lucchese Family through turbulent times, climaxed by their removal with life sentences in 1991 and 1994, respectively. At this writing, the family is reportedly run by the triumvirate of Joseph 'Joey Dee' DiNapoli (indicted in October 2009 for gambling, gun-running, loan-sharking and extortion, presently awaiting trial), Matthew Madonna and Aniello 'Neil' Migliore.

Lucky Luciano

The godfather of America's national crime syndicate was born in the sulfur-mining town of Lercara Friddi, Sicily, on November 24, 1897. Christened Salvatore Lucania, he emigrated to New York with his parents and four siblings in 1906. His first arrest, for shoplifting, followed in 1907. As a young tough man on Manhattan's Lower East Side, Lucania – calling himself 'Charles Luciano' – befriended future business partners Frank Costello, Meyer Lansky and Bugsy Siegel. His willingness to work with non-Sicilians set Luciano apart from old-line mafiosi at the time and shaped the future of America's underworld. Conviction for possessing heroin sent Luciano to prison in 1915, but he emerged in 1920 to a world of new opportunities.

LEFT: Lucky Luciano pictured (right) following the first day of his trial for vice offenses in 1936. He was later convicted.

RIGHT: Luciano exits a police wagon en route to New York's Supreme Court on June 2, 1936.

Prohibition made Luciano and his partners rich, while drawing the attention of Manhattan mafiosi Giuseppe 'Joe the Boss' Masseria and Salvatore Maranzano. Both courted Luciano while demanding that he shed his non-Sicilian allies. In 1929, Maranzano's soldiers kidnapped Luciano for a 'one-way ride,' leaving him scarred and near death, but he survived to earn his 'Lucky' nickname. Thereafter, Luciano joined Masseria's clique while plotting to rid the Mafia of all archaic 'Mustache Petes.' On April 15, 1931, he invited Masseria to lunch, then excused himself as four gunmen entered to kill Joe the Boss. Five months later, Luciano arranged Maranzano's murder, thus eliminating the last 'Boss of Bosses.'

With advice from Lansky and others, Luciano first revolutionized the Mafia, admitting non-Sicilian members and creating a commission of seven bosses

to settle disputes nationwide. Next, he and his partners applied the same structure to a national syndicate led by a 'board of directors' including mobsters of various ethnic backgrounds. That syndicate was well established by 1936, when New York prosecutor Thomas Dewey indicted Luciano on white slavery (compulsory prostitution) charges. Jurors convicted him, based on testimony now widely regarded as false, and Lucky received a sentence of 30 to 50 years.

World War II rescued Luciano from prison. Fearing sabotage on New York's waterfront, the Office of Naval Intelligence sought Mafia aid in policing the docks.

ABOVE: Luciano was placed under police surveillance in November 1954 on suspicion of narcotics trafficking and horse race fixing.

Luciano agreed to help in exchange for early parole, and some reports claim he went even further, persuading Old World mafiosi to cooperate with the Allied invasion of Sicily in July 1943. Whatever his actual contributions to 'Operation Underworld,' Luciano was paroled and deported to Italy in February 1946, after a lavish *bon voyage* party attended by numerous high-ranking mobsters. Ten months later, he hosted another gangland bash – this time a welcoming reception in

Havana, Cuba. Entertained by singer Frank Sinatra, 21 delegates rallied to discuss the international drug trade, mob investments in Nevada and other issues.

American narcotics agents learned of Luciano's presence in Havana and pressured President Ramón Grau San Martín to expel him, resulting in Lucky's deportation on February 23, 1947. Back in Italy once more, Luciano maintained his global connections, though his influence in the US gradually waned. Collaboration on a memoir with American authors Martin Gosch and Richard Hammer prompted an attempt on Luciano's life, for which he blamed Lansky. Plans for a film based on his life were proceeding when a heart attack killed Luciano at Naples International Airport, on January 26, 1962. The syndicate he helped to build remains as Lucky's legacy.

RIGHT: A portrait of mobster, Lucky Luciano, with the facial scars that he was named for clearly visible.

Owney Madden

New York City's future 'Duke of the West Side' was born to parents of Irish ancestry in Leeds, England, on December 18, 1891. Christened Owen Vincent Madden and nicknamed 'Owney,' the boy lost his father in 1902, then emigrated to New York with his mother and elder brother. Soon after arriving, he joined the Gophers – a Hell's Kitchen gang fond of meeting in basements – and committed his first armed robbery at age 14.

Ferocious battles with rival street gangs, including the notorious Hudson Dusters, earned Madden a new sobriquet: 'The Killer.' Suspected of five murders by 1910, he extorted an average $200 per day from neighborhood merchants. Three Hudson Dusters ambushed Madden on November 6, 1912, shooting him 11 times, but he survived and refused to name his attackers, settling the score himself upon his release from hospital. Finally, on November 28, 1914, Madden killed another Duster – William Moore, alias 'Little Patsy Doyle' – in a crowded

saloon, receiving a term of 10 to 20 years in Sing Sing prison. Paroled in January 1923, he found Manhattan gone 'dry' under Prohibition, but wetter than ever.

Madden plunged immediately into bootlegging, acquiring a string of nightclubs with partners Larry Fay, George 'Big Frenchy' De Mange and William 'Big Bill' Dwyer. Their flagship establishment was the Cotton Club in Harlem, featuring black talent and a wealthy, all-white clientele. Near the end of Prohibition, Madden joined De Mange and 'Broadway Bill' Duffy to promote prize fighters, including world heavyweight champions Primo Carnera (1933–34) and Max Baer (1934–35). Madden's lovers included actress Mae West, who later called him 'sweet, but oh so vicious.'

In 1931, Madden tried to mediate a truce between warring gangsters Dutch Schultz and Vincent 'Mad Dog' Coll, but lost his patience after Coll kidnapped George

De Mange and held him for $35,000 ransom. Crime historians suggest that Coll was talking to Madden, perhaps trying to extort more cash from Owney, when a machine-gunner surprised the Coll in a pharmacist's phone booth on February 8, 1932.

New York authorities belatedly noticed Madden in July 1933, returning him to Sing Sing for parole violations. Released later that year, shortly before the end of Prohibition and Manhattan's nightclub era, Madden decamped to Hot Springs, Arkansas, a wide-open haven of gambling and vice that cried out for a stern manager. Marrying the local postmaster's daughter, Madden invested his millions in casinos, brothels and political protection. He ran Hot Springs as a Mecca for high-rollers and a sanctuary for mobsters on the run until 1961, when Arkansas Senator John McClellan's 'rackets committee' summoned Owney for a grilling in Washington, DC. Still, another three years passed before state police closed his casinos. Madden died from emphysema in Hot Springs on April 24, 1965.

LEFT: Owney Madden (left) leaves Sing Sing prison in 1933 after several months behind bars for parole violation.

Carlos Marcello

Calogero Minacore was born to Sicilian parents living in Tunis, Tunisia, on February 6, 1910, emigrating to New Orleans, Louisiana, eight months later. As a youth, he ran wild through the French Quarter, committing petty crimes, then led a team of teenage bandits pulling armed robberies in nearby small towns. Jurors convicted Minacore – now known as 'Carlos Marcello' – in one such case, but their verdict was quashed on appeal. In May 1930, new charges of assault and robbery earned him a nine-year sentence, of which he served five.

By 1935, Marcello was affiliated with the Mafia family run by Sylvestro 'Silver Dollar Sam' Carollo, assisting in management of gambling enterprises shared with New York mobster, Frank Costello. Police caught Carlos with 10 kg (23 lb) of marijuana in 1938, slapping him with another prison sentence and a $76,830 fine, but his connections liberated him within ten months. Carollo, convicted in the same case, was deported after two years in jail, leaving Marcello in charge of the New

Orleans family. By 1947, Marcello controlled organized crime throughout Louisiana, with outposts from Florida and Tennessee to Dallas, Texas, where he worked closely with transplanted Chicago gangster Jack Ruby. Immigration officials ordered his deportation in 1953, but strangely took no further action even after Marcello was called to testify before the US Senate in March 1959.

Those hearings introduced Marcello to committee counsel Robert Kennedy, whose brother was elected

ABOVE: Carlos Marcello (center) and his son Joe (left) leave federal court on October 7, 1966.

president of the United States in 1960. Installed as attorney general in January 1961, 'Bobby' made Marcello a priority target, arranging his surprise deportation to Guatemala – falsely listed by Marcello as his birthplace – on April 4, 1961. Marcello soon returned to the US, stalling further deportation proceedings in court, but he never forgave the Kennedys. In September 1962, an informer told FBI agents that Marcello had 'clearly stated that he was going to arrange to have President Kennedy killed in some way,' adding that he would take out 'insurance' by 'setting up some nut to take the fall for the job, just like they do in Sicily.' That script was realized

in Dallas on November 22, 1963.

Relieved for the moment, Marcello served six months in jail for assaulting a federal agent, and was released in March 1971. While reporters and congressional investigators pursued tales of his involvement in JFK's murder, Marcello was indicted for racketeering in June 1980, and in August 1981 for conspiracy to bribe a federal judge. Conviction in both cases produced an aggregate sentence of 17 years, with Marcello's appeals rejected in April 1983. Two years later, while incarcerated, Marcello allegedly confessed his role in the JFK assassination to fellow inmate Jack Van Landingham.

After serving time in several prisons, Marcello was moved to a federal hospital in Rochester, Minnesota, suffering from Alzheimer's disease and the effects of

multiple strokes. Released to his family in 1990, Marcello died at home in Metairie, Louisiana, on March 3, 1993. No charges were filed against him, or anyone else, in the JFK case.

ABOVE: Marcello ponders questions posed by the Senate Rackets Committee in September 1961. He repeatedly invoked the Fifth Amendment.

Juan Ramón Matta-Ballesteros

A future drug lord and key figure in the 1980s Iran-Contra scandal, Juan Ramón Matta-Ballesteros was born on January 12, 1945, in Tegucigalpa, Honduras. Nothing is known of his life before 1970, when agents of the US Drug Enforcement Administration caught him with 24 kg (54 lb) of cocaine at Dulles International Airport, outside Washington, DC. Sentenced to five years for passport violations and illegal entry into the United States, Matta-Ballesteros spent a year in custody before escaping from a federal prison camp at Eglin Air Force Base in Florida.

By 1978, the DEA recognized Matta-Ballesteros as a major cog in the 'Mexican Trampoline' network, which 'bounced' Colombian cocaine from the Medellín Cartel to the US via a base in Guadalajara, Mexico. In his native Honduras, Matta-Ballesteros served as a partner of General Policarpo Paz García, whose 'cocaine coup' of August 7, 1978, established Paz as dictator through January 1982. That powerful connection in Honduras gave Matta-Ballesteros a ringside seat to the Sandinista revolution that deposed Anastasio Somoza Debayle as president of neighboring Nicaragua in July 1979.

While Somoza's brutality and corruption were legendary, US president-elect, Ronald Reagan, did not approve of his displacement by revolutionary leftists. Beginning in January 1982, the Central Intelligence Agency bankrolled ex-soldiers from Somoza's regime, dubbed 'Contras,' to destabilize the Sandinista government. Reagan compared the Contras to America's founding fathers, but their atrocities against unarmed civilians sparked outrage in Congress, producing a ban on further official support in December 1982. Reagan and the CIA then turned to other channels, including illegal arms sales to Iran and smuggling cocaine into the States. The primary drug traffickers employed were Juan Matta-Ballesteros and Oscar Danilo Blandón Reyes, formerly President Somoza's minister of agricultural imports.

A US Senate report published in April 1989 says that Matta-Ballesteros established the Honduran airline SETCO – short for Services Ejecutivos Turistas Commander – in 1983 to transport Contra supplies and cocaine shipments that earned him recognition as 'a Class I DEA violator.' By 1985, the DEA accused Matta-Ballesteros of importing one-third of all cocaine consumed in the United States. Oscar Blandón handled distribution in California and channeled profits to the Contras. Official involvement is confirmed by a handwritten entry in the diary of White House National Security Council member Oliver North, dated July 9, 1984, reading 'wanted aircraft to go to Bolivia to pick up [coca] paste, want aircraft to pick up 1,500 kilos [1.6 tons].' Another entry, from July 12, 1985, read: '$14 million to finance [weapons] Supermarket came from drugs.'

DEA leaders blamed Matta-Ballesteros for collaborating with Mexican traffickers in the February 1985 torture-slaying of Agent Enrique Camarena, but official stonewalling blocked all moves against Matta-Ballesteros and Blandón until 1986, when both were finally arrested. Matta-Ballesteros paid $2 million to Colombian jailers, who closed their eyes while he escaped and fled to Honduras. US marshals arrested him in April 1988, at his Tegucigalpa home, and flew him to the States for trial. Upon conviction in 1991 he received 12 life terms.

Frank McErlane

A Chicago native, born in 1894, Frank McErlane logged his first arrest at 17 and received his first prison sentence in June 1913 for auto theft. Paroled in March 1916, he was jailed again in November for the June 1916 murder of Oak Park police officer Herman Malow Jr. Despite the crime's severity, McErlane received a three-year sentence, with another year added for a prison break.

Released in the early days of Prohibition, McErlane teamed with Joseph 'Polack Joe' Saltis to quench illicit thirsts on Chicago's South Side. Alcoholic McErlane consumed a fair percentage of his own bootleg product, earning a reputation for homicidal rages when intoxicated. Allied with The Outfit run by Johnny

Torrio and Al Capone during Chicago's 'beer wars,' McErlane personally murdered three members of rival Myles O'Donnell's West Side Gang within ten days, in September 1923. Two months later, McErlane hijacked a pair of O'Donnell's booze trucks and shot both drivers, killing one. Arrested in that case, he beat murder charges at trial when key witnesses suddenly developed amnesia.

On May 4, 1924, while drunk in a Crown Point, Indiana, saloon with friends Alex McCabe and John O'Reilly, McErlane answered a challenge to his marksmanship by killing total stranger Thaddeus Fancher. McCabe and O'Reilly served time in that case, while McErlane went on the run. War with the O'Donnell gang resumed in 1925, with McErlane named as a suspect in the July 23 slaying of George Karl Jr. and William Dickman's murder on September 3. Three weeks later, on September 25, McErlane made gangland history by strafing Edward 'Spike' O'Donnell with a Thompson submachine gun — that famous weapon's first appearance in Chicago. O'Donnell survived, but McErlane did better on October 3, scoring the city's first Tommy gun fatality with victim Charles Kelly. Two more human targets survived their machine-gun wounds on February 10, 1926.

Police finally nabbed McErlane for Thaddeus Fancher's murder on April 22, 1926. Extradited to Indiana in August, he was acquitted on November 3, 1927 after a key witness withdrew. Frank next surfaced in Chicago, with a gunshot wound, on January 28, 1930. Three gunmen tried to finish the job on February 24, in McErlane's hospital room, wounding him three more times, but he drove them off with pistol fire. Blaming mobster John 'Dingbat' Oberta for the attacks, McErlane killed him — with companion Sam Malaga — on March 6, 1930.

McErlane finally cracked on October 8, 1931, capping a drunken quarrel with gunfire that killed common-law wife Elfrieda Rigus and her two dogs on a public street. While never prosecuted, he was forced into retirement by The Outfit with a small pension. Constantly drunk during his final year, McErlane died from pneumonia on October 8, 1932, the one-year anniversary of his final homicide. An anonymous acquaintance told reporters, 'I don't remember that he ever did anything good in his life. I don't believe he had a friend left.'

Jacques Mesrine

Jacques Rene Mesrine, ranked as 'Public Enemy No. 1' in France, was born near Paris, in Clichy-la-Garenne, on December 28, 1936. His doting parents enrolled him at the Collège de Juilly, a prestigious local school, but he was expelled for assaulting the headmaster. Married at age 19 and divorced the following year, Mesrine joined the French army in 1956 and spent three years battling anti-colonial guerrillas in Algeria, during a brutal conflict marked by terrorism and atrocities on both sides. Although he won a medal for valor, Mesrine's parents claimed he was 'never quite right' afterward. Mesrine himself later said that he returned to France in 1959 to punish 'society' for blighting his 'humanity' in defense of a 'false cause.'

The punishment consisted of serial armed robbery, leading to Mesrine's 1962 arrest with three accomplices for looting a bank in Neubourg. He received an 18-month sentence and was released in 1963, trying his hand at architectural design before he was made redundant in 1964 and returned to criminal pursuits. Arrested in Palma, Majorca, in December 1965, while burglarizing the military governor's villa, Mesrine served six months in jail, then left to run a restaurant in the Canary Islands.

Honest work paled beside thievery, and Jacques was soon back on the game, robbing a jewelry store in

Geneva, Switzerland, during December 1966, moving on in the new year to raid a hotel in Chamonix, France, and a posh fashion shop in Paris. February 1968 found Mesrine and mistress Jeanne Schneider in Montreal, Canada, employed as chauffeur and chef for millionaire Georges Deslauriers. After bungling a bid to kidnap their boss for ransom, on June 26, 1969, the couple fled southward, allegedly strangling elderly June Evelyne Le Bouthillier after she gave them shelter. Police in Arkansas arrested the fugitives on July 16 and shipped them back to Montreal for trial.

Convicted of attempted kidnapping, Mesrine received a ten-year sentence, escaped from custody several weeks later, and was recaptured after one day on the run. Jurors acquitted Mesrine and Schneider of Bouthillier's slaying in 1971, but Jacques escaped from Saint-Vincent-de-Paul

RIGHT: The many different faces of fugitive and 'Public Enemy No 1' Jacques Mesrine.

BELOW: French gangster Jacques Mesrine in the high security quarters of Sant□ prison in 1978. He escaped on May 8.

prison with five other convicts on August 21, 1972. He thereafter teamed with fugitive killer Jean-Paul Mercier for a series of Montreal bank heists, wounded two policemen in a botched attempt to liberate more prisoners from Saint-Vincent-de-Paul and murdered two forest rangers to avoid apprehension. Once, Mesrine and Mercier drove to Manhattan for a weekend of high living at the luxurious Waldorf Astoria Hotel. Later in 1972, they traveled to Colombia and Venezuela, but December found Mesrine back in France and up to his old tricks.

More bank holdups followed, climaxed by Mesrine's arrest in March 1973. Held for trial in Compiègne, he used a smuggled pistol to take the judge hostage and flee the courthouse. Recaptured in September by legendary Commissaire Robert Broussard, Mesrine was lodged in Santé maximum-security prison pending trial, which produced a conviction and 20-year sentence on May 18, 1977. Before escaping from Santé with three other convicts on May 8, 1978, Mesrine penned a memoir titled *L'Instinct de Mort* (*The Death Instinct*) and smuggled it out of prison for publication.

Free once more, Mesrine traveled widely, with stops in Sicily, Algeria, London and Brussels. His documented crimes include kidnappings, gun-running junkets, holdups and multiple murders, often committed in disguise. Mesrine dubbed himself 'The Man of a Hundred Faces' and boasted of 39 murders, although that tally remains unconfirmed. In

ABOVE: The disguised face of heavily-armed Jacques Mesrine, who eluded French police for many years.

August 1978, Mesrine sat for an interview with *Paris-Match* magazine, in which he threatened to kidnap and murder Minister of Justice Alain Peyrefitte. 'I will never surrender,' he declared. 'Now, it is war.' Two months later Mesrine bungled the kidnapping of a Parisian judge, but succeeded in snatching French real estate mogul Henri Lelièvre on June 21, 1979, collecting a ransom of six million francs (£600,000 aprox $1,200,000).

While some journalists romanticized Mesrine's exploits and courted interviews with the fugitive-at-large, policeman-turned-reporter Jacques Tillier branded Mesrine a traitor to his criminal cohorts, because he cheated them of revenue from robberies. Furious, Mesrine lured Tillier to a remote cave with a promise of an exclusive interview, then shot him three times: once in the face 'to stop him talking crap,' once in the arm 'to stop him writing crap' and once in the leg 'for the pleasure of it.' Against all odds, Tillier survived his wounds.

In October 1979, Commissaire Broussard received a tip that Mesrine and new mistress Sylvia Jeanjacquot had occupied an apartment in Paris, near the Porte de Clignancourt. On November 2, 50 officers in 15 vehicles converged on the address, surrounding the couple in their car, as they prepared to leave. Broussard later testified that his men demanded Mesrine's surrender, while civilian eyewitnesses say the police opened fire

without warning. In either case, 19 bullets shattered the BMW's windshield, killing Mesrine instantly and blinding Sylvia Jeanjacquot in one eye. A search of the car revealed a Browning automatic pistol and two hand grenades.

Ten days after Mesrine's death, an attorney retained by his family filed a civil lawsuit charging unnamed police defendants with 'assassination.' Marathon litigation and investigations spanned the next quarter-century, involving ten separate judges. In September 2000, Judge Baudouin Thouvenot screened an 8mm film shot by a member of the 1979 ambush party and reported finding no evidence of deliberate murder. Finally, on October 14, 2004, Judge Thouvenot closed the inquiry with a ruling that Mesrine's executioners had 'legitimately interpreted' his final movements as a bid to draw a weapon and resist arrest.

While controversy still surrounds Mesrine's death and the motivation for his crimes, Jacques had the last word on his own blood-stained career. 'Some people like golf, or skiing,' he told eager reporters. 'My relaxation is armed robbery. If I have rubbed the word pity from my vocabulary, it is because I have seen so many injustices.'

Sergei Mikhailov

The cofounder of Russia's most violent crime syndicate was born on February 7, 1958, in the Solntsevo area of Moscow's Western Administrative District. As a young man Sergei Mikhailov sampled honest labor, waiting tables, but the long hours and low pay launched him along a different path. His first arrest, in 1984, cost him six months in jail for petty theft. While imprisoned, he studied the *vory v zakone* ('thieves in law') who worked in organized gangs. Befriended by fellow Solntsevo native Viktor Averin, Mikhailov joined him after their release to create the Solntsevskaya Brotherhood, consciously discarding the 'Thieves Code' of older mobs to follow a more Western style.

Mikhailov's brotherhood was a full-spectrum criminal syndicate, immersed in arms smuggling (including claims of weapons-grade nuclear material offered for sale), arson for hire, art theft, contract murders, drug dealing, extortion, all manner of frauds, human trafficking, pornography and prostitution.

Competition from the Chechen Mafia and other outside groups prompted a merger with Sergei Timofeyev's Orekhovskaya Gang for mutual defense, but Timofeyev severed the alliance in 1990, pursuing an independent course that climaxed with his car-bomb murder on September 13, 1994.

Meanwhile, Sergei Mikhailov was arrested and convicted on extortion charges in 1989, spending 18 months in prison. In his absence, rivals challenged the Solntsevskaya Brotherhood, killing lieutenant Alexander Bezuvkin in 1990 and five more prominent members in 1993. Mikhailov convened a gangland summit meeting in Vienna, Austria, during October 1994 and, while peace was restored, some loose ends remained. Sergei Timofeyev's stubborn successor, Igor 'Max' Maksimov, was killed in February 1995, clearing the way for Mikhailov to annex the Orekhovskaya Gang's various rackets while expanding his influence abroad. A newly purchased castle near Geneva, Switzerland, stood literally as his symbol of success.

But while the Swiss have discreetly welcomed blood money for generations, they grew tired of Mikhailov's public extravagance. Police raided his castle in October 1996, arresting Mikhailov and seizing records of far-flung money laundering activities. Held without bond pending trial, he issued orders for a purge of potential witnesses throughout Europe. After a father and son were found murdered in Holland, both stabbed in the eyes, authorities imposed tighter security. As Mikhailov's trial convened on November 30, 1998, 90 surviving witnesses attired in body armor stood ready to testify against him.

Mikhailov smoked and sneered in court, disdaining the proceedings, and his scorn proved justified when he was acquitted of all charges on December 12, 1998. 'My heart is full of gratitude,' he cried out to the jurors when their verdict was announced. 'I love you, I love you, I love you.' After praising the trial's result as an example of democracy at work, Mikhailov returned to business as usual. At last report, his Solntsevskaya Brotherhood claimed 5,000 active members worldwide. Police linked the group to five corpses pulled from New Melones Lake near Sonora, California, in March 2002, while a report from 2008 tied the brotherhood to drug-dealing gangs in San Francisco.

Semion Yudkovich Mogilevich

Russia's alleged 'Boss of Bosses' was born to a middle-class family in Kiev, Ukraine, on June 30, 1946. He studied at Lviv University, earning an advanced degree in economics during 1968, then moved to Moscow's Lyublino district and immersed himself in crime with the Lyuberetskaya Brotherhood. Mogilevich spent most of the 1970s in prison, serving seven years on two consecutive convictions for illegal currency dealing.

Paroled with a new plan in the 1980s, the 'Brainy Don' victimized Russian Jews emigrating to Israel. Mogilevich promised to sell any property they could not transport and forward the money, but kept it instead to bankroll his other rackets. A millionaire by 1990, Mogilevich himself moved to Israel with several top aides, investing in various legitimate firms while maintaining control of his international narcotics, gun-running and human trafficking networks. In 1991, he married girlfriend Katalin Papp and settled in her native Hungary to sire three children at a fortified villa outside Budapest.

New acquisitions included an armament factory that produced anti-aircraft guns and surface-to-air missiles.

In 1993, Mogilevich joined forces with the Solntsevskaya Brotherhood led by Sergei Mikhailov, creating a kind of super-syndicate. A year later, he gained control of Inkombank, one of Russia's largest private banks, and used it to acquire a major share of Sukhoi – Russia's leading military aircraft manufacturer – in 1996. Two years later, Inkombank collapsed amid charges of fraud and money laundering. In May 1995, authorities in Prague banned Mogilevich from the Czech Republic for ten years, while Hungary declared him *persona non grata* and British police branded him 'one of the most dangerous men in the world.'

Undeterred by bad press, Mogilevich created a public corporation, YBM Magnex International, headquartered in Newtown, Pennsylvania, supervised by Russian immigrant Yakov Bogatin. Investors sank $400 million into YBM, on shares inflated from 10 cents to $20 each, and lost at least $150 million to the mob before FBI agents raided the firm on May 13, 1998. Indictments issued on May 24, 2003, charged three defendants – Mogilevich, Igor Fisherman and Anatoly Tsura – with stealing some $22 million from YBM. Specific charges included 45 counts of racketeering, securities fraud, wire fraud, mail fraud and money laundering. All remained

at large in Russia, demonstrating what one reporter described as Mogilevich's 'knack for never being in the wrong place at the wrong time.'

In 2006, Jonathan Winer, former US Deputy Assistant Secretary of State for International Narcotics Matters, advised reporters, 'I can tell you that Semion Mogilevich is as serious an organized criminal as I have ever encountered and I am confident that he is responsible for contract killings.' Moscow police arrested Mogilevich on January 24, 2008, then released him on July 24, 2009, with an announcement from Russia's Ministry of Internal Affairs that the charges 'are not of a particularly grave nature.' With no prosecution in sight, FBI headquarters added Mogilevich to its list of 'Ten Most Wanted' fugitives on October 22, 2009.

Diego Montoya Sánchez

Drug lord Diego León Montoya Sánchez was born at Trujillo, in western Colombia's Valle del Cauca Department. In different statements to authorities, he claimed a birth date of January 11, 1958 and 1961. While no record survives of his early criminal activities, the 1990s found him ranked among leaders of the Norte del Valle drug cartel, rising to prominence after leaders of the rival Cali Cartel were jailed in June and July 1995. According to the US Department of Justice, the Norte del Valle Cartel smuggled 500 tonnes (550 tons) of cocaine – valued in excess of $10 billion – from Colombia through Mexico and into the United States between 1990 and 2004.

That kind of traffic requires protection. In addition to his own gunmen and legions of corrupt police, Montoya – dubbed *El Señor de la Guerra* ('The Warlord') – enlisted guerrillas from both the right and left wings of Colombian extremist politics. His most prominent associates were members of the far-right *Autodefensas Unidas de Colombia* (United Self-Defense Forces of Colombia), a self-declared band of law-and-order vigilantes formed in April 1997, whose leaders saw no contradiction in protecting shipments of illegal drugs. Designated a terrorist group by the US State Department in 2001, the AUC still collected $1.7 million from Chiquita, the international fruit company, to 'protect' its workers from unionization through 2004.

Montoya needed every soldier he could find during 2003–04, as internal dissension split the Norte del Valle Cartel into warring camps. Trouble began when lieutenants Hernando Gómez and Wilber Varela Fajardo sought to negotiate surrender terms with the US Drug Enforcement Administration. Montoya responded with a failed attempt to kill Varela, sparking mayhem which claimed more than 1,000 lives between October 2003 and April 2004. Colombian police jailed 100 assassins, then extradited Varela lieutenant Julio César López to New York, where he received a 45-year prison term on June 4, 2008.

Montoya himself was indicted by American prosecutors in 1999, for drug trafficking. A new indictment, issued

on May 6, 2004, charged Montoya and nine associates with cocaine trafficking; money laundering; bribing Colombian police and politicians; kidnapping, torturing and murdering informants, rival drug traffickers and others; and wiretapping both Colombian and US law enforcement officials to monitor their activities. FBI headquarters immediately added Montoya's name to the 'Ten Most Wanted' list, with a $5 million reward offered for information leading to his capture.

Eugenio Montoya Sánchez, Diego's brother and second in command, was caught first, on January 15, 2007. Shipped off to Miami, Florida, he pled guilty in January 2009 on charges of drug trafficking and obstruction of justice (through murder of police informer Jhon Jairo Garcia Giraldo in August 2003). On April 27, 2009, he received a 30-year prison term.

ABOVE: Diego Montoya Sⵔnchez arrives at Bogotⵔ Air Force base after his capture on September 10, 2007.

Seven months after Eugenio's arrest, on August 26, 2007, the Bogotá newspaper *El Tiempo* revealed that Colombian police and military officers had been bribed to deactivate radar units and thus grant safe passage to smuggling ships owned by the Norte del Valle Cartel. Colombia's navy had been thoroughly infiltrated, including alleged cooperation from Admiral Gabriel Arango Bacci. A 2008 military tribunal convicted Arango of accepting $115,000 from drug traffickers, but Colombia's Supreme Court overturned that verdict in December 2009 and reprimanded US Ambassador William Brownfield for exerting 'undue influence' on navy prosecutors.

While that case wound its way through the courts, Colombian police arrested Diego Montoya Sánchez at Zarzal, in the Valle del Cauca Department, on September 10, 2007. Carlos Holguin, Minister of Interior and Justice, announced on May 19, 2008, that Montoya would be extradited within 'the coming few days,' yet another seven months elapsed before 'Don Diego' boarded a DEA helicopter bound for Miami on December 12, 2008. Faced with 12 charges including drug trafficking, obstruction of justice, money-laundering and murder, Montoya pled guilty to three counts on August 10, 2009.

On October 21, Judge Cecilia Altonaga sentenced Montoya to 45 years in prison, acknowledging his statement of 'remorse' and intent to pursue a 'new transition' in life. Aside from prison time, Montoya was ordered to pay relatives of murder victim Jhon Jairo Garcia $500,000 in compensation for his death. In accepting the judgment, Montoya offered the court his 'sincere hope to be able to bring relief to my family and the families of the victims and bring their nightmare to a conclusion.'

DEA spokesmen publicly hailed Montoya's incarceration as the end of the Norte del Valle Cartel, but successor Carlos Alberto Rentería Mantilla remains at large with a $5 million price on his head, labeled 'one of Colombia's most powerful and sophisticated narcotics traffickers' by Adam Szubin, Director of the US Treasury Department's Office of Foreign Assets Control.

Lewis Moran

The patriarch of Australia's most notorious crime family, Lewis Moran, was born in Melbourne, Victoria, on July 7, 1941. He subsequently married Judy Cole, ex-wife of mobster Leslie Cole (killed in a Sydney gang war on November 10, 1982) during 1966 and adopted her son, Mark. Their own child, Jason Matthew Patrick Moran, was born on September 20, 1967. While the boys grew to manhood in a criminal environment, Lewis and brother Des 'Tuppence' Moran handled the gang's affairs with Judy's help. Associate Graham 'The Munster' Kinniburgh, based in suburban Kew, collaborated with the Morans in racketeering on Melbourne's waterfront through the Painters and Dockers Union. Rivals included the Williams family, the Italian 'Ndrangheta, a Mafia faction led by Alphonse Gangitano, the 'Sunshine Crew' led by Dino Dibra and a Russian gang led by Nikolai Radev.

That volatile mix produced no less than 35 murders in Melbourne between January 16, 1998 and June 15, 2009. Alphonse Gangitano died first, shot at home during a visit by Kinniburgh and Lewis Moran, but no charges were filed. Dino Dibra shot Reshad Mladenich, a Bosnian associate of Mark Moran, in suburban St. Kilda on May 16, 2000. Carl Williams executed Mark Moran a month later, on June 15, outside his home in Aberfeldie. Jason Moran and bodyguard Pasquale Barbaro were shot dead in their car at a soccer stadium in Essendon, on June 21, 2003. Six months later, on December 13, Graham Kinniburgh died in an ambush outside his Kew home, firing a shot from his own pistol as he fell.

In the midst of that carnage, Melbourne police slapped Lewis Moran with drug trafficking charges, then released him on bond with an unnecessary warning that his life was in danger. On March 31, 2004, while Moran and colleague Bertie Wrout were drinking at the Brunswick Club on Sydney Road, two masked gunmen entered the bar. Wrout was severely wounded by the first shots, but survived. Moran leapt over a poker machine and smashed through a window before one of the shooters overtook him and fired a point-blank shot into the back of his head, killing him instantly.

Police charged three suspects in Moran's slaying. Keith Faure pled guilty in May 2006 and received a life sentence, while jurors convicted Evangelos Goussis in May 2008. He received a 30-year sentence in February 2009. Four months later, on June 15, Des Moran suffered a fatal gunshot outside his home in Ascot Vale. Authorities charged Judy Moran and two other defendants – Geoffrey Amour and Suzanne Kane (sister-in-law of Jason Moran) – with that slaying, naming Judy as an accessory after the fact. None of the defendants had faced trial as this book went to press, but Judy Moran – held in jail without bond – issued a statement on March 25, 2009, that accused Des Moran of stealing millions from her late husband's estate. Despite receiving $4,000 per month from her brother-in-law, Judy Moran reported that 'all the investments had gone bad and there was nothing in the pot.'

Nam Cam

Truong Van Cam was born in Saigon, French Indochina, in 1947. Upon departure of the French in 1954, their territory was split into the nations of Laos and Vietnam, with Vietnam temporarily divided along the 17th parallel. Communists ruled the northern half from Hanoi, while dictator Ngo Dinh Diem ran the 'democratic' south from Saigon, refusing to hold nationwide elections scheduled for 1956. In 1963, the same year Diem was assassinated in a military coup, Truong Van Cam was sentenced to prison for fatally stabbing a man in a fight.

Paroled in 1966, as American forces dominated the war against North Vietnamese regular troops and their Viet Cong guerrilla allies, Truong changed his name to Nam Cam ('Cam the fifth sibling') and joined the South Vietnamese army. A rabid anti-communist, he refused to surrender when North Vietnamese troops captured Saigon on April 30, 1975, subsequently renaming the city in honor of revolutionary leader Ho Chi Minh. Nam Cam fought on against the victors until he was captured and interned for 're-education.'

Whatever Nam Cam learned in custody, the lessons did not include respect for law. At liberty once more, the ex-soldier established himself as 'Vietnam's Godfather,' ruling an illegal gambling and prostitution empire with the aid of thugs and corrupt public officials. Arrested in 1994, he was convicted on charges including assault, gambling, organizing gambling, organizing bribery, organizing illegal emigration and abetting criminals. Despite that list of felonies, Nam was released in May 1995, thanks to intervention from Tran Mai Hanh, head of Vietnam's state radio network. And, as before, his time in jail produced no reformation.

Nam Cam's final conflict with the law began when Dung Ha, a female mobster from Haiphong known in gangland circles as 'Dung the Lesbian,' extended her operations to Ho Chi Minh City in 2000. Nam Cam initially hoped to collaborate with Dung Ha, thereby expanding his casinos into northern Vietnam, but she rejected his offer by sending a box filled with feces-smeared rats to one of Nam's posh restaurants. Furious, Nam ordered her execution, carried out by hitmen at a Haiphong marketplace on October 2, 2000.

Mindful of Nam's connections in Ho Chi Minh City, Vietnamese authorities sent police from Hanoi to arrest Nam and nine associates in December 2001. Those jailed with him included accused killers Bui Anh Viet, Chau Phat Lai Em, Ho Thanh Tung, Nguyen Huu Thinh, Nguyen Van Nha, Nguyen Viet Hung, Nguyen Xuan Truong, Pham Van Minh and Van Cong Tien. Before Nam and his cohorts finally faced trial in March 2004, another 140 defendants were slapped with various charges related to his life of crime, including 80 public officials and high-ranking members of the Vietnamese Communist Party.

Most prominent among Nam's indicted accomplices were Ho Chi Minh City's chief of police, Bui Quoc Huy and Tran Mai Hanh, whose intercession had freed Nam Cam from custody in 1995. In July 2002, Bui was

convicted of negligence for permitting Nam's syndicate to operate without interference, while Tran was found guilty of accepting bribes, including $6,000 in cash and an Omega watch priced at $2,500. Another defendant, deputy national chief prosecutor Pham Sy Chien, was convicted of accepting an $1,800 stereo system after he approved Nam Cam's early parole in 1995. Upon conviction, all three men were expelled from the Communist Party's powerful Central Committee.

On June 4, 2003, after a three-month trial, the People's Court of Ho Chi Minh City convicted Nam Cam and his four gang members of murder and bribing officials. Prior to sentencing, Nam asked Judge Bui Hoang Danh

ABOVE: Nam Cam learns of his death sentence at Ho Chi Minh People's Court on June 5, 2003.

to consider the fact that his crimes had been tacitly approved by corrupt officials, but Bui rejected the argument, sentencing Nam and five cohorts to death.

Vietnam's Court of Appeals began considering petitions from Nam and 69 codefendants in September 2003. In his appeal Nam denied giving orders for Dung Ha's murder. He told reporters, 'At first I admitted my responsibility for the murder of Dung Ha because my lawyer said I could then be eligible for clemency. But I think the death penalty handed to me is unjust and so I am appealing.' The court affirmed all convictions on October 29, 2003, while commuting Ho Thanh Tung's death sentence to life imprisonment. Vietnamese President Tran Duc Luong rejected Nam's final appeal for executive clemency on May 7, 2004. A month later, at dawn on June 3, Nam Cam was executed by a military firing squad at the army's District 9 rifle range in Ho Chi Minh City with condemned codefendants Chau Phat Lai Em, Nguyen Huu Thinh, Nguyen Viet Hung and Pham Van Minh.

Frank Nitti

Future Chicago gang lord Francesco Raffaele Nitto was born on January 27, 1881, at Angri, in the Italian province of Salerno. His father died in 1888 and his mother remarried the following year. Stepfather Francesco Dolendo emigrated to New York in July 1890, sending for his family in June 1893. Stepson Francesco quit school after the seventh grade to work as a barber, spending his free time with friends who included older brothers of neighbor Al Capone. Nitto – calling himself 'Frank Nitti' – left Brooklyn in 1910 and surfaced in Chicago three years later, adopting a criminal lifestyle with cronies including Irish gangster Dean O'Banion and ex-New Yorker John Torrio. Capone and Prohibition both arrived in 1920, launching Chicago on its wild ride through the 'Roaring Twenties.'

Nitti found his niche in the gang as Capone's **administrative aide,** earning his nickname – 'The Enforcer' – by dispatching gunmen to eliminate The Outfit's enemies. In 1931, both he and Capone were convicted of tax evasion, but Nitti's 18-month sentence saw him paroled in 1932, hailed in headlines as Capone's heir apparent. Historians still debate the true extent of his authority, compared to fellow mobsters Paul Ricca and Tony Accardo, but local authorities clearly viewed Nitti as the man in charge.

On December 19, 1932, corrupt mayor Anthony 'Ten-Percent Tony' Cermak sent Detective Sergeants Harry Lang and Harry Miller to kill Nitti. Lang shot Nitti three times, then gave himself a minor flesh wound to excuse the shooting, but Nitti amazed his foes by surviving to seek revenge. At Nitti's trial for attempted murder, in February 1933, Sgt. Miller admitted that Lang received $15,000 to murder Nitti. Jurors acquitted Nitti, while Lang and Miller were fined $100 each for assault. On February 15, 1933, Mayor Cermak was 'accidentally' shot in Florida, allegedly by a deranged gunman trying

LEFT: Chicago gangster Frank Nitti was a member of The Outfit and was seen by many as Al Capone's heir apparent.

to assassinate president-elect Franklin Roosevelt. He died on March 6, while his slayer – former Italian army marksman Giuseppe Zangara – was swiftly executed two weeks later.

Nitti's downfall came in 1943, when federal prosecutors indicted him and seven other Outfit leaders on charges of extorting millions from five major Hollywood film studios. On March 19, the day before his scheduled grand jury testimony, Nitti allegedly walked from his home to a nearby railroad yard and there shot himself in the head. Authorities described his death as suicide, blaming a claustrophobic fear of returning to prison, but gambler George Redston, in his 1965 memoir *The Conspiracy of Death,* claims that he saw plainclothes police force Nitti into an unmarked car shortly before his body was 'discovered' by the railroad tracks. Considering local police corruption and the department's prior attempt to kill Nitti, his death may well have been murder.

LEFT: Detective Sergeant Harry Lang, who claimed to have been the victim of attempted murder by Frank Nitti.

Manuel Noriega

Manuel Antonio Noriega Moreno was born in Panama City, Panama, on February 11, 1934, the son of an accountant who impregnated his maid. Given up for adoption to a local schoolteacher at age five, he attended the prestigious National Institute in hope of becoming a doctor, but his adoptive family could not afford medical school. Granted a scholarship to Peru's Chorrios Military Academy, Noriega graduated with an engineering degree in 1962, then went home to serve as a sublieutenant in Panama's National Guard.

Lieutenant Colonel Omar Torrijos befriended Noriega, sending him off for special training at the US Army's School of the Americas at Fort Bragg, North Carolina. That course, run in conjunction with the Central Intelligence Agency, specialized in teaching interrogation techniques and theories of psychological warfare to Latin American soldiers and police. While at Fort Bragg, Noriega became a CIA contract agent, remaining on the agency's payroll until February 1988.

Elevated to command of Chiriquí Province in 1968, Noriega aided Lieutenant Colonel Torrijos and Colonel Boris Martínez in their coup of October 11, which removed President Arnulfo Arias from office. Torrijos ruled as Panama's dictator until 1978, then installed Aristides Royo Sánchez as nominal president while maintaining control behind the scenes. Noriega defeated a bid to oust Torrijos in 1969, thereafter receiving promotion to lieutenant colonel with appointment to

serve as the dictator's chief of military intelligence, suppressing insurgent guerrillas and doing away with political rivals.

Colonel Torrijos remained in command of the National Guard – renamed the Panamanian Defense Forces – until a still-mysterious plane crash claimed his life on July 31, 1981. Colonel Florencio Flores Aguilar succeeded Torrijos, but was forced to retire in March 1982 by Colonel Rubén Darío Paredes del – who in turn ceded command to Noriega in August 1983.

Noriega's last obstacle was President Ricardo de la Espriella Toral, inaugurated on July 31, 1982. On February 13, 1984, while de la Espriella and his family vacationed in Chiriquí Province, Noriega sent a military plane to fetch the president. Confronted with a list of Noriega's demands and a warning to 'think of your family,' de la Espriella resigned on the spot. Vice President Jorge Illueca filled the president's post for nine months, succeeded by Nicolás Barletta Vallarino on October 11. Barletta in turn resigned under pressure on September 27, 1985, two weeks after assassins tortured and beheaded Noreiga critic Hugo Spadafora

ABOVE: An undated photograph of Panamanian leader Manuel Noriega, who collaborated with Ronald Reagan in his illegal 'Contra' war.

Franco near the Costa Rican border. Panama's next two presidents – Eric Delvalle Cohen-Henríquez and Manuel Solís Palma – were essentially front men for Noriega.

ABOVE: Noriega at a ceremony commemorating the death of former leader, Omar Torrijos, in 1987.

BELOW: US Army troops arrive in Panama to depose former ally Manuel Noriega in December 1989.

As a salaried CIA agent, Noriega collaborated with President Ronald Reagan's illegal 'Contra' war against the government of Nicaragua, permitting use of Panama as a conduit for cash and weapons. Since the covert war was supported with drug money, Noriega also found himself in partnership with leaders of Colombia's cocaine cartels, milking the trade for fabulous profits. A US Senate report published in 1988 declared that 'the saga of Panama's General Manuel Antonio Noriega

ABOVE: Noriega gestures to his supporters from his command HQ in October 1989 after surviving a coup.

represents one of the most serious foreign policy failures for the United States. Throughout the 1970s and the 1980s, Noriega was able to manipulate US policy toward his country, while skillfully accumulating near-absolute power in Panama. It is clear that each US government agency which had a relationship with Noriega turned a blind eye to his corruption and drug dealing, even as he was emerging as a key player on behalf of the Medellín Cartel.'

Noriega's regime was not without critics at home. From 1981 onward, he faced opposition from a 'Civic Crusade' financed by *rabiblancos* ('white-tails'), wealthy Panamanians of European ancestry who dominated politics before the coup in 1968. While the Civic Crusade staged protest rallies, Noriega fielded paramilitary 'Dignity Battalions' to beat, arrest and sometimes kill dissenters. When Noriega staged his own rallies, the ranks were filled with taxi drivers, cheering under threat of losing licenses that let them stay in business.

In June 1987, Noriega's disgruntled former chief of staff, Colonel Roberto Díaz Herrera, accused Noriega of killing Hugo Spadafora and rigging the 1984 election. Díaz also suggested that Noriega had murdered Colonel

Torrijos in 1981. On February 5, 1988, a federal grand jury in Miami, Florida, indicted Noriega and 15 codefendants – including Medellín Cartel leader Pablo Escobar – on multiple charges of narcotics trafficking and money laundering. While President Reagan and the US Senate called for his resignation, Noriega sought a compromise. In May 1989, he declined to run for president, supporting front man Carlos Duque. Members of the rival Panameñista Party, bankrolled with $10 million from US President George H.W. Bush, nominated Guillermo Endara Galimany. On election day, as the returns favored Endara, Noriega's troops seized ballot boxes and violently dispersed the resulting protests.

When economic sanctions imposed by Washington failed to crack Noriega's regime, and Noriega's legislature declared 'a state of war' with the US on December 15, 1989, President Bush launched 'Operation Just Cause' to unseat Noriega. American troops invaded Panama on December 20 and laid siege to Noriega's headquarters. He surrrendered on January 3, 1990, and was extradited to Miami for trial, convening in September 1991. On April 5, 1992, jurors convicted Noriega on eight counts of

BELOW: Panama's Vatican Embassy, where Noriega took refuge during 'Operation Just Cause.' He surrendered on January 3, 1990.

drug trafficking, racketeering and money laundering. He received a 40-year prison term on July 10, with an order to repay $44 million to the Panamanian government.

More charges followed. In March 1994, a Panamanian court convicted Noriega of murder *in absentia,* finding that he ordered the death of military rival Major Moises Giroldi in October 1989. Five years later, a French court

tried Noriega and his wife *in absentia,* on charges of laundering drug money. Both were convicted, sentenced to ten years in prison and a $33 million fine. In August 2007, a federal judge authorized Noriega's extradition to France upon his release. On April 26, 2010, he was extradited.

Khozh-Ahmed Noukhayev

Chechen Mafia founder Khozh-Ahmed Tashtamirovich Noukhayev was a member of the Yalkhoi clan from Geldagan, in the Shalinsky District of the Soviet Union's Chechen Autonomous Oblast. His parents were in exile, somewhere in Central Asia, when Noukhayev was born on November 11, 1954. In 1974, Noukhayev enrolled at Moscow State University, where he studied law. During that same year, with fellow student Said-Khasanom Abumuslimov, he founded the Obshchina ('commune'), described in conflicting reports as the first Chechen organized crime syndicate and a secret committee pledged to liberate Chechnya from Russian rule. In fact – like the Chinese Triads – it was a hybrid of both. Abumuslimov handled the Obshchina's political affairs, while Noukhayev used any means available to raise money.

In 1980, Noukhayev received an eight-year prison term for banditry. Paroled in 1987, he collaborated with Moscow gangster Nikolay Suleimanov to forge working alliances with local syndicates, including the Balashikha, Lyubertsy and Solntsevo crime families. Suleimanov dominated automobile sales in the Southern Port of Moscow, while Obshchina troops divided their time between terrorist acts and more conventional crime, such as cigarette smuggling and drug trafficking. In time, they controlled a lucrative share of heroin flowing westward from the 'Golden Crescent' of Afghanistan, Iran and Pakistan.

The collapse of Russian communism sparked independence movements in various former Soviet republics. Chechnya's first rebellion, between December 1994 and August 1996, claimed some 40,000 lives. Said-Khasanom Abumuslimov served as vice president of the breakaway Chechen Republic of Ichkeria during 1996–97, while Noukhayev recuperated from combat wounds in Turkey, then held office as first deputy prime minister. He also directed the Caucasian-American

Trade-Manufacturing Chamber, founded in spring 1997, collaborated with British leaders to form a private holding company dubbed the Caucasian Common Market and co-founded the Caucasian Investment Fund.

Those initiatives foundered with the outbreak of the Second Chechen War on August 26, 1999. Russian troops invaded Chechnya on October 1, and Noukhayev soon withdrew to Baku, Azerbaijan, continuing a war of words through the underground press. At least 50,000 lives were lost in Chechnya before the war's official end in May 2000, while guerrilla raids and suicide bombings continued through 2010.

Noukhayev continued his underground activities during the war, and granted interviews to journalist Paul Klebnikov, published in 2003 as *Conversation with a Barbarian.* Drive-by gunmen killed Klebnikov in Moscow on July 9, 2004, with some observers blaming Noukhayev for the murder. (Others suspected Boris Abramovich Berezovsky, a millionaire Russian expatriate profiled in Klebnikov's earlier book, *Godfather of the Kremlin.*) Five ethnic Chechens were indicted for Klebnikov's murder in November 2004, but jurors acquitted them all on May 5, 2006.

Meanwhile, unconfirmed reports alleged that Khozh-Ahmed Noukhayev was killed somewhere in the Republic of Georgia, during February 2004, while fighting Russians with soldiers of Ruslan Gelayev's Chechen separatist guerrilla army. If true, Noukhayev's death might absolve him in the Klebnikov murder. Obshchina members remain active in drug trafficking, allegedly through contacts with the Taliban in Afghanistan and Pakistan.

Raymond Patriarca Sr.

Raymond Loreda Salvatore Patriarca was born to Italian immigrant parents in Worcester, Massachusetts, on March 17, 1908. When he was three years old, his family moved to Providence, Rhode Island, where Patriarca spent the rest of his life except for prison time. His first arrest, by Connecticut police in May 1926, resulted in a $350 fine for an unspecified offense. Arrested twice in Massachusetts for suspicious behavior, in August 1926, Patriarca escaped from jail the second time and received a 30-day sentence in February 1927. Eight months later, in Worcester, he paid a $100 fine for transporting illegal liquor. A Providence break-in, committed in February 1928, cost him a two-year sentence on January 21, 1929.

Paroled in January 1930, Patriarca was arrested twice in April – for 'suspicion' (dismissed) and for a Rhode Island prison break that claimed two lives. That case languished until June 1945, when the state supreme court dismissed Patriarca's indictment on grounds that the statute of limitations had expired. Returned to prison for parole violations in September 1930, Ray emerged once more in November, then received a one-year federal term on December 30 for violating the Mann Act (transporting women across state lines for 'immoral purposes'). Released again in October 1931, Patriarca logged 15 more arrests by August 1938, when he was convicted of burglary, receiving a sentence of three to five years. An identical sentence for auto theft followed in September 1938, but Governor Charles Hurley pardoned Patriarca that December.

By November 1941, when Patriarca returned to prison on a robbery conviction, he was well established as a member of Phillip Bruccola's Boston-based Mafia family. Paroled in May 1944, he advanced through the ranks and was named as New England's 'king of the rackets' by US Senate investigators in 1950. Bruccola returned to Sicily in 1954, leaving Patriarca to run the family from his Providence headquarters. Summoned before the McClellan Committee in February 1958, Patriarca denied any knowledge of strong-arm tactics employed by distributors of his National Cigarette Service vending machine company.

In June 1967, federal prosecutors charged Patriarca with conspiring to murder independent gambler William Marfeo in July 1966. Convicted on that charge in March 1968, thanks to testimony from hitman-informer Joe Barboza, Patriarca received a five-year sentence and a $10,000 fine. In August 1969, Patriarca and six codefendants were charged with killing Marfeo's brother and a companion in April 1968. Jurors convicted all seven in March 1970, resulting in ten-year sentences. Parole freed Patriarca once again in January 1975.

In December 1980, police charged Patriarca with the 1965 murder of a drug addict who burglarized his brother's home. Failing health barred his trial on that charge, and on a Florida racketeering indictment filed in September 1981. While prosecutors tried to overturn that ruling and proceed with trial, Patriarca languished in Providence. A heart attack claimed his life on the morning of July 11, 1984.

Quirino Paulino Castillo

Quirino Ernesto Paulino Castillo was born in 1969, raised in the Dominican Republic's Elías Piña Province. No record of arrests charts his entry into the world of drug trafficking, where he earned millions and was known among his cohorts as 'El Don.' By 2000, Paulino Castillo was wealthy enough to favor the Dominican Revolutionary Party with a donation of DOP2 million ($55,000) for construction of gates for the elementary and high schools in Comendador, capital of his home province. He also donated a car to the Dominican Liberation Party's municipal committee and gave cash to the Christian Social Reformist Party in Elías Piña Province. When Henry Duval, director of the **Dominican Republic's** National Water Resources Institute, lost his government job in 2000, Paulino hired him as chief of irrigation for one of Paulino's farms. Four years later, Duval had a new government post under President Leonel Fernández Reyna. Farmer Paulino's chief veterinarian, Esvelti Edmond, was director of cattle ranching for the government in San Juan de la Maguana during the first Fernández regime, and returned to office with Fernández in 2004.

Those connections may have aided Paulino Castillo in his ultimate career move, merging crime with military service. On March 9, 2002, he joined the Dominican Army as a sergeant major, but his tenure was short lived, as General Manuel Ernesto Polanco Salvador dismissed him on August 1. General Jorge Radhamés Zorrilla Ozuna succeeded Polanco as commander of the army in 2003, and reinstated Paulino with the elevated rank of first lieutenant. The order for Paulino's reinstatement and promotion, Memorandum No. 32070, was signed by Major General Soto Jiménez, Secretary of the Dominican Armed Forces, under orders from President Rafael Hipólito Mejía Domínguez – leader of the same Dominican Revolutionary Party that accepted Paulino's DOP2 million contribution.

Thus protected from above, with troops at his command, Paulino expanded the scope of his cocaine shipments. He drew attention from the US Drug Enforcement Administration, which contacted Major General Furcy Castellanos, chief of intelligence for the Dominican Army, in April 2004. Furcy himself alerted President Mejía, but Mejía declined to take disciplinary action of the eve of impending May primary elections. Defeated in his bid for re-election, Mejía left office on August 16, 2004, branded an *azaroso* ('jinx') by his party's disappointed leaders.

On December 18, 2004, DEA agents and Dominican police arrested Paulino in Santo Domingo with a truck bearing 1,386 kg (3,051 lb) of cocaine valued at $26.4 million. Indictments swiftly followed, as a federal grand jury in New York charged Paulino with five counts of drug trafficking and money laundering. Under terms of a newly adopted criminal code in the Dominican Republic, he was extradited to New York on February 19, 2005, and charged in federal court three days later. In conjunction with Paulino's indictment, more than 60 other Dominicans were also arrested and extradited for trial in the US.

June 2007 brought reports that Dominican prosecutors were 'studying a proposal' from Paulino, under which the government would receive DOP100 million ($2.8 million) in exchange for dropping all charges against Paulino and any of his relatives still in the country. The offer – representing 5 per cent of Paulino's estimated DOP2 billion ($55.1 million) personal fortune – was apparently rejected, since the National District Office of the Prosecutor indicted six Paulino family members on August 12, 2008. Those charged with laundering more than DOP400 million ($11 million) included Paulino's wife Diomaris Marmolejos, his mother Zaira Castillo, his brother Quirilio, his son Anderson, his brother-in-law Luis Marmolejos and another relative by marriage, Ricardo Encarnación. In February 2009, authorities charged Paulino's nephew, Pedro Alejandro Paniagua Castillo, with the December 2007 kidnap-murder of two victims – Adolfo Justo Cervantes Arellano and Victor

ABOVE: Dominican drug enforcement officers burn more than 1,800 kg (2 tons) of cocaine seized from Quirino Paulino Castillo.

Manuel Mella Terrero – who allegedly stole DOP60 million ($1.7 million) from Paulino's syndicate.

Paulino's military connections proved embarrassing in March 2010, when the US State Department canceled visas held by ten retired Dominican generals, citing their links to Paulino. One of those singled out, ex-general Manuel de Jesus Perez, was director of the country's prisons when hundreds of phone calls from various jails were made in connection to narcotics shipments in transit. With that furor underway, Dominican businessman Faustino Perozo surrendered to police in Ciudad Nueva, pending extradition for trial in America.

Thus far, the only defendant convicted in Paulino's case is Fátima Henríquez, a Dominican national found guilty of laundering more than $300,000 for Paulino. On June 19, 2009, she received a one-year sentence from Judge Kimba Wood in New York.

Santiago Luis Polanco Rodríguez

A native of the Dominican Republic, born in Santiago on June 16, 1961, Santiago Polanco Rodríguez reached Washington, DC, in 1969, when his family arrived as illegal immigrants. After dabbling in juvenile crime, he organized a gang in 1982 that sold powdered cocaine outside his apartment complex in the Washington ghetto, paying $43,000 cash for his first limousine. Three years later, in June 1985, Polanco switched to selling crack cocaine, marketed as 'Based Balls' with price discounts offered on weekends. His dealers advertised with business cards bearing the slogan 'Cop and Go.' Today, spokesmen for the Drug Enforcement Administration consider Polanco the first mass-marketer of crack in the United States.

His product came from the Dominican Republic, where Polanco established a financial empire with his profits, laundering drug revenue through a nightclub, pharmacy and finance company. His preferred 'mules' were elderly women who carried cocaine from Polanco's homeland to the States, then returned with bundles of cash. Other funds were shipped out through a wire-transfer office Polanco ran from a Washington storefront. At the top, his operation was a family affair, including brothers Elvis and Santiaguito as couriers, half-brother Chiqui serving as manager in Polanco's absence, while sister Dulce Elizabeth and mother Luisa Ordalina kept the books and supervised the crack labs. Over time, Polanco expanded to New York City, recruiting street gang members in Manhattan, Brooklyn and the Bronx. DEA agents blamed Polanco's network for at least five murders in New York, but lacked sufficient evidence for an indictment.

In 1986, the DEA launched an anti-crack drive in New York, jailing hundreds of dealers, recruiting some as informers. On July 30, 1987, a federal grand jury indicted Polanco on 58 counts of drug trafficking, racketeering and money laundering. DEA agents raided his Bronx headquarters, seizing automatic weapons, bulletproof vests and 100,000 empty crack vials. While six suspects were jailed, Polanco escaped to the Dominican Republic with a false passport.

His luck seemed to sour in 1988. Wounded in a gunfight over a woman, he was arrested and sent to La Victoria prison without trial. Brawls with fellow inmates brought a transfer to the Monte Plata jail in 1990, where prison guards furnished a cell phone, cable television and takeout restaurant meals. Released in 1992, he returned to Santiago and spent millions on a casino and clothing factory, hotels and discotheques, banana plantations and a mansion shaded by fruit trees. Polanco cultivated the image of a community benefactor. Touring Santiago with a *New York Times* reporter, he pointed out trash cans he purchased and placed on the streets as a public service, declaring, 'I'm helping my people, but I haven't received a single thank-you from the government, or anybody.'

Thanks of a sort, however, were delivered by President Leonel Fernández Reyna in November 1996, when New York Police Commissioner Howard Safir visited Santo Domingo, seeking extradition of Polanco and other indicted drug smugglers. Fernández spurned the request as 'absurd' and 'totally impossible.'

Bernardo Provenzano

Bernardo Provenzano was born in Corleone, Sicily, on January 31, 1933. The third of seven sons in an impoverished peasant family, he left primary school to work the fields, then joined the Mafia for better prospects in his teens. Dr. Michele Navarra ruled the Corleonesi crime family in those days, but Provenzano cast his lot with upstart Luciano Leggio, fomenting rebellion against the boss. On August 2, 1958, Provenzano joined the 14-man firing squad that killed Navarra and another physician during a house call outside Corleone.

Over the next five years Provenzano tracked and killed various Navarra loyalists, prompting Leggio to remark that, 'He shoots like a god. It's a shame he has the brains of a chicken.' During that period, Provenzano earned his nickname 'Bennie the Tractor,' for his efficiency in 'mowing people down.' A botched murder contract in May 1963 sent him into hiding, first from rival gunmen, then from an arrest warrant issued on September 10. On December 10, 1969, he led the hit team that killed Michele Cavataio and three associates in Palermo, as retribution for their role in Sicily's so-called 'First Mafia War.'

Provenzano was still a fugitive in May 1974, when Leggio's imprisonment placed Salvatore Riina in charge

ABOVE: Mafia fugitive Bernardo Provenzano is arrested on April 11, 2006, after more than 40 years on the run.

of the Corleonesi, with Provenzano elevated to the post of underboss. Operating behind the scenes, Bernardo earned another nickname – 'The Accountant' – for his relatively low-key approach to Mafia administration. His role in the 'Second Mafia War' of 1981–82 is obscure, but the Corleonesi emerged triumphant. At the 'Maxi Trial' held in Palermo between February 1986 and December 1987, both Riina and Provenzano were sentenced to life prison terms *in absentia*. Riina's capture by police on January 15, 1993, left Provenzano in command of the Corleonesi – and, at least in theory, of the whole Sicilian Mafia.

He lived well for a convicted murderer in hiding, spending most of his time (unknown to the authorities) with family at an 18th-century villa in the Palermo suburb of Bagheria. Mafiosi Leoluca Bagarella and Giovanni Brusca reportedly challenged Provenzano for leadership, but their respective arrests in June 1995 and May 1996 removed both from circulation. Provenzano remained at large by shunning telephones and issuing orders through hand-delivered notes called *pizzini*, some signed with the benediction 'May the Lord bless and protect you.' When meetings of the Mafia Commission were convened, he sometimes arrived by ambulance, disguised as a patient in transit. At one meeting, in 1992, Provenzano appeared in the purple robes of a Roman Catholic bishop.

Meanwhile, Provenzano continued to mow down opponents, informers and anyone else who threatened his Cosa Nostra. Aside from standard contract murders, Provenzano launched a terrorist car-bombing campaign

ABOVE: Italian police inspect the farmhouse near Corleone where Provenzano was finally captured.

Health Service. DNA testing confirmed the patient's identity, but it brought police no closer to their man after 39 years on the run.

On January 25, 2005, authorities raided various homes and hideouts in Sicily, jailing 46 mafiosi on suspicion of helping Provenzano elude capture. Two months later, additional raids netted 80 more suspects, while once again missing the godfather. Informers in the latest batch described Provenzano's habit of shifting incessantly between safe houses, but another 13 months elapsed before detectives followed a shipment of clean laundry to a farm outside Corleone, finally bagging their man on April 11, 2006. No trial was required, since Provenzano already faced a life sentence imposed in 1987.

soon after his ascension to the Corleonesi throne in 1993. The first blast – apparently targeting Maurizio Costanzo, a television talk-show host in Rome who publicly denounced the Mafia – injured 18 people on May 14. Two weeks later, on May 26, a second bomb outside the Uffizi Gallery in Florence killed six persons, wounded 26 and destroyed priceless works of art. The final spasm, three explosions on the night of July 27–28, struck a modern-art gallery in Milan and two Catholic churches, San Giovanni in Laterano and San Giorgio in Velabro, leaving five more victims dead. An individual victim, anti-Mafia Catholic priest Giuseppe Puglisi, was gunned down on his 56th birthday (September 15) in Palermo. Motives in some of the attacks remained obscure, though observers speculated vaguely on a budding Mafia alliance with Silvio Berlusconi's right-wing Forza Italia ('Forward Italy') Party, or Pier Ferdinando Casini's Union of Christian and Centre Democrats.

In 2002, diagnosed with prostate cancer, Provenzano traveled to France and underwent surgery in Marseille, subsequently billing the operation to Italy's National

With Provenzano safely locked away, rumors surfaced that he may have led a double life in hiding, as a fugitive and an informer for the Carbinieri. Turncoat mafiosi Giovanni Brusca and Massimo Ciancimino claimed that Provenzano 'sold' Salvatore Riina to police in 1993, in exchange for delivery of compromising evidence Riina maintained on Provenzano, at his home in Palermo. Once that bargain was struck, the informers contend, Provenzano gave detectives a map pinpointing Riina's lair.

Two months after Provenzano's arrest, on June 20, prosecutors launched 'Operation Gotha,' issuing 52 arrest warrants for Palermo's top-ranking mafiosi, comprising leaders of 13 families grouped into four clans. Those netted in the sweep included Antonio Rotolo, Dr. Antonio Cinà (named as Provenzano's personal physician) and builder Francesco Bonura. Simultaneously, speculation began concerning Provenzano's successor as Mafia 'Boss of Bosses.' Prominent candidates included Salvatore Lo Piccolo, Matteo Denaro and Domenico Raccuglia. Of the three, only Denaro remained at large as this book went to press. Lo Piccolo was captured in

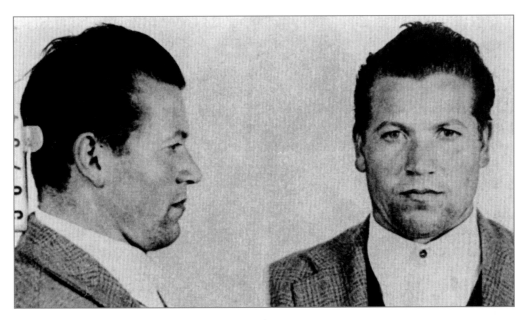

Giardinello on November 5, 2007, while police nabbed Raccuglia at Calatafimi-Segesta on November 15, 2009.

Provenzano's 'New Mafia' remains a covert power in Italy, as witnessed by claims from informer Antonino Giuffrè that mafiosi cultivated ties with Prime Minister Silvio Berlusconi, inaugurated on May 8, 2008. Critics note that Berlusconi employed mafioso Vittorio

ABOVE: A police mugshot of Provenzano taken in 1959, four years before he went into hiding.

Mangano at his Villa San Martino near Milan, and that close friend Marcello Dell'Utri was convicted at a Mafia extortion trial in 2004.

Chotta Rajan

Future mobster Rajendra Sadashiv Nikalje was born during 1956 in Maharashtra, India's third-largest state. As a young man he joined the gang led by Rajan Mahadeo Nair in the Tilaknagar district of Chembur, a Mumbai suburb. A turf war with rival Abdul Kunju climaxed with Nair's assassination on September 21, 1983. Nikalje promptly adopted the name Chotta Rajan ('Little Rajan') in honor of his mentor, vowing retribution against Nair's killers. In 1985, Rajan and two other gunmen killed Kunju in the middle of a cricket match, while Kunju's teammates watched, aghast. Triggerman Chandrashekar Safalika soon followed, kidnapped and tortured to death by a hit team including Chotta Rajan and a younger brother of Mumbai mobster Dawood Ibrahim.

By that time, Rajan had joined Ibrahim's syndicate, trafficking in drugs, running extortion rackets and infiltrating the 'Bollywood' film community, where his brother produced motion pictures financed by Rajan. Along the way, he was linked to 17 murders and several more unsuccessful murder attempts. One alleged victim, a brother of Mumbai gangster Arun Gulab Gawli, vanished from a wedding ceremony held for Dawood Ibrahim's brother, reportedly killed for a drug deal gone sour.

Rajan followed Ibrahim's lead in 1988, fleeing legal heat in India to hide out in Dubai. Their formal rift occurred on March 12, 1993, when Ibrahim's agents coordinated 12 car-bomb blasts in Mumbai, killing 257 victims and wounding 713. In fact, some observers suggest that the split occurred earlier, sparked by religion: Dawood is a Muslim, while Rajan is a Hindu, a frequent cause of bloodshed in post-colonial India. After the bombings, Rajan organized his own separate gang to pursue all the rackets he formally ran on behalf of Rajan Nair and Dawood Ibrahim.

War erupted in 1994, when Rajan's men lured Ibrahim loyalist Phillu Khan to a hotel in Bangkok, Thailand, and tortured him to death for his role in the Mumbai bombings. Other bombing suspects – Saleem Kurla, Mohammad Jindran and Majid Khan – fell before Chotta's guns in April 1998, June 1998 and March 1999. Ibrahim's assassins struck at Rajan's associates in the legitimate world: hotelier Ramanath Payyade; film producer Mukesh Duggal; East West Airlines managing director Thakiyuddin Wahid; Nepalese legislator Mirza Dilshad Beg; and Mohammad Saleem, a leader of the far-right Shiv Sena political party endorsed by Rajan. In September 2000, Ibrahim's gunmen botched an attempt on Rajan's life in Bangkok, killing Chotta's lieutenant Rohit Varma and his wife while Rajan escaped through a window. Rajan struck back in 2001, murdering Ibrahim aides Vinod Shetty and Sunil Soans in Mumbai. Next, on January 19, 2003, Rajan's men killed Ibrahim's chief financial manager – Sharad Shetty – at the India Club in Dubai.

These days, Rajan complains about his treatment in the press. 'Is something the matter?' he asked a reporter from *Indian Express*. 'Why are you upset with me? I haven't threatened anybody in the last several months, leave alone kill anybody. These reports projected me in a very poor light. In fact, I am doing good work for the country.'

Željko Ražnatović

Serbian mobster and militant Željko Ražnatović was born in Brežice, in the Lower Styria region of northeastern Slovenia, on April 17, 1952. He loathed life at home, later telling a reporter that his father 'didn't really hit me in a classical sense, he'd basically grab me and slam me against the floor.' Ražnatović ran away the first time at age nine, spending six weeks on his own in Dubrovnik, Croatia. When his parents divorced, in his teens, Ražnatović went to live in Belgrade with Stane Dolanc, a friend of his father and one of Yugoslavian president Josip Broz Tito's closest advisors. At some uncertain point, Ražnatović chose his own later-famous nickname – 'Arkan' – from a popular comic strip character.

By then, he was involved in juvenile crime, snatching purses and looting kiosks, later graduating to robbery. Ražnatović made good grades during his rare appearances at school, but preferred kick-boxing lessons to academic subjects. He logged his first arrest in 1966 and spent a year in juvenile detention. Next, his father packed him off to join the Yugoslav navy at Kotor, Montenegro, but Ražnatović fled to Paris. French police nabbed him in 1969 and sent him home, where waiting burglary charges sent him to jail at Valjevo in western Serbia.

Upon release in 1972, Ražnatović emigrated illegally to Western Europe, joining forces with other expatriate felons including future Serbian Guard founder Đorđe Božović Giška, gangster Ranko Rubežić, murderer Goran Vuković and future 'Serbian Godfather' Ljuba Zemunac. Over the next two years, Ražnatović dodged police in Austria, Belgium, Germany, Italy, the Netherlands, Sweden and Switzerland. Swedish authorities alone charged him with 20 burglaries, seven bank robberies, attempted murder and aiding a prison break. On the side, Ražnatović and his cronies did various shady favors for the UDBA – Tito's secret police. That service, and his childhood ties to Stane Dolanc, would later serve Ražnatović well.

Belgian police nabbed Ražnatović for bank robbery on December 28, 1974, resulting in a ten-year prison term. He escaped on July 4, 1979, and was recaptured on October 24, after pulling two more holdups in Sweden and three in Holland. He escaped once more on May 8, 1981, committing more heists before German police wounded and captured him on June 5, during a raid on a Hamburg jeweler's shop. Lodged in a prison hospital, Ražnatović leapt from a window on June 9, attacked a pedestrian to steal his clothes and fled to Switzerland. Officers in Basel arrested Ražnatović during a routine traffic stop on February 15, 1983, but they couldn't hold him. After his next escape, on April 27, he returned to Yugoslavia. Tired of a bandit's life, Ražnatović established a syndicate dealing in drugs, prostitution and gambling. In November 1983, he shot and wounded two policemen who attempted to interrogate him, but Stane

ABOVE: Ražnatović poses with the sword of Montenegrian King Nikola in May 1999, eight months before his assassination in Belgrade.

Dolanc's intercession secured his release two days later.

Ethnic Serbian uprisings rocked Yugoslavia in August

1990. On October 11, Ražnatović recruited 20 members of the Red Star Belgrade soccer club to form a private militia, the Serb Volunteer Guard, to patrol rebel territories of Croatia under command of the Yugoslav army. On November 29, following a council of war of the Republic of Serbian Krajina (now Eastern Slovenia), Ražnatović was arrested in Dvor na Uni, Croatia, on charges of gun-running and conspiring to assassinate newly-elected Croatian president Franjo Tuđman. Tried in Zagreb, he was acquitted and released on June 14, 1991.

Tired of official supervision, Ražnatović next organized a paramilitary force – Arkan's Tigers – that waged wide-ranging guerrilla warfare from 1991 through 1995 in Croatia, Eastern Slovenia and Bosnia-Herzegovina. A report from the United Nations on 'ethnic cleansing' in Bosnia later named Arkan's Tigers as some of the worst offenders, particularly active in terrorizing Albanian residents of Kosovo. Operating from a mansion in the elite Belgrade neighborhood of Dedinje, home to many high-ranking Yugoslavian officials and foreign diplomats, Ražnatović maintained his powerful connections while casting himself as a hero to fellow Serbs. On November 3, 1993, he played a key role in founding the Party of Serbian Unity.

Through it all Ražnatović maintained his role as a crime lord in Belgrade, liquidating rivals such as 'Gypsy king' Iso Lero Dzamba, murdered on September 23, 1992. Arkan's Tigers formally disbanded in April 1996, whereupon Ražnatović took command of Belgrade's FK Obilić soccer club, guiding it to national championships in 1997–98. According to some reports, members of opposing teams were threatened with death if they scored against FK Obilić.

On September 30, 1997, the International Criminal Tribunal for the former Yugoslavia indicted Arkan on 24 counts of crimes against humanity and grave breaches of the Geneva convention, though his arrest warrant was not publicized until March 31, 1999. Specific events included civilian massacres and rape of Muslim women. Before he could be tried, Ražnatović was assassinated by a rogue policeman at Belgrade's InterContinental Hotel, on January 15, 2000.

Paul Ricca

Future Chicago mobster, Felice DeLucia, was born in Naples, Italy, in 1897. He joined the Mafia at age 15 and three years later murdered one Emillio Parillo – either on orders from his boss, or because Parillo jilted DeLucia's sister. After two years in prison, he emerged to kill Vincenzo Capasso, the prosecution's key witness against him, and fled through France to Cuba. There he met a fellow Neapolitan, Chicago bootlegger 'Diamond Joe' Esposito, who invited DeLucia to join him in the Windy City. DeLucia landed in New York on August 10, 1920, giving his name as 'Paul Ricca,' and soon reunited with Esposito in Chicago.

A fter a brief apprenticeship smuggling moonshine liquor from Kentucky, Ricca served as maitre d' at Esposito's flagship restaurant, the Bella Napoli, earning his lifelong nickname as 'Paul the Waiter.' One frequent guest was Al Capone, who recognized Ricca's potential and wooed him away from Esposito. In 1928, Ricca became a naturalized US citizen under the name 'Paul DeLucia,' while filing tax returns as 'Paul Maglio.' That ploy, designed to confuse authorities, would later come back to haunt him. That same year, on March 21, Joe Esposito was killed by Capone-allied mobster, Frank McErlane, for buying liquor from the rival Sheldon gang.

In 1930, Capone sent Ricca to New York City as an arbitrator in the Mafia war between Giuseppe 'Joe The Boss' Masseria and Salvatore Maranzano. The mission failed, but introduced Ricca to rising stars of the future national crime syndicate – Lucky Luciano, Meyer Lansky, et al. – who warned Ricca of Capone's impending downfall and advised him to keep a low profile. Capone's subsequent imprisonment for tax evasion left Frank Nitti in charge of the Chicago Outfit,

RIGHT: Paul Ricca strides gleefully from a Chicago courtroom in June 1957, after winning a delay in his trial for income tax evasion.

though some observers viewed Ricca as the brain behind 'The Enforcer.'

Things ran smoothly without Capone until The Outfit discovered Hollywood. Mobsters, Willie Bioff and George Browne, got things rolling in the mid-1930s, when they seized control of the International Alliance of Theatrical Stage Employes, Moving Picture Technicians, Artists and Allied Crafts. Command of

BELOW: When Paul Ricca was summoned before the Senate Labor Rackets Committee in 1958, he predictably pled the Fifth Amendment.

the union allowed them to call strikes against theaters and film studios – an expensive inconvenience which management paid handsomely to avoid. Chicago's gang lords noticed the racket and cut themselves in for a lion's share of the profits, thrilled with the arrangement until the gravy train derailed in October 1941, when Bioff and Browne were convicted of extortion, racketeering and tax evasion. Averse to prison, both turned state's evidence against their bosses, resulting in federal indictments of Nitti, Ricca, Louis 'Little New York' Campagna, Philip D'Andrea, Charles 'Cherry Nose' Gioe, Louis Kaufman,

ABOVE: An aerial view of the sprawling estate in Long Beach, Indiana (featuring tennis court and swimming pool) owned by Italian mobster, Paul Ricca.

Frank Maritote, Ralph Pierce and John Rosselli on March 18, 1943.

Nitti was found shot to death the next day, an alleged suicide, though evidence suggests assassination. The remaining defendants faced trial on October 5, 1943, with Ralph Pierce's charges dismissed by the court soon thereafter. Browne and Bioff testified for the prosecution, as did extortion victims Louis B. Mayer of Metro-Goldwyn-Mayer studios, Harry and Albert Warner of Warner Brothers, Joseph Schenck of 20th-Century Fox and his brother Nicholas Schenck, president of the Loews theater chain. Jurors convicted the remaining defendants on December 22 and they were sentenced on December 31. Chicago's Outfit leaders each received ten-year prison terms, while Kaufman (from New Jersey) was sentenced to seven years, all accompanied by $10,000 fines.

FBI agents soon reported that Ricca and Campagna retained control of The Outfit from their prison cells, though Phil D'Andrea fared worse, beaten by guards in Atlanta, Georgia, after he threatened a prison orderly.

Ricca sought a transfer to Leavenworth, Kansas, for closer proximity to Chicago, a move granted in May 1945 despite opposition from wardens at both prisons. Next, he reached out to Paul Dillon, a lawyer in St. Louis, Missouri, who had managed President Harry Truman's 1934 race for the US Senate. On August 13, 1947, an unprecedented early-release order freed Ricca, Campagna, D'Andrea, Gioe and Rosselli. While prosecutors seethed in outrage, FBI director J. Edgar Hoover collected – and suppressed – evidence of payoffs channeled through Dillon to Attorney General Thomas Campbell Clark. Two years later, in August 1949, President Truman named Clark to a seat on the US Supreme Court. Truman – whose political career was launched in the 1920s and nurtured thereafter by boss Tom Pendergast's Mafia-allied Jackson County Democratic Club – later called Tom Clark 'my biggest mistake,' but he raised no objection to the 1947 payoff.

Back in Chicago, Ricca resumed his post as *consigliere* to new boss Tony Accardo, avoiding public contact with The Outfit to escape parole violation by consorting with known criminals. In September 1950, he and Louis Campagna were questioned regarding the murders of ex-police lieutenant, William Drury, and attorney Marvin Blas, but no charges were filed and the crimes remain officially unsolved.

Meanwhile, Immigration officials pursued Ricca, first locating the real Paul Maglio whose name he had borrowed decades earlier, thus discovering the lie on Ricca's tax returns. They also found a sister of 1915 murder victim Emillio Parillo, who identified Ricca as her brother's convicted killer. In April 1957, prosecutors secured a deportation order against Ricca, but a federal judge reversed it on appeal. Next came the tax men, indicting Ricca for income tax evasion in 1959. Jurors convicted him, resulting in a nine-year prison sentence. Ricca served 27 months, then was indicted on the same charge once again, in 1965. At trial, Ricca argued that his total income for 1963 – $80,159 – was derived from gambling and that filing a return would constitute self-incrimination banned by the Fifth Amendment to the US Constitution. Jurors bought the line and acquitted Ricca. He resumed duties as The Outfit's elder statesman, serving until a heart attack killed him on October 11, 1972.

Salvatore Riina

Born in Corleone, Sicily, on November 16, 1930, Salvatore 'Totò' Riina joined the local Mafia at age 19 after killing a man on orders from boss Michele Navarra. A second homicide in 1950, committed during a quarrel, sent Riina to prison for six years on a manslaughter charge. Insider assessments of Riina varied during those years, as he earned conflicting nicknames as 'The Short One' and 'The Beast.' During the course of his career, Riina allegedly killed 40 victims with his own hands, while ordering the deaths of hundreds more. As informer Antonino Calderone explained it, Riina was 'unbelievably ignorant, but he had an intuition and intelligence and was difficult to fathom, very hard to predict. His philosophy was that if someone's finger hurt, it was better to cut off his whole arm just to make sure.'

Paroled in 1956, Riina found the Corleonesi clan in turmoil. Insurgents Luciano Leggio and Bernardo Provenzano recruited Riina for their rebellion against Dr. Navarra, killing him and another physician during a house call on August 2, 1958. The rebellion cost 153 lives overall, leaving Leggio in command of the family. Next came Sicily's so-called 'First Mafia War' of 1962–63, climaxed with a bombing that killed seven lawmen at Ciaculli on June 23, 1963. Riina and Leggio were among 117 suspects held for trial in 1968, on charges related to that struggle, but they were acquitted with most of the rest thanks to bribery and intimidation of jurors and witnesses.

Slapped with another murder charge in 1970, Riina fled into hiding. Prosecutors convicted Leggio of murder that December, *in absentia,* and finally arrested him in May 1974, thus clearing the Corleonesi throne for Riina. He forged ties with Calabria's 'Ndrangheta crime syndicate and expanded the Mafia's heroin trafficking network, while orchestrating liquidation of rivals in Sicily. The 'Second Mafia War' of 1981–82 pitted Riina's Corleonesi against Palermo's Mafia clans, producing 800 known murders, while another 160 mafiosi simply vanished. Riina emerged victorious, the presumed 'Boss of Bosses,' and was nowhere to be found when prosecutors charged him as one of 474 defendants slated for Sicily's 'Maxi Trial' of 1986–87. Convicted of murder and sentenced to life *in absentia,* he audaciously declared war on the government itself.

Prominent victims in Riina's terrorist campaign included Judge Rosario Livatino, shot in Agrigento on September 21, 1990; anti-Mafia clothing manufacturer Libero Grassi, murdered in Palermo on August 29, 1991; Salvatore Lima, ex-mayor of Palermo and a member of the European Parliament, killed in a drive-by shooting on March 12, 1992; prosecutor Giovanni Falcone, killed with his wife and three

RIGHT: Salvatore Riina shortly after his arrest in Palermo in January 1993.

bodyguards by a Mafia bomb near Capaci, on May 23, 1992; magistrate Paolo Borsellino, slain in another Palermo bombing with five police guards, on July 19, 1992; and wealthy businessman Ignazio Salvo, shot in Santa Flavia on September 17, 1992.

Such public murders sparked outrage throughout Sicily and provoked yet another government crackdown. On January 15, 1993, an anonymous tip sent Carabinieri officers to a Palermo neighborhood where they found Riina sitting in a car stopped at a traffic light. Riina initially gave a false name, posing as an innocent accountant, but refused to name his firm. Fingerprints soon confirmed his identity, and Riina provoked laughter at his court appearance, claiming he had 'no idea' that he was Italy's most-wanted fugitive from justice.

Controversy still surrounds Riina's arrest. Salvatore himself suspected ex-chauffeur Baldassare Di Maggio of selling him out to police, a supposition that resulted in murder of several Di Maggio family members. In fact, Di Maggio *was* an informer, whose tales included a report of Riina greeting Giulio Andreotti with a Mafia 'kiss of honor' in September 1987, at the Palermo home of later murder victim Ignazio Salvo. At the time, Andreotti was Italy's Minister of Foreign Affairs, having served two terms as prime minister in 1972–73 and 1976–79, with a third term still to come in 1989–92. Andreotti denied the allegations and was never charged with any Mafia-related crime.

BELOW: The wrecked car of anti-mafia police chief General Carlo Alberto Dalla Chiesa, who was murdered in September 1982 on the orders of Salvatore Riina.

Despite his outstanding life sentence, Riina was tried once more and convicted in October 1993 on more than 100 counts of murder. Victims named in that indictment included Giovanni Falcone and Paolo Borsellino, with mafiosi brothers Vincenzo and Pietro Puccio, killed in separate, but coordinated attacks, on May 15, 1989. In 1998, another life sentence was added to Riina's list, for the slaying of Salvatore Lima. Riina survived two heart attacks in 2004, and was tried in April 2006 for the presumed murder of journalist Mauro De Mauro, missing since September 1970. At last report, that trial was still in progress, with no verdict in sight.

John Rosselli

Filippo Sacco was born at Esperia, in the mainland Italian province of Frosinone, on July 4, 1905. His father soon emigrated to the United States, settling in Somerville, Massachusetts, and sent for his family in 1911. Filippo made the journey with his mother and a female friend. Sacco graduated from petty crime to murder at age 17, after killing a man in a quarrel, and fled westward to Chicago. On arrival there, he changed his name to 'John Rosselli,' reportedly in honor of Florentine Quattrocento artist, Cosimo Rosselli.

With Prohibition in full swing, Rosselli soon found work with the Chicago Outfit, led by Johnny Torrio and Al Capone. In 1924, he pled guilty to bootlegging beer, then struck off for Los Angeles, California, as Chicago's ambassador to the Mafia family run by Joseph Ardizzone, then by successor Jack Dragna after Ardizzone vanished in 1931. Rosselli was particularly fond of Hollywood, befriending producer-director Bryan Foy. Rosselli's Hollywood-Chicago ties subsequently produced Rosselli's federal indictment in March 1943 – with various high-ranking Outfit mobsters – on charges of extorting money from major film studios and the Loew's theater chain via threats of strikes by the mob-controlled International Alliance of Theatrical Stage Employes, Moving Picture Technicians, Artists and Allied Crafts. Convicted with his codefendants in New York, on December 22, 1943, Rosselli received a ten-year sentence and a $10,000 fine. Payoffs to US Attorney General Tom Clark sprang the convicted gangsters from custody well ahead of schedule, on August 13, 1947.

In the 1950s and 1960s Rosselli divided his time between LA and Las Vegas, Nevada, with mixed results. He was tolerated in Vegas by kingpin Moe Dalitz, but never 'ran the town', as some historians suggest. Once, he was beaten, jailed and deloused for offending Sheriff Ralph Lamb. Rosselli had better luck with the Central Intelligence Agency, which recruited him in 1960 to kill Cuban dictator Fidel Castro. Rosselli in turn sought aid from mafiosi Sam Giancana and Santo Trafficante, but their efforts were a fruitless comedy of errors. In November 1968, Rosselli was convicted of cheating card players out of $1 million at the exclusive Friar's Club in Los Angeles, receiving a five-year prison term and a $55,000 fine, plus six additional months for failure to register as an alien.

Released in September 1973, still facing possible deportation to Italy, Rosselli drew unwelcome attention from media exposure of the plots against Castro. He testified twice before the US Senate's Select Committee to Study Governmental Operations with Respect to Intelligence Activities on June 24 and September 22, 1975, then received another subpoena on April 23, 1976, to return and discuss possible Mafia involvement in the murder of President John Kennedy. Before he could testify a third time, Rosselli vanished from Miami, Florida, on July 28, 1976. His dismembered remains were found floating in an oil drum, in Florida's Dumbfounding Bay, on August 9. Mafioso Salvatore Bonanno, jailed with Rosselli in the early 1970s, later said that Rosselli admitted shooting JFK in November 1963.

Arnold Rothstein

Arnold Rothstein's lawyer once described him as 'a man who waits in doorways – a mouse, waiting in the doorway for his cheese.' His business acumen, unfailingly applied to crime, earned him a reputation as 'The Brain,' 'The Fixer' and 'The Man Uptown.' To others who sought favors, or a grubstake in the rackets, Rothstein was 'The Big Bankroll,' the man to see for sponsorship in gambling, bootlegging, or the narcotics trade.

The son of a respectable businessman, born in New York City on January 17, 1882, Rothstein excelled at mathematics and applied his knowledge in gambling. By 1910, he owned a thriving, if illegal, casino in Manhattan's seedy 'Tenderloin' district. Nine years later, he allegedly bribed members of the Chicago White Sox to let the Cincinnati Reds win the World Series. A Chicago grand jury grilled Rothstein in that case, but accepted his denials of involvement in the scandal and released him without charges. Novelist F. Scott Fitzgerald alluded to the incident in *The Great Gatsby,* referring to Rothstein as 'Meyer Wolfsheim.'

Two years after the 'Black Sox' fiasco, Rothstein won $500,000 on the Travers Stakes at New York's Saratoga Race Course, amid allegations that the thoroughbred race was somehow 'fixed.' Once again, he banked the money and escaped indictment, despite persistent rumors of conspiracy.

Already a millionaire by age 30, Rothstein increased his wealth greatly during Prohibition. Would-

RIGHT: Arnold Rothstein's renowned business acumen made him a lot of money in the underworld of 1920s America.

be bootleggers and rum-runners besieged him with pleas for start-up money, sage advice and access to his various official connections. Rothstein was always glad to oblige, for a price, and served as a mentor for such rising underworld stars as Meyer Lansky, Lucky Luciano, Frank Costello and Dutch Schultz. Whenever possible, Rothstein restrained the violent impulses of his young protégés, mediating in gangland turf wars to minimize counterproductive bloodshed. Operating from a table

ABOVE: Arnold Rothstein's funeral on November 7, 1928. His murder remains officially unsolved.

'office' in Lindy's Restaurant, at Broadway and 49th Street, 'The Brain' knew everyone worth knowing in Jazz Era Manhattan and beyond.

Still, despite his best efforts, life in the Roaring Twenties was dangerous for gangsters, even at the top. Rothstein surrounded himself with bodyguards, led by Jack 'Legs' Diamond. He recognized the risks and spared no sentiment for his competitors or 'marks.' He constantly advised his underworld apprentices, 'Look out for Number One. If you don't, no one else will. If a man is dumb, someone is going to get the best of him, so why not you? If you don't, you're as dumb as he is.'

On November 5, 1928, an unknown gunman shot Rothstein at Manhattan's Park Central Hotel. When questioned by police at Stuyvesant Polyclinic Hospital, Rothstein refused to name his assailant, finally telling detectives, 'Me mudder did it.' He died on November 6 and was buried at Union Field Cemetery in Ridgewood, Queens, in a Jewish Orthodox ceremony.

And the question remains: who killed Rothstein?

On the night he was shot, Rothstein received a call from gambler George McManus, asking Rothstein to meet him at the Park Central. In September 1928, McManus had hosted a poker game where Rothstein lost $322,000 and left without paying. Two months later, the debt remained unpaid and Rothstein's creditors – Joe Bernstein, Nate Raymond and Alvin 'Titanic' Thompson – were furious. Police charged McManus with Rothstein's murder in 1929, but Judge Charles Nott Jr. directed jurors to acquit him on December 5, citing lack of evidence.

Another theory, touted in the *New York Times,* suggests that a rift between Rothstein and Legs Diamond claimed five lives in 1928 before Rothstein's murder ended the feud. Indeed, the *Times* was still reporting aftershocks from that alleged gang war in June 1930, when police found Anna Urbas, ex-lover of murdered Rothstein bodyguard Eugene Moran, floating in the Harlem River.

A third hypothesis, raised by Dutch Schultz biographer Paul Sann in 1971, blames Schultz for Rothstein's death. Noting that Legs Diamond shot Schultz partner Joe Noe on October 15, 1928, inflicting wounds that killed Noe seven weeks later, Sann surmises that Schultz blamed Rothstein for the ambush and reacted accordingly. No evidence was forthcoming, and the murder remains officially unsolved.

Rothstein lived and died a gambler, shot the night before one of his biggest scores. He had bet heavily on the year's presidential election – held on the day he died – and favored Republican Secretary of Commerce Herbert Hoover to defeat New York's Catholic governor Al Smith. Hoover won by a margin of 6.4 million votes, meaning that Rothstein would have won $570,000, if he had lived. Death canceled his wager, however. New York's State Tax Department assessed Rothstein's estate at $1,757,572 in March 1934, but it swiftly dwindled. By April 1938, his total worth stood at $286,232.

Alex Rudaj

A native of Montenegro, born to ethnic Albanian parents in 1968, Alex Rudaj came to the United States in 1991, after the collapse of Albania's communist regime relaxed American immigration quotas. Settling in Yorktown Heights, New York, 60 km (38 miles) north of Manhattan, he worked briefly for the Gambino Mafia family, then gathered a clique of Baltic felons in a bid to challenge New York's five established Cosa Nostra clans. Leading members of the so-called 'Sixth Family' included Nikola 'Nicky Nails' Dedaj, Prenka 'Frankie' Ivezaj, Gjelosh 'Joey' Lelcaj and Nardino Colotti – a protégé of late mafioso 'Skinny Phil' Loscalzo.

Prosecutors later claimed that Rudaj and Colotti tried to kill Bonanno family member Gaetano Peduto during a high-speed chase through Manhattan, in December 1993, though jurors would acquit both men of that charge in January 2006. Next, Rudaj targeted gambling operations run by Greek mobsters Antonios Balampanis and Fotios Dimopoulos for the Lucchese Family in Astoria, Queens. In June

2001, the Albanians lured Balampanis from his Stimatis gambling club and beat him severely. Two months later, on August 3, Rudaj and his gunmen invaded another club, Soccer Fever, pistol-whipping proprietor Mikhail Hirakis and driving his patrons out of the club.

Such activities sparked resentment in gangland. Mikhail Hirakis turned police informer in fear of his life. In September 2004, gang member Nikola Nuculovic approached FBI agents, offering to 'squeal' on Rudaj and company in exchange for immunity from prosecution. On October 6, 2004, a federal grand jury indicted Rudaj and 21 associates on racketeering charges that included attempted murder, extortion, illegal gambling and loan-sharking.

Prior to commencement of trial in October 2005, Lelcaj pled guilty to extortion, gambling and illegal entry into the US. On January 5, 2006, federal jurors convicted defendants Rudaj, Colotti, Dedaj, Ivezaj, Angelo DiPietro and Ljusa Nuculovic on multiple charges including extortion, firearms offenses, illegal gambling, loan-sharking and racketeering. DiPietro received a 59-year sentence in May 2006. In June, Rudaj and Colotti received 27-year prison terms, Dedaj was sentenced to 26 years and 7 months, while Ivezaj and Nuculovic got 22 years each.

All six defendants appealed their convictions, claiming that FBI agents seized evidence illegally in 2004 and that Nuculovic's defense attorney fell asleep during the trial in 2005. The US Court of Appeals for the Second Circuit affirmed all six convictions on June 11, 2009, noting that the sleepy lawyer in question simply sat in a 'lounging position' and, in fact, was 'a careful observer of the proceedings and an active participant, conducting some of the most memorable cross-examinations' of prosecution witnesses. Alex Rudaj is presently incarcerated at Fort Dix, New Jersey, with a presumed release date of May 2, 2028.

Nicky Scarfo

Nicodemo Domenico Scarfo was born in Brooklyn, New York, on March 8, 1929. His father was a 'made' member of the local Mafia family led by Giuseppe 'Joe The Boss' Masseria, while three maternal uncles – Joseph, Michael and Nicholas Piccolo – worked for mafioso Salvatore Sabella in Philadelphia, Pennsylvania. After boxing for a time in the 1940s, Scarfo moved to Philadelphia as a bookmaker working for his uncle Nicholas. By then, the Philly Mafia was under the command of Joseph Ida, who inducted Scarfo as a formal member of the family. Following Ida's retirement in 1959, power passed to Angelo Bruno.

Scarfo proved to be a thorn in Bruno's side, first declining to marry *consigliere* Joe Rugnetta's daughter on grounds that she was ugly, then defending a friend who seduced the niece of family members Alfonse and Guarino Marconi. Bruno – dubbed 'the gentle don' for his reluctance to grant murder contracts – rejected pleas for Scarfo's execution from Rugnetta and the Marconis. While tension simmered, Scarfo stabbed a longshoreman to death in 1963 and served a year in prison for manslaughter, emerging in 1964. Bruno then sent Scarfo off to manage Mafia affairs in Atlantic City, New Jersey.

There, Scarfo supervised illegal gambling and loan-sharking, and invested in an adult bookstore owned by Alvin Feldman, while dabbling in con games with swindler Nicholas 'The Crow' Caramandi. In June 1973, Scarfo was jailed for contempt, after spurning questions from New Jersey's State Commission of Investigation, but he changed his mind in July and answered a limited range of inquiries. Around the same time, Alvin Feldman vanished forever, accused of embezzling from Scarfo at their porn outlet. When asked about his missing partner, Scarfo told associates, 'You won't see him no more.'

In 1976, New Jersey voters approved legal casino gambling in Atlantic City. Rather than bemoan a loss of gaming revenue, Scarfo increased loan-sharking, prostitution and drug trafficking, while acquiring control of the local Hotel Employees and Restaurant Employees International Union. Soon, Scarfo was earning an average $20,000 per month from the union via labor racketeering operations and embezzlement. He also established relations with City Commissioner (later Mayor) Michael Matthews, until Matthews himself pled guilty to extortion and received a 15-year prison term. Meanwhile, Scarfo ran a semi-legitimate concrete firm – Scarf Inc. – which gave him a piece of Atlantic City's booming construction business. Partner Vincent Falcone was gunned down in 1979, after criticizing Scarfo and nephew Phillip 'Crazy Phil' Leonetti. FBI agents charged

Scarfo and Leonetti with murder, but jurors acquitted them on October 1, 1980, after a local policeman testified in the mobsters' defense.

Meanwhile, Angelo Bruno was shot dead by persons unknown outside his home, on March 21, 1980. Successor Philip 'Chicken Man' Testa suspected *consigliere* Antonio Caponigro of ordering the hit, an offense that resulted in the murders of Caponigro and brother-in-law Alfred Salerno, found dead in the Bronx on April 18, 1980. Testa led the family with Scarfo as his *consigliere* until a nail bomb killed him on March 15, 1981. Scarfo then ascended to the local throne and executed Testa's presumed assassins. Suspect Frank 'Chickie' Narducci

BELOW: Nicodemo Scarfo (right) – with Lawrence Merlino (left) and Phillip Leonetti (center) – during their murder trial in September 1980.

died from ten gunshot wounds on January 7, 1982, while Rocco Marinucci was found on the first anniversary of Testa's death, shot repeatedly, his mouth packed with firecrackers. April 1982 saw Scarfo convicted of firearms possession (banned for ex-convicts), but sentencing was deferred until August. Meanwhile, he faced rebellion in the ranks.

On May 13, 1982, associates of mafioso Harry 'The Hunchback' Riccobene killed Scarfo loyalist Frank Monte. Riccobene survived an ambush on June 8 and retaliated by wounding Phil Testa's son, Salvatore, on July 31. Riccobene dodged more bullets on August 21, while Scarfo killed Pasquale 'Pat the Cat' Spirito on April 29, 1983, for bungling a contract on Riccobene's brother Robert. Riccobene soldiers Frank Martinez and Salvatore Tamburrino fell on October 14 and November 3, 1983, while shotgun blasts killed Robert Riccobene on December 6. Salvatore Testa escaped a drive-by shooting four days later, then was murdered on September 14, 1984. Between those shootings, Harry Riccobene's nephew Enrico committed suicide, on December 3, 1983, in fear that he was being stalked by Scarfo's soldiers.

Scarfo spent the war's latter months in prison, serving his firearms sentence, then returned to active duty in March 1984, but new charges multiplied. Philadelphia jurors convicted him of extortion on May 6, 1987, resulting in a 14-year sentence. On January 11, 1988, a federal grand jury indicted Scarfo and 18 associates on racketeering charges including ten

murders, four attempted murders, extortion, drugs, illegal gambling and loan-sharking. Conviction on November 19 brought Scarfo a 45-year sentence. On April 5, 1985, another jury convicted Scarfo in the 1985 murder of mobster Frank D'Alfonso, producing a life sentence later overturned on appeal. He will be eligible for parole on January 5, 2033.

RIGHT: 'Thank God for an honest jury,' said Nicky Scarfo, after his acquittal on murder charges on October 1, 1980.

Dutch Schultz

Arthur Simon Flegenheimer was born in the Bronx, New York, to German-Jewish immigrant parents, on August 6, 1902. His father abandoned the family in 1916, whereupon Arthur quit school to support himself and his mother. Crime paid more than the menial jobs reserved for adolescents, and Flegenheimer soon attached himself to local mobster Marcel Poffo, a bank robber and extortionist who claimed a share of Arthur's loot from robbing crap games. Imprisoned for the first and only time at 17, for burglary, Flegenheimer was a combative inmate, nicknamed 'Dutch Schultz' after a legendary brawler from the 19th-century Frog Hollow Gang.

A dozen more arrests would follow, but Schultz would never hear another court pronounce him guilty. By the time he was released from custody, America had plunged into the 'dry' experiment of Prohibition and the gangs of every city nationwide were busy quenching thirsts with bootleg beer and liquor. Schultz joined Lucky Luciano, Meyer Lansky and other young gangsters in learning the tricks of their new trade from Arnold Rothstein. He later struck off on his own with partner Joey Noe in 1928 as proprietors of a speakeasy called the Hub Social Club. They gathered a troupe of street soldiers – including Abraham 'Bo' Weinberg and two Irish brothers, Peter and Vincent Coll – to hijack booze from rival gangs and push their liquor into other clubs. Opposition was ruthlessly crushed, as when Schultz kidnapped competitor Joe Rock and blinded him by taping gauze saturated with gonorrhea bacteria over Rock's eyes.

Joey Noe suffered fatal wounds in a drive-by shooting on October 15, 1928. Noe killed one of his assailants – Louis Weinberg (no relation to Bo) – but Schultz blamed Irish rival Legs Diamond for the attack. At the time, Diamond worked as a bodyguard for Arnold Rothstein, and some historians believe Schultz was responsible for Rothstein's murder

LEFT: Dutch Schultz pictured in 1934, less than a year before he was gunned down and killed in a New Jersey restaurant.

RIGHT: Charles Workman, a suspect in the slaying of Dutch Schultz, is questioned by police in Brooklyn in 1941.

on November 4. In any case, Schultz's war with Diamond would span the next three years, ending at last with Diamond's murder in Albany, New York, on December 18, 1931.

A second war distracted Schultz from business in 1931, as the Coll brothers defected to form their own gang and raid Schultz's supplies. Dutch's gunmen killed Peter Coll on May 30, sparking retaliation by his 'mad dog' brother that claimed at least five lives by June 8. Nine days later, Schultz and bodyguard Danny Iamascia mistook two plainclothes policemen for Coll hitmen, sparking a gunfight that left Iamascia dead and Schultz briefly detained on charges of felonious assault and packing a concealed weapon. The first count was dropped when police could not prove they had identified themselves; the second fell when Dutch produced a pistol permit signed by a friendly local judge. Freed from jail, Schultz went into hiding once more, emerging only after Coll was caught in a phone booth and riddled with machine-gun bullets on February 8, 1932.

By then, Schultz had realized that Prohibition's time was limited. Franklin Roosevelt campaigned for the White House with a promise of repeal in 1932, as savvy gangsters sought new sources of income. One that appealed to Schultz was the 'numbers', or 'policy' racket, in Harlem, an illicit lottery whose daily winning numbers were selected from the tote boards of specific racetracks. The Harlem numbers racket earned millions

of dollars per month – and Schultz wanted it all. Despite some initial resistance, brute force weeded out Harlem's

ABOVE: Dutch Schultz (left) leaves a New Jersey court hearing in October 1935, accompanied by bail bondsman Max Silverman.

main operators and consolidated the rest under the thumb of Schultz governor Ellsworth 'Bumpy' Johnson. Never one to miss a trick, Schultz soon discovered that he could improve his profit margin by having gang accountant Otto 'Abbadabba' Berman place strategic last-minute bets, thus ensuring that popular numbers always lost.

Aside from numbers, Schultz also tried his hand at extortion, terrorizing restaurateurs and their employees into joining his Metropolitan Restaurant & Cafeteria Owners' Association. Their dues fattened Schultz's war chest, but he later caught his front man in the racket, one Jules Modgilewsky, skimming $70,000 from the take. Confronted by Schultz on March 2, 1935, Modgilewsky admitted stealing 'only' $20,000, whereupon Dutch shot him in the mouth, then stabbed him repeatedly, later telling lawyer Richard 'Dixie' Davis, 'I cut his heart out.'

On November 1, 1933, a federal grand jury indicted Schultz for tax evasion. Dutch went into hiding, then surrendered on November 28, 1934. One jury deadlocked on April 29, 1935, then Schultz obtained a change of venue to tiny Malone, New York, where his lavish spending thrilled locals. They cheerfully acquitted Dutch on August 2, but prosecutor Thomas Dewey persevered. Beaten on the felony charge of willful tax evasion, Dewey rebounded on October 10, 1935, with misdemeanor counts of failing to file tax returns for 1929, 1930 and 1931. Furious, Schultz hatched a plan to kill Dewey.

Assassination of a public figure required approval from the national crime syndicate's board of directors. They voted against Schultz, and when he threatened to act alone the die was cast. On October 23, 1935, a team of gunmen from Lepke Buchalter's 'Murder Incorporated' troupe found Schultz at the Palace Chop House in Newark, New Jersey, blasting him along with Otto Berman and two bodyguards, Abe Landau and Bernard 'Lulu' Rosenkrantz. All four were fatally wounded, Schultz raving incoherently in hospital until he died at 8:35 p.m. on October 24.

Lucky Luciano, in particular, had reason to regret the vote that spared Tom Dewey's life. Seven months after Schultz's murder, Dewey persuaded a jury to convict Luciano and eight associates on charges of compulsory prostitution, earning Lucky a sentence of 30 to 50 years in prison. Mafioso Michael Coppola claimed Schultz's numbers racket in Harlem, while the Cleveland syndicate, led by Moe Dalitz, took over his River Downs racetrack in Cincinnati, Ohio.

Bugsy Siegel

Benjamin Hyman Siegelbaum was born in Williamsburg, Brooklyn, on February 28, 1906. His parents were Jewish immigrants from Letychiv in Russia's Podolia Governorate (now the Khmelnytskyi Oblast of modern Ukraine). As a youth, he joined fellow delinquent Moe Sedway to operate a protection racket, extorting money from merchants on Manhattan's Lower East Side, where Siegelbaum's erratic violence earned him the 'Bugsy' ('crazy') nickname he despised. Friendship with Meyer Lansky expanded his horizons into gambling, while acquaintance with Lucky Luciano paved the way for a bootlegging empire during Prohibition. Along the way, Siegelbaum shortened his surname to 'Siegel,' cultivating parallel reputations as a killer and a ladies' man. When persuasion failed to charm a prospective lover, he used force, resulting in a 1926 rape charge. Lansky persuaded the victim to recant, and the case was dismissed.

In 1927, Siegel and Lansky – leading the 'Bug and Meyer Mob' – formed one component of the Eastern Seaboard's 'Big Seven' bootlegging syndicate. Two years later, when war between mafiosi Salvatore Maranzano

and Giuseppe 'Joe The Boss' Masseria divided New York's Italian-American underworld, the partners joined Luciano in a scheme to modernize the American Mafia by eliminating stodgy 'Mustache Pete' bosses. Luciano joined Masseria's gang, then betrayed him, inviting Joe the Boss to lunch on April 15, 1931. During the meal, Siegel appeared with Joe Adonis and Albert Anastasia to execute Masseria. Lepke Buchalter arranged Maranzano's murder five months later, clearing Luciano's path to reorganize the Mafia and build a multi-ethnic crime syndicate spanning the United States.

Arrested for bootlegging and gambling in 1932, Siegel escaped with a fine. Meanwhile, an underworld 'War of the Jews' erupted between Waxey Gordon and the Siegel-Lansky combine. Siegel personally dispatched several of Gordon's soldiers before federal agents jailed Gordon on tax-evasion charges in 1933, allegedly aided by Lansky. Three years later, the Mob sent Bugsy to Los Angeles, where he fell in love with Hollywood while bringing independent gamblers under syndicate control. His presence sparked tension with local Mafia boss Jack Dragna, but Dragna's family was no match for Siegel, his lieutenant Mickey Cohen, or their allies in the East. While moving his wife and daughters to LA, Siegel continued his extravagant lifestyle, spending his days at racetracks and film studios, while many of his nights were spent with celebrity lovers including actresses Wendy Barrie, Ketti Gallian and Marie 'The Body' MacDonald. Another Siegel lover, Countess Dorothy DiFrasso, briefly encouraged Siegel's fantasy of traveling to Italy and killing dictator Benito Mussolini.

Nothing came of that plot, but Siegel's trigger finger still got plenty of exercise. On November 22, 1939, he joined brother-in-law Whitey Krakower and Benjamin Tannenbaum to kill Harry 'Big Greenie' Greenberg, a New York mobster-turned-informer on the run from Lepke Buchalter. LA authorities charged Siegel with the murder in December 1940, but Tannenbaum and Krakower were slain in February and July 1941, respectively, leaving jurors to acquit Siegel for lack of witnesses.

In 1945, Siegel 'discovered' Las Vegas, a tiny Nevada town with little to recommend it besides a 1931 statute that legalized casino gambling. In November, he bought land outside of town, with visions of building a luxury resort. New lover Virginia Hill – mistress of countless gangsters before Siegel – encouraged that dream with an eye on personal profits. Siegel called his project 'The Flamingo,' based on Hill's nickname, and persuaded his New York partners to bankroll construction of Nevada's first lavish 'carpet joint.'

Cost overruns made Siegel's partners nervous even before the unfinished Flamingo opened to players on December 26, 1946. Rain grounded many high-rollers in LA, and the casino lost $300,000 in its

BELOW: The gravestone of Bugsy Siegel at the Hollywood Forever Cemetery, California.

first week, before Siegel closed it. Reopened on March 1, 1947, the Flamingo started earning profits, but it was too late for Siegel. Moe Dalitz had confirmed Virginia Hill's embezzlement of some $2.5 million, banked in Switzerland.

Hill was out of the country on June 20, 1947, when Siegel and associate Allen Smiley met at her mansion in Beverly Hills, California. They were seated on a couch together when a still-unknown gunman fired nine shots from a .30-caliber M1 carbine through a nearby window, obliterating Siegel's face. Moments later, mobsters Moe Sedway and Gus Greenbaum appeared at the Flamingo in Las Vegas and took command of the resort. Two decades later, federal prosecutors indicted Meyer Lansky, Sam Cohen (of Detroit's old Purple Gang) and Morris Landsburg on charges of skimming $27 million from the Flamingo between 1960 and 1967. Cohen and Landsburg pled guilty and received one-year sentences, while poor health spared Lansky from trial.

Klaus Speer

While commercial sex has been legal in Germany since the early 19th century, providing that both prostitutes and brothels are registered and subject to inspection, any act 'in furtherance of prostitution' – including simple advertising of legal bordellos – was banned by law until 2001. Klaus Speer, the so-called 'Godfather of Berlin,' ignored that law and thereby made himself a multi-millionaire over three decades, from the 1960s through the early 1990s.

Born in Berlin during 1944, Speer was an infant when Soviet forces and their former allies divided Germany, leaving his occupied hometown adrift within the communist-controlled German Democratic Republic. He barely understood the Berlin Blockade and subsequent airlift of 1948–49, but Speer was 17 when Red forces began erecting the Berlin Wall in June 1961. Within a year, or two, he started pimping, luring warehouse workmen to seedy brothels in Berlin's red-light district. By the decade's end, he was wealthy enough to open his own establishment on Potsdamer Straße – the Apollo 11 Club, named for America's first mission to the moon in July 1969. Bribing police to avoid arrest, Speer expanded his repertoire to include gambling, loan-sharking, fraud and extortion.

That expansion placed Speer in competition with Hans Helmcke, unofficial boss of Berlin's red-light district. A more immediate threat, however, was posed by a band of Iranian immigrant pimps with designs on the West Berlin flesh trade. Speer led a squad of gunmen who fought the invaders on June 27, 1970, in a battle that left one man dead and three wounded on the Bleibtreustraße.

Police took their time building a case against him, but in 1972, the shootout cost Speer a 27-month jail term. In his absence, on August 16, 1973, police found Hans Helmcke dead outside Hamburg, strangled with his own necktie and set on fire.

Upon release, Speer opened a boxing school, soon graduating from the role of trainer to that of a fight promoter. Berlin's public prosecutor still suspected him of criminal activity, but Germany was reunited with the Berlin Wall dismantled before Speer was arrested again, on June 16, 1992. The 21 counts filed against him included bribery of public officials, coercion, extortion, fraud, illegal gambling and illegal possession of firearms. Speer's trial began on March 22, 1993, and continued until February 27, 1995, when jurors convicted him on five counts, resulting in a prison sentence of 5½ years. Paroled once more in 1998, Speer resumed his career as a boxing promoter, with a lucrative sideline in real estate. Granting a press interview in 2004, he announced severance of all underworld ties and denied ever filling a 'godfather's' role in Berlin.

Tony Spilotro

Anthony John Spilotro was born in Chicago on May 19, 1938, the fourth of six children produced by immigrant parents from Triggiano, in the mainland Italian province of Bari. He was raised in a neighborhood known as 'The Patch,' where his father ran a restaurant favored by mafiosi including Frank Nitti and Sam Giancana. A stroke killed Spilotro's father in 1954, and Anthony quit high school that same year to pursue a life of crime with brothers John, Victor, Vincent and Michael. Arrested for the first time on January 11, 1955, for shoplifting, he paid a $10 fine and was placed on probation. By 1960, Spilotro had 13 arrests on his record and boasted the nickname 'Tough Tony.' Local FBI agent William Roemer preferred to call him a 'pissant,' shortened by reporters to 'The Ant.'

By that time Spilotro was working for 'Mad Sam' DeStefano, a notorious loan-shark and hitman with the Chicago Outfit. Tony participated in the 1962 torture slayings of gang victims Billy McCarthy and Jimmy Miraglia, crushing McCarthy's head in a vise, and allegedly joined DeStefano in killing loan collector Leo Foreman on November 19, 1963. Such services led to Tony's induction as a 'made' mafioso, overseeing bookmakers on Chicago's northwest side and working as a bail bondsman with Irwin Weiner – a longtime friend of Florida mobster Santo Trafficante and Jack Ruby, slayer of alleged JFK assassin, Lee Harvey Oswald.

In 1964, the Outfit sent Spilotro to Miami, where he spent three years as 'muscle' for transplanted Chicago gambler Frank 'Lefty' Rosenthal. Rosenthal left Florida in 1967, after the *Miami Herald* exposed his 1963 no-contest plea on charges of fixing a college basketball game, and wound up in Las Vegas, Nevada, running a sports book for Moe Dalitz at the Stardust casino. Spilotro returned to Chicago, performing more violent

Mafia chores until 1971, when he followed Rosenthal to Vegas. While Rosenthal supervised skimming from the Stardust, Fremont and other mob-infested casinos, Spilotro bought a gift shop at the Circus Circus hotel for $70,000, selling it three years later for $700,000.

BELOW: Tony Spilotro in court in 1983 accused of the murders of Billy McCarthy and Jimmy Miraglia 21 years previously.

Chicago authorities indicted Spilotro for Leo Foreman's murder in August 1972, but jurors acquitted him on May 22, 1973, while convicting Sam DeStefano. A year later, the *Los Angeles Times* noted that Las Vegas had suffered more gangland-style murders since Tony's arrival than in the prior quarter-century. Matters went from bad to worse in 1976, when Spilotro opened a jewelry store, the Gold Rush, which served as headquarters for a burglary ring dubbed 'The Hole-in-the-Wall Gang' after their method of entering stores. In December 1979, as a result of statements from informer Jimmy Fratianno, Nevada authorities added Spilotro's name to their 'Black Book,' banning him from casino premises under threat of having his license revoked.

And Tony's troubles kept expanding. Unknown gunmen fired at Spilotro's home and his brother's, next door, on April 9, 1981. On May 23, a federal grand jury indicted Spilotro, Joseph 'Joey the Clown' Lombardo and Teamsters consultant Allen Dorfman for conspiracy to defraud the union's pension fund and bribe Nevada senator Howard Cannon. On July 4, FBI agents caught six members of Spilotro's burglary gang in the act of looting a Las Vegas jewelry store. During those same hectic months, Spilotro's affair with Lefty Rosenthal's wife soured their relationship and caused Chicago mafiosi to question Tony's judgment. On January 27, 1983, a Chicago grand jury charged Spilotro with the 'M&M murders' of McCarthy and Miraglia. September 1983 saw Spilotro indicted in Las Vegas for the murder of police informer Sherwin Lisner, based on statements from turncoat gang member Frank Culotta.

BELOW: Mourners attend the funeral of Tony Spilotro and his brother Michael on June 27, 1986.

Through it all, Spilotro displayed a talent for dodging conviction on a par with that of 'Teflon Don' John Gotti in New York. He pled poor health to defer trial on the Teamster charges, then was acquitted after the shotgun murder of the state's key witness. Chicago judge Thomas Maloney – convicted of bribery nine years later – acquitted Spilotro of the McCarthy-Miraglia murders, and a Vegas jury did likewise, thanks in large part to attorney (later mayor) Oscar Goodman. Police suspected Tony in the car bombing that failed to kill Lefty Rosenthal on October 4, 1982, but that crime remains officially unsolved. Despite such luck, Spilotro had drawn too much attention for his overlords to tolerate.

Tony and brother Michael vanished, following a meeting with their lawyers on June 14, 1986. Nine days later, their battered corpses were unearthed from an Indiana cornfield. On April 25, 2005, federal prosecutors charged 14 Outfit members with 18 murders, including those of the Spilotros. Mafioso Nicholas Calabrese pled guilty on May 18, 2007, and turned state's evidence against his codefendants. Trial began on June 19, 2007, in Chicago and concluded on September 10 with conviction of five defendants, including loan-shark Frank Calabrese Sr., Joseph Lombardo Sr., James 'Jimmy Light' Marcello, Paul 'The Indian' Schiro and ex-Chicago policeman Anthony 'Twan' Doyle.

ABOVE: Tony Spilotro (right) and Irvin Weiner (left) head into court in February 1975, charged with stealing money from a Teamsters Union pension fund.

Marcello was specifically convicted of killing the Spilotro brothers, receiving a life prison term on February 5, 2009.

According to authorities, Spilotro was replaced by Donald 'The Wizard of Odds' Angelini as Mafia overseer of Las Vegas. White-haired and soft-spoken, Angelini was the polar opposite of Spilotro, but he still faced problems with the law. In 1989, he received a 37-month federal prison sentence for attempting to infiltrate casino gambling at the Rincon Indian Reservation near San Diego, California. Paroled in October 1994, Angelini died of natural causes in 2000.

Spilotro was memorialized in 1995 with the film *Casino*, in which Joe Pesci portrayed mobster Nicholas 'Nicky' Santoro, opposite Robert De Niro cast in the Lefty Rosenthal role as Sam 'Ace' Rothstein. Actress Sharon Stone, cast as Rosenthal/Rothstein's wife, received Academy Award and Golden Globe nominations for Best Performance by an Actress, while Martin Scorsese was nominated for a Golden Globe as Best Director.

Stanko Subotić

Stanko Subotić was the sixth child of middle-class parents, born on September 9, 1959, in Kalinovac village, in Serbia's Kolubara District. After childhood service in his father's carpentry shop, he attended Ub's High School of Economics, then struck off to work as a tailor in France, later founding a chain of boutiques. Communism's collapse brought him home in 1991, founding a tailor's shop in Belgrade, then expanding into textile production by 1993.

Thus far, Subotić's businesses appeared to be legitimate. That changed in 1995, when he began smuggling cigarettes into the Federal Republic of Yugoslavia in defiance of a three-year-old United Nations trade embargo. From two duty-free shops in Đeneral Janković, near the Macedonian border, Subotić proceeded to become his homeland's sole distributor of foreign smokes manufactured by Philip Morris and other major Western firms. Competition surfaced in 1997, but was ruthlessly suppressed with the February 20 murder of rival Vlada Kovaćević and the April 11 slaying of Radovan Stojićić – Serbia's deputy chief of police and an ex-member of the paramilitary Arkan's Wolves, led by mobster Željko Ražnatović. It proved more difficult to deal with Marko Milošević, whose father – Slobodan Milošević – took office as the FRY's president on July 23, 1997, subsequently issuing a warrant for Subotić's arrest.

Subotić promptly moved his headquarters to Montenegro and established ties to all the right people – Prime Minister Milo Đukanović, National Security Advisor Goran Žugić, Democratic Party of Socialists president Svetozar Marović and wealthy businessman Duško Ban. He thrived in virtual anonymity until May 2001, when Croatia's weekly *Nacional* magazine exposed his ties to mobsters and public officials, branding him the godfather of a 'Tobacco Mafia,' lately granted Croatian citizenship under suspicious circumstances. *Nacional* pegged Subotić's net worth at $500 million, and Prime Minister Đukanović's at $130 million. The revelations scuttled British American Tobacco's plan to build a factory at Kragujevac, valued in excess of DM150 million ($104 million).

Subotić responded with denials, 26 libel suits and claims that *Nacional* served his main competitor, the Rovinj Tobacco Factory. Meanwhile, Subotić associate Blagota Sekulic died in a machine-gun ambush at Budva, Montenegro, on May 30, 2001 – allegedly because he 'knew too much' about Subotić's business. Subotić moved to Cyprus in 2005, while maintaining interests in Montenegro. On June 6, 2007, Serbian police detained three of his employees and four police officers, said to smuggle cigarettes for Subotić. Interpol then issued a 'red notice' on Subotić, resulting in his arrest at Moscow's Sheremetyevo International Airport on April 28, 2008. Despite submission of a formal extradition request from Serbia, Subotić was released on June 27.

Subotić remains free today, proceeding with plans to build a new cigarette factory in collaboration with British American Tobacco. In March 2007, his Villa Montenegro on Sveti Stefan island received a 'Five Star Diamond Award' from the American Academy of Hospitality Sciences. Three years later, in an interview with Belgrade's B92 broadcasting network, Subotić blamed dishonest rivals for his 'persecution' in Montenegro and Serbia.

Omid Tahvili

Omid Tahvili was born in Tehran, Iran, on October 31, 1970, and emigrated to Canada in 1994, settling in Vancouver, British Columbia. Little is known of his activities before 1999, when he established a fraudulent telemarketing firm that targeted senior citizens, swindling them out of some $3 million by 2002. At the same time, Tahvili was active in drug trafficking. On November 30, 2000, a team of Vancouver detectives and Royal Canadian Mounted Police officers caught Tahvili and brother-in-law, Alvin Royhit Pal, with 8 kg (17.5 lb) of opium, 3 kg (6.5 lb) of cocaine, a ½ kg (1 lb) of methamphetamine and 113 g (4 oz) of Ecstasy. The case seemed airtight until Pal pled guilty and absolved Tahvili of any involvement, prompting Tahvili's acquittal at trial.

Undeterred, investigators continued their pursuit of Tahvili and his mostly-Persian accomplices. Alvin Royhit Pal had served 11 months and was paroled by January 30, 2003, when a federal grand jury in California indicted Tahvili on charges of mail fraud, wire fraud, telemarketing fraud and aiding and abetting criminal activity. Canada's Immigration Board convened a detention hearing on Tahvili in 2003, reviewing evidence that his clique of 20 to 30 Iranian expatriates were involved in drug trafficking, fencing of stolen cars, fraud and robbery. Formal deportation proceedings began in July 2004 and were still underway a year later, when Tahvili and Alvin Royhit Pal faced new felony charges.

As reconstructed by police, Tahvili discovered that $350,000 of the gang's drug money had vanished from Purolator Courier's warehouse in Richmond, British Columbia, apparently stolen by a Purolator employee who suddenly quit his job and flew home to Vietnam. On June 20, 2005, Tahvili and another man kidnapped the missing suspect's brother-in-law, drove him to an auto detailing shop, once purchased in the name of Tahvili's wife, then tortured and sexually abused him in a futile effort to learn where their money had gone. Finally released, the victim contacted police, identifying his assailants as Tahvili and Pal.

Officers soon seized another $200,000 from Purolator and $109,000 from Toronto gang members. They charged Tahvili and Pal with kidnapping, sexual assault, possession of an imitation firearm, assault causing bodily harm, uttering a threat and proceeds-of-crime charges. A judge acquitted Pal, ruling that the victim's identification was unreliable, but Tahvili was still awaiting trial when he escaped from custody on November 21, 2007. Investigation revealed that Tahvili had paid guard Edwin Ticne $50,000 to open prison doors, while Tahvili fled in the guise of a janitor.

Tahvili remains at large today, listed by *Forbes* magazine as one of the world's ten most-wanted fugitives in April 2008. Four months later, Tahvili allegedly called the RCMP in British Columbia. September brought an anonymous claim that Tahvili was dead, but no evidence was forthcoming.

Ömer Topal

Ömer Lütfü Topal, often called 'Lütfi,' was born in 1942 at Doğan ehir, in Turkey's Eastern Anatolia Region. By age 20, he was known to the police as an extortionist, adding arrests for assault with a deadly weapon in 1969 and suspicion of murder in 1971. On June 14, 1978, police in Antwerp, Belgium, caught him with 6 kg (13 lb) of heroin and a passport in the name of 'Sadik Sami Onar,' issued to Topal by authorities in Gaziantep Province, Turkey.

He was still incarcerated on January 13, 1981, when Dutch police launched a five-week series of raids in the Netherlands, capturing multiple smugglers with 'vast amounts' of heroin. Some of those arrested turned state's evidence, resulting in Topal's indictment on federal drug-running charges in the United States. On July 23, 1981, Belgian authorities extradited Topal to New York, where he was subsequently convicted and sentenced to five years in prison. Released on November 7, 1984, he was promptly deported to Turkey.

Back on his native soil, with no thought of going straight, Topal continued narcotics trafficking while plunging headlong into gambling, quickly earning a reputation as Turkey's 'casino king.' Starting with Istanbul's Caddebostan Grand Club, Topal expanded nationwide and looked beyond Turkey's borders for new realms to conquer. President Heydar Alirza oglu Aliyev satisfied his son's $6 million gambling debt by allowing Topal to build a casino in Azerbaijan, while corrupt Turkish officials bore the construction costs of three gambling resorts in Turkmenistan. At home, Topal claimed a loss of $6 billion Turkish lira ($546,493) in 1993, but revenue agents claimed that he actually turned a profit of TL473 billion ($39 million) for the year. Meanwhile, on May 5, 1989, officers of the Istanbul Narcotics Branch arrested Topal on charges stemming from the 1981 investigation, then released him on orders from the State Security Council.

Suspected of murdering business partner Hikmet Babata in early 1996, Topal fled to Antalya on the Mediterranean coast of southwestern Turkey, but later returned to his home in Yeilköy, 9.5 km (6 miles) from downtown Istanbul on the Sea of Marmara. It was there that time ran out for the casino king, cut down by AK-47 fire outside his house on July 28. Topal left a TL100 trillion ($1 billion) estate, including 22 companies, passed to his son, daughter and two wives. Associate Ömer Gultekin took charge of Topal's casino empire. A 1999 report from Turkey's Ministry of Finance claimed that Topal had withdrawn several trillion Turkish lira from various banks using both legitimate and stolen credit cards, while filling 137 personal accounts with millions of Turkish, American and Germany currency. At his death, Topal owned 452 properties, many acquired in payment of gambling debts.

Johnny Torrio

John Torrio was born at Matera, in the mainland Italian province of the same name, during February 1882, emigrating with his family to Manhattan's Lower East Side at age two. As a youth, he formed the James Street Gang, later joining with the larger Five Points Gang led by pseudo-Irishman 'Paul Kelly' (né Paolo Vaccarelli). Despite a ferocious reputation, Torrio preferred profit to violence and left the Five Pointers with colleague Frankie Yale in his early 20s, to run the Harvard Inn on Coney Island. Young Al Capone worked the club as a bouncer, doubling as muscle for a chain of brothels owned by Torrio and Yale.

In 1909, Torrio struck off for Chicago, summoned by cousin-in-law Vincenzo 'Big Jim' Colosimo. 'Black Hand' extortionists were terrorizing Colosimo's 200 brothels and gambling dens until Torrio arrived and killed enough of them to make the rest back off. Torrio's courage – coupled with business acumen that earned him recognition as 'The Fox' – soon placed him in charge of Colosimo's vice empire, leaving Colosimo more time for young mistress, Dale Winter. The dawn of Prohibition found Colosimo besotted by love and doggedly resistant to bootlegging. When persuasion failed, Torrio arranged for Colosimo's murder on May 11, 1920, and seized control of his gang, soon importing Capone from New York as his chief enforcer.

ABOVE: Chicago gangster Johnny Torrio was one of many underworld figures to grow rich from Prohibition in the 1920s.

O'Banion. On May 19, 1924, he offered to sell Torrio a brewery, then sent federal agents to the meeting in his place. They seized the property and charged Torrio with his second liquor violation, which meant jail time. The prank cost O'Banion his life, gunned down on November 10. Torrio received a nine-month sentence in January 1925, but O'Banion's gang struck back before he entered prison, critically wounding him at home on January 24. Upon recovering and finishing his jail term, Torrio left Chicago to Capone and embarked on a leisurely cruise to Hawaii before returning to live in New York.

There, Torrio forged an alliance with Arnold 'The Brain' Rothstein and various rising stars of gangland including Lucky Luciano, Frank Costello and Meyer Lansky. He collaborated in formation of the 'Big Seven' bootlegging combine in 1927 and attended the May 1929 conference in Atlantic City, New Jersey, which laid the foundation for America's first national crime syndicate. A month before repeal of Prohibition, in November 1933, Torrio used a brother-in-law as his front man to create Pendergast-Davies Inc., a wholesale liquor distributor.

Treasury agents shadowed Torrio, arresting him for tax evasion on April 22, 1936. Formally indicted on September 10, 1937, Torrio stalled for 19 months, then pled guilty on April 11, 1939, and received a two-year sentence. Upon release, he effectively retired from criminal pursuits. On April 16, 1957, Torrio suffered a fatal heart attack in a Brooklyn barber's chair.

The 1920s roared in Chicago, as rival gangs fought for control of bootleg millions. Torrio's primary competitors were members of the North Side Gang led by Dean

Roger Touhy

The 'Terrible Touhys' – five brothers raised in Chicago by their widowed policeman father – comprised the leadership of an unusual gang in the 1920s and early 1930s. While most local gangs of the Prohibition era focused primarily on bootlegging and related rackets, the Touhys alternated between rum-running, labor racketeering and the kind of armed robberies normally practiced by 'disorganized' criminals in the mold of John Dillinger and 'Baby Face' Nelson.

Roger Touhy, born in 1898, was the acknowledged brains of the outfit, although he quit school after eighth grade. A late starter in crime, he joined the navy when the US entered World War I, and thus missed the 1917 robbery that saw brother James Jr. killed by police. On leaving the service, he worked as a taxi driver, then as an auto salesman, before joining brothers Eddie and 'Terrible Tommy' to run a trucking company in Des Plaines, Illinois. The trucks were useful in 1920, when Roger Touhy joined partner Mathias Kolb to supply Chicago's northwest suburbs with beer and liquor, soon expanding into gambling and loan-sharking. By 1926, the gang was grossing more than $1 million per year from slot machines alone, paying tribute to Al Capone for permission to operate in peace.

That relationship began to fray in summer 1927, when Capone opened brothels on Touhy turf. Roger and Tommy led police to raid and close the whorehouses. Next, Capone claimed that 50 of 800 barrels in a Touhy beer shipment were leaky, withholding $1,900 from the payment due. Touhy confronted Al and got his money, but harsh feelings lingered. Capone soldiers were the prime suspects when John Touhy and companion Charles Miller were gunned down on December 28, 1927. Next, Capone slashed beer prices to steal Touhy customers. Joseph Touhy died in June 1929, accidentally shot by one of his own men while raiding a turncoat proprietor's speakeasy.

LEFT: Chicago bootlegger Roger Touhy in handcuffs in August 1954, following his re-arrest in connection with the kidnapping of John Factor.

ABOVE: Roger Touhy (far right) and other members of his gang on trial for the kidnapping of William Hamm in November 1933.

Jurors convicted Capone of tax evasion on October 17, 1931, but the war continued. One day later, gunmen killed Mathias Kolb at his saloon in Morton Grove, Illinois. On May 5, 1932, as Capone left Chicago on a train bound for prison, Roger Touhy and three associates invaded the local Teamsters union headquarters, kidnapping two officials hired by Capone to take over it. Both were released without injury two days later, but blood spilled on June 16, in two separate incidents. Touhy gangsters killed Capone labor racketeer George Barker in Chicago, while others suffered wounds in a gunfight with Outfit soldiers at a local speakeasy. Mayor Anton Cermak – a Touhy ally – sent police to kill Capone heir Frank Nitti on December 19, 1932, but Nitti survived his wounds and Cermak paid with his life in March 1933.

Meanwhile, on January 3, 1933, Tommy Touhy and others robbed a US mail train in Minneapolis, escaping with $74,714. He was still at large on July 19, when Roger and three cohorts – Eddie McFadden, Gus Schafer and Willie Sharkey – crashed their car outside Elkhorn, Wisconsin. Police found a machine gun in the vehicle and delivered the four to FBI agents in Chicago, where the prisoners were charged with two kidnappings. One abduction, of Minnesota brewer William Hamm, had been committed by the roving 1930s gang led by the Barker brothers and Alvin Karpis in June. The other, of British swindler John Factor (brother of cosmetics mogul Max Factor), was a hoax concocted by Frank Nitti specifically to frame Touhy and company.

Indicted for the Hamm kidnapping on August 12, 1933, Touhy and company faced trial in St. Paul on November 9. Jurors acquitted them on November 28, whereupon they were remanded for trial in the Factor case. Sharkey committed suicide in jail on November 30, while the rest went to trial in Chicago on January 11, 1934. Jurors deadlocked on February 2, but a second panel convicted Touhy on February 23, resulting in a 99-year sentence. Over the next eight years Touhy spent most of his fortune on fruitless appeals.

On October 9, 1942, Touhy and five other inmates escaped from prison. FBI agents killed two of the fugitives in Chicago on December 28, then captured Touhy and the other survivors the following day. Tried for the escape, Touhy received an additional 199 years.

On August 9, 1954, a federal judge ordered Touhy's release, declaring that Factor's kidnapping had been a hoax. Free for barely two days, Touhy returned to prison when a higher court reversed the district judge's order. The US Supreme Court upheld that judgment in February 1955. Finally, on July 31, 1957, Governor William Stratton commuted Touhy's sentences, permitting his release in November 1959. Hitmen blasted him with shotguns just weeks later, on December 16. As he lay dying, Touhy said, 'I've been expecting it.'

Santo Trafficante Jr.

Born in Tampa, Florida, on November 15, 1914, Santo Trafficante Jr. was the son of Florida's top-ranking mafioso. Santo Senior, a Sicilian native, had arrived in Tampa during 1904 and joined the Mafia family led by Ignacio Antinori, rising through the ranks until a shotgun ambush killed Antinori on October 22, 1940. Suddenly in charge, the elder Trafficante expanded Mafia narcotics trafficking, seized control of the state's illegal *bolita* lottery and bought a share of syndicate gambling interests in Cuba. He sent Santo Jr. to New York for an apprenticeship with boss Tommy Lucchese, and then to Havana, where he learned the casino business first-hand. By the time Santo Senior died from natural causes, on August 11, 1954, his son was ready to succeed him.

Schooled in collaboration with non-Italian syndicate allies, Trafficante profited from Florida gambling clubs run by Meyer Lansky, Moe Dalitz and others. Police charged Trafficante with two counts of bribery in May 1954. One charge resulted in acquittal on September 14; a second jury convicted him on September 27, resulting in a five-year sentence, but that verdict was reversed on appeal in January 1957. Meanwhile, a June 1954 arrest for gambling produced another not-guilty verdict on November 8. Trafficante was charged with gambling again on April 1, 1955, acquitted at trial after many delays on December 12, 1959.

Author Hank Messick claimed that Trafficante swore a 'blood oath' to Lansky in 1956, witnessed by Dalitz partner Sam Tucker, and that he subsequently played a role in the assassination of New York mafioso Albert Anastasia. It is known that Trafficante paid a visit to Anastasia on October 24, 1957, then hastily returned to Tampa the next morning, before Anastasia was gunned

LEFT: Santo Trafficante was a suspect in the still unsolved murder of US President John F. Kennedy in 1963.

down in a hotel barbershop.

On November 14, 1957, Trafficante was one of 63 mafiosi detained by police at Apalachin, New York. Grand jury subpoenas related to that arrest and Anastasia's murder prompted Trafficante's flight to Havana, where Cuban National Police questioned him on January 3, 1958. American inquiries in Cuba revealed that Trafficante had been listed as a resident alien since October 3, 1957. Fidel Castro's revolutionary government arrested Trafficante on June 8, 1959, later deporting him as an undesirable alien. Before his expulsion, Trafficante received two jailhouse visits from Texas mobster Jack Ruby. Trafficante's embarrassment and financial losses in Cuba made him eager to cooperate in 1960, when the Central Intelligence Agency sought Mafia aid in killing Castro. Operating in conjunction with Chicago's Sam Giancana and John Rosselli, Trafficante sponsored several failed assassination bids over the next four years.

Trafficante was also a prime suspect in the November 1963 slaying of President John Kennedy in Dallas, Texas. Months before the murder, in September 1962, Trafficante told anti-Castro Cuban exile Jose Aleman, 'Mark my word, this man Kennedy is in trouble and he will get what is coming to him. Kennedy's not going to make it to the [1964] election. He is going to be hit.' Mob lawyer Frank Ragano says that Teamster union boss Jimmy Hoffa sent him to meet Trafficante and New Orleans mafioso Carlos Marcello in July 1963, to discuss the impending assassination. On November 24, 1963, Trafficante's friend Jack Ruby killed alleged JFK assassin Lee Harvey Oswald, thus eliminating any possibility of public trial for the man who called himself 'a patsy.' Days later, Hoffa told lawyer Ragano, 'I told you they could do it. I'll never forget what Carlos and Santo did for me.'

Allegations of conspiracy in JFK's murder surfaced during 1966 and proliferated thereafter, but another decade passed before Congress created the US House of Representatives Select Committee on Assassinations in 1976, to review the deaths of Kennedy and Dr. Martin Luther King Jr. Trafficante testifed before the committee on September 28, 1978, specifically denying any prediction of Kennedy's murder. Instead, he claimed that he had told Jose Aleman that JFK would be 'hit by a lot of Republican votes' in November 1964. That explanation failed to persuade conspiracy theorists, who note Trafficante's continuing involvement with the CIA and its cocaine-funded 'Contra' war against the government of Nicaragua under President Ronald Reagan.

That war was still in progress when a grand jury indicted Trafficante and 11 asssociates for racketeering in April 1983. Poor health delayed commencement of Trafficante's trial until June 23, 1986, and Judge William Castagna declared a mistrial on July 9, after prosecutors introduced illegal hearsay evidence. Persistent cardiac problems prevented Trafficante from being retried, as he scheduled heart surgery. Shortly before the operation, Trafficante told Frank Ragano, 'I think Carlos [Marcello] messed up in getting rid of Giovanni [John]. Maybe it should have been Bobby [Kennedy].' Trafficante died on March 19, 1987, three hours after undergoing triple-bypass surgery at the Texas Heart Institute in Houston.

Robert Trimbole

Future narcotics baron Robert Trimbole was born in Australia to Italian immigrant parents on March 19, 1931. Married at age 21, he tried his hand at various seemingly legitimate trades, running an auto body shop that went bankrupt and burned in 1968, then embarking on a four-year stint as a traveling pinball machine repairman and finally opening a restaurant – the Texas Tavern – in 1972. In retrospect, authorities believe that most (or all) of those occupations were covers for Trimbole's marijuana trafficking and other illicit enterprises.

Trimbole sold the Texas Tavern to associate Giuseppe Sergi and discharged his bankruptcy debts in 1973, while purchasing a mansion that his neighbors in Griffith, New South Wales, dubbed the 'Grass Castle.' Trimbole invested his illicit profits in cars and speedboats, several clothing stores, a trucking company, a supermarket and a butcher shop, a liquor store and a wholesale wine business. He also bought several farms, where cannabis was grown to keep the party rolling. Soon recognized as 'The Godfather' of illicit drugs in New South Wales, Trimbole – 'Aussie Bob' to his friends – seemed to lead a charmed life, virtually ignored by the police. Some of them were on Trimbole's payroll, as were various jockeys and horse trainers hired to 'fix' races at tracks where Trimbole often bet $20,000 on a single horse.

One man who noticed him was Donald Bruce Mackay, a Griffith furniture dealer, anti-drug campaigner and perennial losing candidate for parliament from the Australian Liberal Party. Mackay identified a farm where Trimbole grew marijuana, at Coleambally, New South Wales, and tipped police to its location, resulting in

seizures and the conviction of four Trimbole employees. Despite a promise of anonymity, Mackay's name was read out at their trial. On July 15, 1977, Mackay vanished from a hotel parking lot, leaving behind his bloodstained van, vehicle keys and three .22-caliber cartridge cases.

The disappearance prompted a two-year Royal Commission inquiry into the Griffith drug trade. Presiding justice A.E. Woodward finally declared that 'the disposal of Mackay was the result of an organized plan,' naming Trimbole and several associates as prime suspects. While that finding was not a formal charge, police pressed ahead with their investigation. On May 5, 1981, Trimbole fled to the United States, then to France and Ireland, where police arrested him in June. A battery of lawyers foiled extradition, leaving Trimbole free on bond while Australian authorities appealed the decision. He fled Ireland for Spain, and died there in a country villa, from natural causes, on May 12, 1987. Meanwhile, Australian prosecutors convicted Trimbole associates James Frederick Bazley, George Joseph and George Joseph of Mackay's murder in 1986. They received life sentences, with Bazley quietly released in 2001.

Yves Trudeau

Québec native Yves Trudeau was 31 years old when he helped organize a local chapter of the Hells Angels Motorcycle Club in 1977. By then, he was already a veteran killer, the first Canadian to wear a 'Filthy Few' patch on his vest, indicating a biker who had murdered for the club. Later, in conversations with police, Trudeau – nicknamed 'Apache' – could not recall how many victims he had slain. While listing 43 hits between September 1973 and July 1985, he also acknowledged killing his first man in 1970. That victim, Jean-Marie Viel of Trois-Rivières, was shot for stealing one of the club's motorcycles.

Other acknowledged victims include Jeanne Desjardins, beaten to death in February 1980 for harboring her son, ex-Angel Andre Desjardins and his girlfriend (both also slain by Trudeau); Donald McLean, a member of the rival Outlaws Motorcycle Club, killed with his girlfriend in May 1980, when Trudeau wired a bomb to McLean's motorcycle; Hugh McGurnaghan, killed in an October 1981 car bombing commissioned

by Westmount, Québec, gangster Frank Ryan; Michel Desormiers, brother-in-law of Montreal mafioso Frank Cotroni, shot in July 1983; Hells Angel Charlie Hachez, slain over a $150,000 drug debt; and four suspects in the November 1984 murder of Frank Ryan, killed by a television set packed with explosives that also wounded eight others.

The seeds of Trudeau's downfall were sown when he

joined other Montreal Hells Angels to form a breakaway 'North Chapter' based in Laval, Québec, in September 1979. By 1985, leaders of the parent Montreal chapter were fed up with Trudeau's murder spree, his heavy drug use and his efforts to extort $250,000 from the club's chapter in Halifax, Nova Scotia. They decided to clean house. They scheduled a meeting with the North Chapter's leaders in Lennoxville on March 24, and executed five renegade Angels who attended, dumping their bodies into the St. Lawrence River. As luck would have it, Trudeau had entered a drug rehab clinic and missed the meeting, subsequently learning that Montreal Angels had stolen his motorcycle and $46,000 in cash.

Trudeau got his bike back after strangling renegade Angel Jean-Marc Deniger for the club in May 1985, then learned of a $50,000 contract on his life. He turned state's evidence against the club, pled guilty on 43 reduced counts of manslaughter (unintentional homicide) and testified against fellow Angels at trials involving an additional 40 murders and 15 attempted murders. Trudeau's controversial plea bargain included a life sentence with eligibility for parole in seven years, plus $40,000 in cash and $35 per week for cigarettes during his prison term.

Paroled in 1993 and granted a new identity as 'Denis Côté,' Trudeau worked as a nursing home orderly until 2000, when he was laid off and resumed using cocaine. In April 2004, he pled guilty to four counts of sexually molesting a 13-year-old boy, receiving a four-year sentence on July 13. Diagnosed with bone cancer in 2006, Trudeau was released to an outside medical facility by the Canadian National Parole Board on July 15, 2008.

Francis Vanverberghe

Francis Vanverberghe was born in the Belle de Mai quarter of Marseille, France, on March 3, 1946, the son of a French-Flemish carpenter and a 'Blackfoot Andalusian' Spanish mother. An injury at age 16 ended his youthful dream of playing soccer for Olympique Marseille, whereupon he turned to crime, logging his first arrest for theft the same year. In 1965, he was convicted of pimping and drew a 15-month sentence, then left prison to lead a gang in his home neighborhood. Members of the gang included jailbreak artist Antoine 'Tony the Eel' Cossu, Robert Di Russo, Charles Filippi, Victor Funenia, Emile Chessa, Sebastiano Denart, Daniel and Gerard Alesso and Emile and Jean Pardo. All were known 'police characters' with records dating from their teens. They knew Vanverberghe as 'Francis the Belgian.'

On October 26, 1966 two policemen entered a bar in the Old Port of Marseille, seeking to arrest Antoine Cossu for outstanding warrants. In the resultant brawl, one of the officers shot Cossu, then fled to get reinforcements as Vanverberghe's gang trashed the place. That adventure cost Francis a one-year sentence, imposed on June 15, 1967. Eight days later, Marseille godfather Antoine Guerini met a bloody end, gunned down at a filling station by assassins presumed to work for rival gambling czar Marcel Francisci. By the time Vanverberghe left prison in February 1968, he felt ready to tackle the big time. He was also recognized by Belgian authorities, whose criminal file identified him as a 'dangerous individual living from theft and pimping.' New additions to his crew included mobsters Nonce Ashiero, Noël Filippi, Albert Franconi and Michel Hadjilouloudes.

The big time, for Vanverberghe, meant drugs. Marseille had long been a processing and shipping center for heroin from Central Asia's 'Golden Crescent,' dominated by Corsican mobsters, and Vanverberghe wanted his share. Joining forces with Charles Laurent Fiocconi and Jean Claude Kella, he forged a smuggling network

Jurors convicted Fiocconi and Kella on May 24, 1972, and they received prison terms of 19–25 years on October 24.

Vanverberghe escaped indictment with his cohorts, although he was arrested on April 25, 1971, and spent the next four months in jail, following a Casablanca meeting with Sicilian mafiosi active in the 'smack' trade. At home in Marseille, he faced competition from Jacques 'Mad Jacky' Imbert and Gaetan 'Tani' Zampa, rising stars in the city's drug, prostitution and protection rackets. On March 31, 1973, after Zampa's gang hijacked a heroin shipment valued at 600,000 francs ($122,000), Vanverberghe's soldiers raided a Zampa hangout and killed three of the opposition, plus the bartender. At year's end, Francis drew another three-year sentence for aggravated pimping, possession of illegal firearms and carrying false identification. Soon afterward, French police seized a shrimp boat loaded with 425 kg (935 lb) of heroin, slapping Vanverberghe with new charges of drug trafficking. Conviction in that case earned him 12 years in prison, plus five years banishment from Paris.

Paroled in 1984, Vanverberghe seemed to be a changed man. He sought respectability by dabbling in the fashion industry and professional soccer, occupying a luxurious villa in Vitrolles. Still, he felt the draw of crime, reuniting with former gang members and recruiting new ones including Boglietti 'Lolo' Lawrence and Jean-Jacques Maillet. Focused on the Bouches-du-Rhône district of southern France, Vanverberghe found himself in conflict once again with Tani Zampa. A series of

later immortalized on film as 'the French Connection.' On November 20, 1969, a federal grand jury in Boston, Massachusetts, indicted Fiocconi and Kella for smuggling heroin into the US between September 15, 1968, and April 22, 1969. Both were arrested in Italy, in August 1970, and extradited to Boston on October 6, 1971.

bombings and murders ensued between 1986 and 1993. One victim was Vanverberghe's brother Joseph, slain on September 1, 1989.

Vanverberghe received that news in jail, detained on narcotics charges from April 1988 until his acquittal on December 4, 1992. His release sparked a new round of killings, with five victims identified before his next arrest, on November 25, 1993. Charged for his role in the war against Zampa, Vanverberghe was released for lack of evidence on December 14, 1994. In 1996, the European Court of Human Rights ruled that French authorities had violated Vanverberghe's civil liberties by detaining him from 1988 to 1992 without trial, ordering the government to pay him $11,470 in compensation.

On March 22, 2000, Parisian police jailed Vanverberghe on a new charge of aggravated pimping,

ABOVE: Francis Vanverberghe enters a Marseille court in March 1996. He was later awarded compensation for infringement of his civil liberties.

releasing him on May 16 after he posted 800,000 francs ($162,000) bail. The end came for Francis the Belgian on September 27, 2000, when a gunman mounted on a motorcycle shot him dead outside L'Artois Club, a betting parlor in the eighth arrondissement of Paris. Authorities detained suspect Boualem Talata, a bodyguard of actor-comedian Jamel Debbouze, then released him without filing charges. Unknown gunmen killed Talata in Dreux on November 19, 2000. The Vanverberghe crime family officially ceased to exist on October 15, 2002, when two of Francis's nephews were shot in the Bouches-du-Rhône.

Calogero Vizzini

A son of peasant farmers, Calogero Vizzini was born in Villalba, Sicily, on July 24, 1877. While two of his brothers studied for the Catholic priesthood, Vizzini dropped out of elementary school, married into a modest land-owning family, and joined the local Mafia initially as a means of protecting his newfound relative affluence. By the dawn of the 20th century, mutual defense would be transformed into the same quest for power and profit which other, older Mafia clans had pursued since the 1860s. Vizzini himself compiled a police record including suspicion of 39 murders and six attempted murders, 13 other acts of personal violence, 36 robberies, 37 thefts and 63 cases of extortion. Through it all, he remained philosophical, telling a reporter for Milan's newspaper *Corriere della Sera* in 1949, 'The fact is that in every society there has to be a category of people who straighten things out when situations get complicated. Usually they are functionaries of the state. Where the state is not present, or where it does not have sufficient force, this is done by private individuals.'

In 1914, Vizzini acquired an exclusive contract to supply Italy's army with horses and mules during World War I. He 'taxed' owners of quality animals for keeping their property, while shipping sick and aged beasts to the front. A 1917 investigation climaxed with a 20-year sentence for fraud, but that judgment was soon overturned on appeal. A 1926 police report from Villalba called Vizzini a 'dangerous cattle rustler, the Mafia boss of the province linked with cattle rustlers and Mafiosi of other provinces.'

Benito Mussolini allegedly jailed Vizzini, though no surviving records support that claim. In any case, he was free by July 1943, reportedly using his influence to aid the Allied invasion of Sicily as a favor to Lucky Luciano in New York. Vizzini soon became Villalba's mayor and an 'honorary colonel' in the US Army, ideally positioned to profit from black-market trading. One Sicilian observer reported that Vizzini's men 'robbed the storehouses of the agrarian co-op and the army's storehouses; sold food, clothes, cars and lorries in Palermo on the black market. In Villalba all power was in their hands: church, Mafia, agricultural banks, *latifundia* [landed estates], all in the hands of the same family. One used to go and see [Vizzini] and ask, "Can you do me this favour?" even for a little affair one had with some other person.' Exiled New York mafioso Vito Genovese collaborated in those

RIGHT: A rare photograph of cattle rustler, mayor, US Army 'colonel' and Sicilian godfather Calogero Vizzini.

efforts, while planning his own return to America.

Vizzini also supported Sicilian separatists, founding the Fronte Democratico d'Odine Siciliano and staffing it with men described as 'lieutenants in the high Mafia.' When that movement failed to catch fire, Vizzini shifted his support to the anti-communist Christian Democrat Party, allegedly staging a shootout with leftists that wounded 14 persons in Villalba on September 16, 1944. Police charged Vizzini and one of his bodyguards with attempted murder in that case, but legal proceedings dragged on beyond Vizzini's death.

In 1949, Vizzini and Lucky Luciano bought a candy factory in Palermo, shipping sweets and heroin to Europe and America. The Roman newspaper *Avanti!* published photos of their drug lab on April 11, 1954, prompting public outrage that failed to dent Don Calo's influence. Nature intervened on July 10, 1954, when Vizzini died from natural causes. Thousands of peasants, with scores of priests and politicians, thronged his funeral. An epitaph posted at Villalba's church read: 'Humble with the

humble. Great with the great. He showed with words and deeds that his Mafia was not criminal. It stood for respect for the law, defence of all rights, greatness of character: it was love.' Humble Don Calo left an estate valued at $1.3 million in property and investments. In 1958, as an ironic postscript, Vizzini was acquitted of involvement in the 1944 Villalba shootings.

Vizzini once told the *Corriere della Sera*, 'When I die, the Mafia dies.' Some modern observers believe he was partly correct, as his passing marked a permanent shift from rural Mafia activities toward urbanized racketeering. A meeting held at Palermo's Delle Palme Hotel between October 12–16, 1957, with Lucky Luciano and American mafioso Joseph Bonanno in attendance, laid the groundwork for a commission (or '*cupola*') to rule the Sicilian Mafia and resolve internal disputes without bloodshed. Formally established in 1958, the commission chose Salvatore Greco as 'first among equals.' Shattered by internal warfare during 1962–63, the commission was not restored until 1974, with a dozen members.

Curtis Warren

A merchant seaman's son, born on May 31, 1963, in the inner-city Toxteth neighborhood of Liverpool, England, Curtis Warren quit school at age 11 and received several police cautions for criminal activity before his arrest for auto theft at age 12. That charge placed him on two years' probation, violated with a burglary arrest in 1976. More convictions followed: three months' detention in 1978; a borstal term in 1981 for assaulting police officers; another bust during the July 1981 Toxteth riots; and a two-year sentence imposed in March 1982 for assaulting a prostitute and her client.

Upon release from that charge, Warren found work as a nightclub bouncer in Liverpool. Police initially believed that he had changed his ways, but Warren was simply learning the ropes of the drug trade. Before he could make a name for himself in that racket, however, a 1983 armed robbery arrest earned him another five-year prison term. Paroled once more, Warren forged an alliance with Middlesbrough auto dealer and drug trafficker Brian Charrington. In September 1991, the pair

sailed from France to Venezuela aboard Charrington's yacht, arranging to transport cocaine concealed in lead blocks. On arrival in Britain, HM Customs and Excise officers cut open one block, found nothing, and let the shipment pass.

A second cargo – 907 kg (1,995 lb) of cocaine – was seized in early 1992, resulting in arrest of Warren, Charrington and 26 cohorts, but charges were dismissed on January 28, 1993, following revelation of Charrington's role as a police informer. In the wake of that debacle, one of Charrington's police handlers acquired a £70,000 BMW previously registered to Charrington. Warren left Liverpool to escape police surveillance, settling in a villa at Sassenheim, Holland, in 1995. By then, his profits from drug smuggling had allowed him to purchase some 300 houses in England's northwest, plus office buildings and the Holker Street grounds of the Barrow-in-Furness Association Football Club, casinos in Spain, discothèques in Turkey, a Bulgarian vineyard and property in The Gambia, Western Africa.

On October 24, 1996, Dutch police raided Warren's villa, seizing weapons, 1,500 kg (3,300 lb) of cannabis resin, 60 kg (132 lb) of heroin, 50 kg (110 lb) of Ecstasy, 400,000 Dutch guilders and $600,000 in cash. While that case wound its slow way through the courts, the *Sunday Times* Rich List for 1998 pegged his fortune at £40 million. Convicted and sentenced to prison, Warren killed another inmate – Turkish murderer Cemal Guclu – on September 15, 1999. A manslaughter conviction in that case added four years to his sentence, but he was released and deported to England in June 2007. Conviction on new smuggling charges in Jersey brought Warren a 13-year sentence on December 3, 2009.

Adam Worth

Long before Sir Arthur Conan Doyle created fictional super-villain James Moriarty and dubbed him, 'The Napoleon of Crime,' Scotland Yard detectives applied that title to a real-life mastermind of gangland. Adam Werth was born in 1844, to impoverished Jewish parents in the Kingdom of Prussia, and emigrated with his family to Cambridge, Massachusetts, at age five. In 1854, he ran away from home, living in Boston for six years, then moving on to New York City. When America's Civil War erupted in 1861, Werth – now 'Worth' – lied about his age to join the Union army, winning promotion to sergeant before he was wounded at the Second Battle of Bull Run, on August 30, 1862. Mistaken records listed him as 'killed in action', thus facilitating his desertion. He then became a 'bounty jumper,' hiring on to serve in the place of various wealthy conscripts, deserting again, and so on.

After the war, Worth earned his living as a pickpocket in Manhattan, soon organizing a ring of bandits and burglars. Caught robbing an Adams Express wagon, Worth received a three-year sentence, but escaped after two weeks in Sing Sing prison. Teamed with female fence and mobster Fredericka Mandelbaum, Worth directed bank and shop robberies, helped safecracker Charley Bullard escape from jail in 1869, then joined him to loot a Boston bank on November 20 of that year. With Pinkerton detectives on their trail, Worth and Bullard fled to Liverpool, England, robbing a series of pawn shops before they moved on to Paris. There, Worth ran the American Bar, a café and saloon with an illegal casino downstairs. More heat from the police drove Worth to London in 1873, flush with proceeds from a diamond heist.

On arrival in London, Worth bought West Lodge at Clapham Common, while leasing a Mayfair flat as his launching pad into high society. Financing his lavish lifestyle with holdups and burglaries, Worth maintained buffer layers between himself and his street soldiers, allegedly demanding that they refrain from violence. Inspector John Shore of Scotland Yard learned Worth's identity from informers, but building a case proved frustrating. The first crack in Worth's armor was his brother's arrest for passing a bad check in Paris. Next, four underlings were caught with forged letters of credit in Constantinople.

On October 5, 1892, Worth was captured during a holdup in Liège, Belgium, receiving a seven-year sentence in March 1893. Released in 1897, he returned to London, stole £4,000 (approx $6,000) from a jeweler, then moved on to meet William Pinkerton in New York. In March 1901, Pinkerton arranged the return of a Gainsborough painting Worth stole in 1876, netting Worth a $25,000 reward. Worth died in London on January 8, 1902.

Frankie Yale

The mysteries surrounding New York mobster Francesco Ioele begin with his birth. Some sources claim that he was born at Longobucco, in the Italian province of Cosenza, on January 22, 1893. The *Encyclopedia Britannica* disagrees, asserting that he was a Brooklyn native born in 1885. His headstone at Brooklyn's Holy Cross Cemetery confirms 1893 as the year of his birth, but provides no further details. The *New York Times* called Francesco and his brother Angelo 'Uale,' an error passed on to generations of subsequent scribes despite the family's funeral marker.

Ioele's adoption of an 'American' name was standard gangland procedure, probably occurring when he joined the notorious Five Points Gang led by Paolo Vaccarelli, a Sicilian immigrant who called himself 'Paul Kelly.' In the early 1900s, a perpetual state of war existed between the Five Pointers and two deadly rivals: Monk Eastman's mostly-Jewish gang and the Irish White Hand Gang, allegedly founded to combat Italian 'Black Hand' extortion. Yale and ally Johnny Torrio quit the Five Pointers and moved to Brooklyn in search of a more peaceful atmosphere, managing a string of brothels and gambling dens from headquarters at the Harvard Inn, on Coney Island. Young Al Capone got his start with the mob as a Harvard Inn bouncer.

In 1909, Torrio moved to Chicago, joining forces with vice lord and cousin-by-marriage Vincenzo 'Big Jim' Colosimo. Yale assumed sole ownership of the Harvard Inn and related enterprises, logging one of his many arrests in October 1912 for disorderly conduct. Expansion into legitimate business included restaurant food services and ice delivery to tenements, a funeral parlor and the Yale Cigar Manufacturing Company. The latter produced such disreputable stogies that lousy smokes were nicknamed 'Frankie Yales.' Prohibition's advent offered new opportunities for enrichment through smuggling and sale of illegal beer and liquor.

When Jim Colosimo refused to enter the booze trade, Johnny Torrio called for help. Most crime historians today agree that Yale himself shot Colosimo

ABOVE: Frankie Yale's criminal career came to a bloody end when he fell foul of Al Capone in 1928.

ABOVE: Frankie Yale's funeral on July 5, 1928, in New York was a lavish affair. The gangster's casket was worth $15,000.

in Chicago, on May 11, 1920, thus clearing the path for Torrio's ascendancy and securing a franchise for whiskey shipments to the growing Chicago Outfit. Two months earlier, Yale had secured control of labor racketeering on the Brooklyn waterfront by killing White Hand leader Dennis Meehan on March 31. The Irish retaliated at a Manhattan dance hall on February 6, 1921, wounding Yale in one lung and killing companion Michael Dimesci. Yale blamed Meehan successor William 'Wild Bill' Lovett for the shooting and recognized the triggermen. One, Peter Behan, was beaten to death by a policeman on August 7, 1921. Another, Garry Barry, was fatally stabbed

in November. Lovett survived an ambush on January 3, 1933, but ran out of luck on October 31, when three assailants shot him and split his skull with a cleaver.

Many histories of the Roaring Twenties describe Yale as national president of the *Unione Siciliana*, a support group for Sicilian immigrants founded in 1893 and later infiltrated by mafiosi, but dissenting reporters note that Yale was not Sicilian – and some claim the *Unione* had no chapters in New York. In either case, he was allied with mafioso Giuseppe 'Joe The Boss' Masseria on Manhattan's Lower East Side and enjoyed political protection citywide. Arrested twice for carrying concealed weapons in 1922, Yale escaped prosecution both times thanks to gun permits issued by Supreme Court Justice Selah Strong of Suffolk County. Brother Angelo, detained on a kidnapping charge in August 1922, was also quickly released.

Yale paid another visit to Chicago in 1924, leading the team that executed Capone rival Dean O'Banion on November 10. Chicago police detained Yale for questioning on November 15, then released him for lack of evidence. Irish retaliation may explain the Harvard Inn's destruction by an early morning fire on January 24, 1925. White Hand leader Richard 'Peg Leg' Lonergan, brother-in-law of the late Wild Bill Lovett, certainly craved revenge against Yale and company. On December 26, 1925, he invaded Brooklyn's Adonis Social Club with five companions, interrupting a party hosted by visitor Al Capone. As Lonergan's men began harassing Italian patrons, someone doused the lights and gunfire erupted, killing Lonergan and two of his soldiers, wounding a third. Police detained Capone and company, but ultimately filed no charges.

Yale's relationship with Capone soured in 1927, when liquor shipments from New York began to disappear in transit. Capone sent James 'Filesy' DeAmato to supervise the Brooklyn operation, but unknown gunmen killed him on July 7. Capone bided his time for another year, then struck on July 1, 1928. A phone call lured Yale from his Sunrise Club speakeasy, warning of trouble at home. A carload of assassins overtook Yale's Lincoln coupe in transit, blasting him with shotguns and a Thompson submachine gun – the first use of a 'Tommy gun' in New York City. Police found the murder car abandoned nearby, with the weapons still inside it, and traced the machine gun to a Chicago sporting goods store.

ABOVE: Brooklyn was the birthplace of many later gangsters including Frankie Yale and Al Capone, as this charts shows.

Modern research names Yale's probable slayers as Fred 'Killer' Burke, Louis 'Little New York' Campagna, Fred Goetz (alias 'Shotgun George' Ziegler) and Gus Winkler – all named as suspects in the 1929 St. Valentine's Day massacre.

Yale received an impressive send-off. Thousands of Brooklynites observed his funeral procession, featuring an open hearse bearing Yale's $15,000 silver casket, 110 Cadillac limousines filled with mourners and 23 cars jammed with flowers. Dennis Meehan's widow ran out to spit on the passing coffin, and more drama occurred at graveside, when two women surfaced, claiming to be

Yale's widow. Underboss Gandolfo 'Frankie Marlow' Curto succeeded Yale but was gunned down on June 24, 1929, as Joe Masseria moved to consolidate power in his war with rival Salvatore Maranzano. Masseria placed Anthony 'Little Augie Pisano' Carfano in charge of Yale's gambling and liquor business, while ceding the waterfront rackets to Alfredo 'Al Mineo' Manfredi (killed by Maranzano's soldiers on November 5, 1930).

Yoshio Kodama

Yoshio Kodama was born on February 18, 1911, the fifth son of an unsuccessful businessman in Nihonmatsu City, Japan. To spare his parents the expense of raising him, Yoshio was sent to live with relatives in Japanese-occupied Korea. Forced to work in a factory there as a child, he became sensitized to the plight of impoverished workers. He joined the Kenkokukai, a secret society formed in April 1926 that called for 'the creation of a genuine people's state based on unanimity between the people and the emperor.' The group espoused 'state control of the life of the people in order that among Japanese people there should not be a single unfortunate, nor unfully-franchised individual,' while embracing Pan-Asianism. Kenkokukai spokesmen declared that, 'The Japanese people standing at the head of the coloured people, will bring the world a new civilization.' A far-right group despite its Marxist trappings, by 1928 the Kenkokukai was controlled by 'Shadow Shogun' Toyama Mitsuru, founder of the paramilitary Black Dragon Society.

In addition to his work for the Kenkokukai, Yoshio organized his own ultranationalist Independence Youth Society, pledged to the elimination of Japanese politicians opposed to his cause. Jailed for those activities in 1931, Yoshio was released in July 1937, with the outbreak of the Second Sino-Japanese War. Enlisted to transport war supplies from continental Asia to Japan, he financed the effort with opium sales, creating a network of smugglers known as Kodama Kikan, reaping an estimated fortune of $175 million by trading in cobalt, copper, nickel, radium and heroin. Engaged in espionage after Pearl Harbor, Yoshio finished the war as a rear admiral – and was branded a 'Class A' war criminal by the American victors, held at Sugamo Prison with fascist leader Ryoichi Sasakawa. Both were unexpectedly acquitted and released in December 1948.

Mindful of Yoshio's record, the US Central Intelligence Agency recruited him to battle Asian communism – and, in 1949, to smuggle stolen tungsten out of China. That shipment vanished en route, but Yoshio kept his $150,000 payoff. In Japan, meanwhile, he organized Yakuza gangsters to suppress labor unions and leftist political parties. Another incident from 1949 found Yoshio fielding mobsters from the Meiraki-gumi clan to crush a strike at the Hokutan coal mine.

An estimated 5,200 Yakuza gangs with 184,000 known members ran rampant through Japan during the 1950s, outnumbering the nation's military forces. Yoshio Kodama did his best to bring order out of chaos, negotiating a truce between Kazuo Taoka's powerful Yamaguchi-gumi clan and the Tōa-kai led by Hisayuki Machii, alias 'The Ginzu Tiger.' Encouraged by that success, Yoshio envisioned a super gang ruling all organized crime in Japan and tried to achieve it in 1964, with creation of the Kantō-kai syndicate, but that effort failed when Kazuo Taoka withdrew his Yamaguchi-gumi clan, and the Kantō-kai dissolved in January 1965.

It was a relatively minor setback for Yoshio, known by then as 'The Kingmaker.' In 1972, the Lockheed Corporation hired Yoshio to secure contracts from All Nippon Airways, Japan's largest domestic airline. Lockheed paid a total of ¥2.4 billion ($25.5 million) to clinch the deal, including ¥160 million ($1.7 million) paid to various ANA officials after Yoshio used his underworld contacts to discredit a company president who preferred McDonnell Douglas aircraft. A US Senate investigation broke news of the payoffs in February 1976, leading to the July arrest of Prime Minister Kakuei Tanaka on bribery charges. Meanwhile, a disillusioned Yoshio admirer – ex-porn star Mitsuyasu Maeno – crashed a plane into Yoshio's home in Setagaya, on March 23, 1976. Yoshio, recovering from a stroke suffered in 1975, escaped harm from the crash and was carried to safety by Yakuza guards. That done, the gangsters returned to extinguish the flames in Yoshio's house and assault reporters who flocked to the scene. Afterward, the battered journalists complained that police had ignored the attack, while warning them not to 'excite the young men.'

Yoshio was scheduled for trial in the Lockheed scandal during June 1977, but poor health and legal maneuvers stalled those proceedings indefinitely. Kakuei Tanaka was convicted of bribery on October 12, 1983, and received a four-year prison sentence, deferred pending resolution of various appeals. Yoshio Kodama's trial was still pending when a second stroke claimed his life on January 17, 1984. Ex-prime minister Kanaka likewise never served a day in jail, dying from pneumonia and complications of diabetes on December 16, 1993.

RIGHT: A photograph of Yoshio Kodama from 1961, when the Japanese gangster/politician was at the height of his criminal powers.

Gaetan Zampa

Gaetan Zampa was born on April 1, 1933, in the Le Panier district of Marseille, France. His father, Matthew, was a transplanted Neapolitan gangster, employed by Corsican racketeer Paul Carbone until 1943, when a train derailed by members of the French Resistance crushed Carbone's car. Thereafter, Matthew Zampa worked for the Guerini crime family, packed off to run a bar fronting for heroin traffic in Saigon, French Indochina. The elder Zampa would not return until 1972, leaving Gaetan – dubbed 'Tani' – to raise himself.

Predictably, he turned to crime. First affiliated with Antoine Guerini's gang, Zampa later moved on to the Trois Canards ('Three Ducks') crew led by ex-Marseille policeman Robert Blemant, active in heroin smuggling from Southeast Asia. Dispatched to Paris on Blemant's behalf in 1955, Zampa established

himself as a hotel director while overseeing prostitution, gambling and extortion rackets. Returning to Marseille for a two million-franc ($406,000) burglary on the night of December 31, 1960, Zampa plowed the money back into his Parisian operations. When Guerini soldiers murdered Robert Blemant on May 4, 1965, Tani was suddenly in business for himself.

Surrounded by mobsters including half-brother Jean Toci, underworld strategist Gaby Regazzi, nightclub impresario Gilbert Hoareau, stickup artist Gérard Vigier and Bimbo Roche, Zampa was primed to challenge the Guerinis in Marseille when a five-year prison term put a brake to his plans in 1966. In his absence, on June 23, 1967, two still-unknown gunmen killed Antoine Guerini with 11 close-range gunshots at a Marseille filling station. Released in 1970, Zampa added arms trafficking to his repertoire, supplying weapons to various militant groups including the Basque separatist Euskadi Ta Askatasuna and their Spanish opponents of the vigilante Grupos Antiterroristas de Liberación.

By 1972, Zampa was embroiled with Francis Vanverberghe in a struggle for control of the French heroin trade, hijacking a shipment of Vanverberghe drugs valued at 600,000 francs ($122,000). Zampa followed that coup with a raid at Canet, killing Vanverberghe soldiers Jean-Claude Bonello, Robert Di Russo and Daniel Lamberti. Vanverberghe retaliated with strikes that claimed seven of Zampa's men

ABOVE: Floral tributes at the funeral of French gangster Gaetan 'Tani' Zampa in Marseille in August 1984.

between October 1972 and March 1973. The war ended in November 1973, with Vanverberghe's arrest and later incarceration.

Zampa had legal problems of his own, serving eight months for a weapons violation during 1975. The following year, he was suspected of collaborating in Albert Spaggiari's theft of 60 million francs ($12.2 million) from the Société Générale bank in Nice, but no firm evidence linked him to that epic burglary. Around the same time, Zampa did join forces with Jean-Dominique Fratoni, a casino operator on the Cote d'Azur who vowed to make Nice 'the Las Vegas of the Riviera.' In a similar vein, ally Richard 'The Butcher' Baqué joined Zampa to run slot machines from Marseille to Bordeaux.

In 1977, Zampa's ambitions collided with those of Jacques Imbert, a native of Toulouse and would-be successor to the Guerinis in Marseille. Zampa's soldiers ambushed Imbert on February 1, 1977, but failed to finish the job, one gunman reportedly saying, 'A swine like him isn't worth *le coup de grâce* ("blow of mercy"). Let him die like a dog.' Imbert survived his wounds, albeit with a paralyzed right arm, of which the newspaper *Le Monde* observed: 'Small matter, he learned to shoot with the left.' Subsequently jailed for six months, pending investigation of a gang-related murder, Imbert struck a

truce with Zampa upon his release from custody.

French authorities also suspected Zampa of complicity in a more successful murder contract, which claimed the life of leftist intellectual and convicted robber Pierre Goldman, shot in Paris on September 20, 1979. That crime remains officially unsolved, but police speculated that Zampa may have arranged the killing on behalf of Spanish vigilantes who despised Goldman for his links to the Basque ETA – and perhaps because of Goldman's rumored role in the slaying of Robert Blemant.

August 1980 brought news of raids on heroin labs in Sicily, where French chemist Andre Bousquet was jailed with mafioso Gerlando Alberti and others. A French judge, Pierre Michel, collaborated with Italian authorities in staging those raids, and Zampa was suspected when gunmen killed Michel in October 1981.

Two years later, on October 6, 1983, a gunman executed Gilbert Hoareau. On November 29, police arrested Zampa, his wife and other gang members for complicity in that slaying. Convicted and sentenced to five years in prison, Zampa hanged himself with a jump rope on July 23, 1984. Still alive when found by prison guards, Zampa survived an emergency tracheotomy but never regained consciousness, finally dying on August 16, 1984.

Zhenli Ye Gon

A native of Shanghai, China, born on January 31, 1963, Zhenli Ye Gon joined partner Hongju Ye to organize the firm Unimedic Hong Kong Company Ltd. in 1995, advertised as a supplier of raw materials to the pharmaceutical industry. Launched with a modest $10,000 investment, Unimedic Hong Kong subsequently changed its name to Emerald Import and Export Corporation. In 1997, Zhenli moved to Mexico, where he applied for citizenship (granted in 2002). He spent two years as a technician at Laboratorios Silanes near Mexico City – owned by Antonio López de Silanes Pérez, a longtime friend and supporter of former president Vicente Fox Quesada – and then started yet another firm, United Pharm Chem de Mexico. According to authorities in Mexico and the United States, Emerald Import and Export provided false labels that allowed 54,500 kg (60 tons) of pseudoephedrine – a decongestant used to manufacture methamphetamine – to slip past Mexican customs agents.

On October 18, 2006 Zhenli traveled to Mongolia, where he purchased another 19,500 kg (42,893 lb) of pseudoephedrine from Chifeng Arker Pharmaceutical Technology, a subsidiary of Shanghai Industrial United

Holdings, for $692,895. The shipment sailed from Tianjin, China, but this time authorities seized it at the port of Lázaro Cárdenas, in the Mexican state of Michoacán. Narcotics agents then began to track other shipments along a route stretching from China to Long Beach, California, then onward to Lázaro Cárdenas and Manzanillo on Mexico's Pacific coast. While that investigation was in progress, during February and March 2007, United Pharm Chem imported eight industrial pill-manufacturing machines through the port of Veracruz. Mexican police traced one of them to Toluca de Lerdo, 62 km (39 miles) southwest of Mexico City, where Zhenli Ye Gon was building a 46,000-square-meter (150,000-square-foot) pill factory. The other seven machines – each one capable of spitting out three million methamphetamine tablets per day, valued at $14.9 million

– had vanished.

On March 15, 2007, police raided Zhenli's mansion in the Lomas de Chapultepec district of Mexico City, arresting nine persons. The raiders seized seven vehicles, an incomplete drug lab and an unspecified large amount of jewelry, plus cash in various denominations including $207 million, 18 million Mexican pesos, 200,000 euros, 113,000 Hong Kong dollars and 11 centenarios (Mexican gold bullion coins). Two Chinese nationals, Fu Huaxin and Yen Yongging, were also detained by Mexican authorities on July 23, 1997. That same day, agents of the US Drug Enforcement Administration found Zhenli Ye Gon in Wheaton, Maryland, arresting him on charges of drug smuggling and money laundering. Nine days later, on August 1, two of the federal agents who participated in the raid on Zhenli's home – Josue Hernandez and Anibal Sanchez – were beaten and shot to death in the southern Mexican state of Guerrero.

In custody, Zhenli denied any involvement in the illicit drug trade and explained the huge amount of cash found at his home as a by-product of Mexican politics. According to Zhenli, the money was delivered by Javier Lozano Alarcón, a campaign manager for presidential candidate Felipe de Jesús Calderón Hinojosa, who served as Mexico's Secretary of Labor, following Calderón's inauguration on December 1, 2006. Both Calderón and Lozano dismissed Zhenli's tale as a fabrication, insisting that Zhenli was involved in drug trafficking with members of the Sinaloa Cartel led by Joaquín Guzmán Loera. On July 26, 2007, a federal grand jury in the

District of Columbia indicted Zhenli on a single count of conspiracy to aid and abet the manufacture of 500 grams (1.1 lb), or more of methamphetamine, knowing or intending, that it would be imported into the United States.

In October 2008, Zhenli retained prominent attorneys Eduardo Balarezo and Manuel Retureta, both pledged to resist any move toward extradition from the US to Mexico. Zhenli's trial in Washington, DC, was scheduled to begin in September 2009, but on June 22 of that year, the Justice Department dismissed its case. Explaining that surprise move, prosecutors first cited 'Mexico's interests,' then admitted that a key government witness

BELOW: The defense counsel for Zhenli Ye Gon respond to media questions about their client outside the US District Court House in Washington, DC.

had recanted his testimony. The federal decision frustrated DEA agents, who leaked claims that Zhenli had gambled away nearly $126 million in Las Vegas casinos, while telling an employee at the Mirage Hotel that he was laundering money for Mexican drug traffickers.

Litigation of Mexico's extradition request, filed on June 2, 2008, continues, while many Mexicans appear to accept Zhenli's claims of a frame-up motivated by politics. Bumper stickers reading, 'I believe the Chinaman' decorate many cars in Mexico City.

Abner Zwillman

Abner Zwillman was born in Newark, New Jersey, on July 27, 1904. His father's death in 1918 forced Zwillman – nicknamed 'Longy' for his 1.87-meter (6 ft 2 in) height – to quit school and work in support of his mother and six siblings. First employed as a waiter, then a pushcart peddler and numbers runner, he soon recruited 'muscle' to dominate the local policy racket by 1920. His gang, 'The Happy Ramblers,' also defended Jewish merchants from anti-Semitic harassment, while collecting tribute for themselves. Prohibition's advent launched Zwillman into bootlegging, using army-surplus trucks from World War I to carry booze from 'Rum Row' to Newark's speakeasies.

By 1927, when he helped found the 'Big Seven' liquor syndicate with Lucky Luciano, Meyer Lansky, Moe Dalitz and others, Zwillman was a multi-millionaire. Two years later, he joined Atlantic City boss Enoch 'Nucky' Johnson to organize the first national summit meeting for leaders of organized crime nationwide. In 1931, Zwillman backed Luciano's violent bid to modernize the American Mafia, while newspapers dubbed him 'the Al Capone of New Jersey.' He monopolized cigarette vending machines in New York, New Jersey and later in Las Vegas, Nevada. Zwillman's other investments included hotels and restaurants in Florida and Cuba, plus Hollywood film studios.

The Hollywood connection had a personal side, as Zwillman enjoyed a torrid affair with 'Blonde Bombshell' Jean Harlow. They often shared a bungalow at West Hollywood's Garden of Allah apartment complex, rubbing shoulders with celebrities whose ranks included billionaire Howard Hughes and novelist F. Scott Fitzgerald. In 1971, author Hank Messick blamed Zwillman for the mysterious death of Harlow's husband, MGM studio executive Paul Bern, found shot at their home on September 5, 1932, barely two months after their wedding. Police ruled the shooting a suicide, and

while Messick claims that Zwillman killed Bern to spare Harlow from physical abuse, FBI wiretaps recorded Longy's derogatory comments to other mobsters concerning Harlow.

Following the murder of Dutch Schultz in October 1935, Zwillman divided Schultz's Newark rackets with mafioso-partner Guarino 'Willie' Moretti. New Jersey's largest illegal casino was the Marine Room, located in Zwillman's Riviera nightclub, atop the Palisades of Fort Lee, at the western end of the George Washington Bridge. While raking in illicit millions, Zwillman still sought to sanitize his public image with generosity. In 1932, he offered a reward for the safe return of kidnap victim Charles Lindbergh Jr. Two decades later, in March 1954, Zwillman donated $250,000 toward slum clearance in Newark's Third Ward, saying he hoped the cash would help 'about 12,000 families who didn't have the luck I've had lately in business.'

Longy's 'luck' in business brought him before the US Senate's Special Committee to Investigate Crime in Interstate Commerce in March 1951, with the panel reporting that 'Zwillman exercises his influence in New Jersey in a manner that makes detection almost impossible. He makes it a practice never to attend any public function